Greek
phrase book

**Berlitz Publishing / APA Publications GmbH & Co.
Verlag KG, Singapore Branch, Singapore**

Contacting the Editors
Every effort has been made to provide accurate information in this publication, but changes are inevitable. The publisher cannot be responsible for any resulting loss, inconvenience or injury. We would appreciate it if readers would call our attention to any errors or outdated information by contacting Berlitz Publishing, 95 Progress Street, Union, NJ 07083, USA. Fax: 1-908-206-1103
email: comments@berlitzbooks.com

Satisfaction guaranteed—If you are dissatisfied with this product for any reason, send the complete package, your dated sale receipt showing price and store name, and a brief note describing your dissatisfaction to: Berlitz Publishing, Langenscheidt Publishing Group, Dept. L, 46-35 54th Rd., Maspeth, NY 11378. You'll receive a full refund.

Layout: Media Marketing, Inc.
Cover photo: ©Steve Outram

Developed and produced for Berlitz Publishing Company by:
G&W Publishing Services, Oxfordshire, U.K.
Greek edition: Dr. Ioanna Psalti

Printed in Singapore

Contents

Pronunciation

This section is designed to make you familiar with the sounds of Greek using our simplified phonetic transcription. You'll find the pronunciation of the Greek letters and sounds explained below, together with their "imitated" equivalents. This system is used throughout the phrase book: simply read the pronunciation as if it were English, noting any special rules below.

The Greek language

Greek is a language with a long history. The language itself has developed over the centuries into the Modern Greek of today spoken by approximately 11 million people in Greece and Cyprus, as well as Greek-speaking communities within other countries.

It is a phonetic language – the sound of each letter does not usually change with its position. Although the characters may appear confusing at first, don't be put off by this. With a bit of practice most people can read Greek in just a few hours. Spelling, however, is a different matter, as certain sounds – such as the sound *i*, as in "lit" – may be written in five different ways.

Stress

Stress, or emphasis on a word, is important in Greek, as often the meaning of the word changes depending upon which syllable is stressed. In written Greek, stress is indicated by a small mark (´) on the syllable to be stressed. In the Greek phonetic transcription we indicate stress by underlining the stressed syllable, for example: πόσο **po**so (how much). If you do not stress a word properly, don't worry. Most people will still understand what you are trying to say – particularly if you point to the word or phrase in this book!

Note: Over the last 10 years, the Greek language has been greatly simplified with the number of stress and breathing marks reduced, although you will still see words written with the more elaborate stress marks.

Pronunciation of Greek letters

The pronunciation of many Greek letters is similar to their English equivalents. However, look out for the Greek letter ν, which is pronounced "n," and ρ, which is pronounced "r."

It is also worth paying some closer attention to the consonant and vowel combinations and to the diphthongs.

Consonants

Letter	Approximate pronunciation	Symbol	Example	Pron.
β	like *v* in *v*oice	v	βάζο	*va*zo
δ	voiced *th*, like *th* in *th*en	TH	δεν	*TH*en
ζ	like *z* in *z*oo	z	ζω	*z*o
θ	unvoiced *th*, like *th* in *th*ing	th	θέλω	*the*lo
κ	like *k* in *k*ey	k	κότα	*ko*ta
λ	like *l* in *l*emon	l	λεμόνι	*lem*onee
μ	like *m* in *m*an	m	μαμά	*ma*ma
ν	like *n* in *n*et	n	νέο	*ne*o
ξ	like *x* in fo*x*	ks	ξένος	*ksen*os
π	like *p* in *p*en	p	πένα	*pena*
ρ	trilled like a Scottish *r*	r	ώρα	*ora*
σ*	like *s* in *s*it	s	σε	*se*
τ	like *t* in *t*en	t	τι	*tee*
φ	like *f* in *f*un	f	φως	*fos*
χ	like *ch* in Scottish lo*ch*	kh	χαρά	*khara*
ψ	like *ps* in to*ps*	ps	ψάρι	*psaree*
γ	a combination of the *w* sound in *w*ere and the *y* sound in *y*ard	gh	γάλα	*ghala*

* if this character falls at the end of a word, it changes to ς

Consonant combinations

Although double consonants are typically pronounced in the same manner as each individual consonant, some two-consonant combinations produce a sound somewhere in the middle of the two individual consonants.

Letter	Approximate pronunciation	Symbol	Example	Pron.
γγ, γκ	like *g* in *g*o, but in some cases a more nasal *ng* as in a*ng*ling	g	γκαρσόν	gar*son*
μπ	like *b* in *b*ath, but in some cases more like *mp* as in la*mp*	b	μπαρ	bar
ντ	like *d* in *d*o, but in some cases more like *nd* as in e*nd* .	d	ντομάτα	do*mata*
τζ	like *j* in *j*azz	tz	τζατζίκι	tzatzeekee
τσ	like *ts* in le*ts*	ts	τσάντα	*tsanda*

Vowels

Letter	Approximate pronunciation	Symbol	Example	Pron.
α	like *a* in t*a*p	a	μα	ma
ε	like *e* in t*e*n	e	θέλω	*thelo*
η, ι, υ	like *i* in t*i*n	ee	πίνω	*peeno*
ο, ω	like *o* in t*o*p	o	πότε	*pote*

Diphthongs

Two vowels are often found next to each other and may be pronounced as separate sounds or as one combined sound. If they are to be pronounced separately either the first vowel bears the stress mark or the second vowel bears the ¨ symbol, similar to the German *umlaut*. For example: ρολόι – *roloee*, μαϊμού – *maeemoo*.

Letter	Approximate pronunciation	Symbol	Example	Pron.
αι	like *e* in t*e*n	e	μπαίνω	*beno*
οι, ει, υι	like *i* in t*i*n	ee	πλοίο	*pleeo*
αυ	*av* or *af*	av/af	αυτός	*aftos*
ευ	*ev* or *ef*	ev/ef	λευκός	*lefkos*
ου	like *oo* in z*oo*	oo	ούζο	*oozo*

Other combinations

Below are other two and three letter combinations. Notice that more than one combination can produce the same sound. For example, the combinations γι, γυ, and γη all produce the sound **ee**.

Letter	Approximate pronunciation	Symbol	Example	Pron.
για, γεια	like *ya* in *yak*	ya	για	*ya*
γε, γιε	like *ye* in *yen*	ye	γερό	*yero*
ειο, γιο	like *yo* in *yoyo*	yo	γιος	*yos*
γι, γυ, γη	like *yea* in *yeast*	yee	γύρω	*yeero*
ια, οια	like *ia* in *piano*	ia	ποια	*pia*

The Greek alphabet

A α	*alfa*		N ν	*nee*
B β	*veeta*		Ξ ξ	*ksee*
Γ γ	*ghama*		O o	*omeekron*
Δ δ	*THelta*		Π π	*pee*
E ε	*epseelon*		P ρ	*ro*
Z ζ	*zeeta*		Σ σ, ς	*seeghma*
H η	*eeta*		T τ	*taf*
Θ θ	*theeta*		Y υ	*eepseelon*
I ι	*yota*		Φ φ	*fee*
K κ	*kapa*		X χ	*khee*
Λ λ	*lamTHa*		Ψ ψ	*psee*
M μ	*mee*		Ω ω	*omegha*

Basic Expressions

ESSENTIAL

Yes.	Ναι./Μάλιστα. *ne/maleesta*
No.	Όχι. *okhee*
Okay.	Εντάξει. *endaksee*
Please.	Παρακαλώ. *parakalo*
Thank you (very much).	Ευχαριστώ (πολύ). *efkhareesto (polee)*

Greetings/Apologies
Χαιρετισμοί/ζητώντας συγγνώμη

Hello./Hi!	Χαίρετε./Γειά σας! *kherete/ya sas*
Good morning.	Καλημέρα. *kaleemera*
Good afternoon/evening.	Καλησπέρα. *kaleespera*
Good night.	Καληνύχτα. *kaleeneekhta*
Good-bye.	Αντίο. *andeeo*
Excuse me! (getting attention)	Παρακαλώ! *parakalo*
Excuse me. (May I get past?)	Συγγνώμη. *seeghnomee*
Excuse me!/Sorry!	Συγγνώμη! *seeghnomee*
It was an accident.	Ήταν κατά λάθος. *eetan kata lathos*
Don't mention it.	Παρακαλώ, τίποτα. *parakalo, teepota*
Never mind.	Δεν πειράζει. *тнen peerazee*

INTRODUCTIONS ➤ 118

Communication difficulties
Δυσκολίες επικοινωνίας

Do you speak English?	Μιλάτε Αγγλικά; *meelate angleeka*
Does anyone here speak English?	Μιλάει κανείς εδώ Αγγλικά; *meelaee kanees etho angleeka*
I don't speak (much) Greek.	Δεν μιλώ (πολλά) Ελληνικά. *then meelo (pola) eleeneeka*
Could you speak more slowly?	Μπορείτε να μιλάτε πιο αργά; *boreete na meelate peeo argha*
Could you repeat that?	Μπορείτε να το επαναλάβετε; *boreete na to epanalavete*
Excuse me? [Pardon?]	Συγγνώμη, δεν άκουσα καλά. *seeghnomee, then akoosa kala*
Please write it down.	Μπορείτε να μου το γράψετε; *boreete na moo to ghrapsete*
Can you translate this for me?	Μπορείτε να μου μεταφράσετε αυτό; *boreete na moo metafrasete afto*
What does this/that mean?	Τι σημαίνει αυτό/εκείνο; *tee seemenee afto/ekeeno*
What do you call this/that in Greek?	Πώς λέγεται αυτό/εκείνο στα Ελληνικά; *pos leghete afto/ekeeno sta eleeneeka*
How do you pronounce that?	Πώς το προφέρετε αυτό; *pos to proferete afto*
Please point to the phrase in the book.	Παρακαλώ δείξτε μου την φράση στο βιβλίο. *parakalo theekste moo tee frasee sto veevleeo*
I understand.	Καταλαβαίνω. *katalaveno*
I don't understand.	Δεν καταλαβαίνω. *then katalaveno*
Do you understand?	Καταλαβαίνετε; *katalavenete*

– *kanee saranda evro.*
– *then katalaveno.*
– *kanee saranda evro.*
– *boreete na moo to ghrapsete? ... A!.*
"40 euros." ... *Oreeste.*

11

Questions Ερωτήσεις

GRAMMAR

Questions in Greek are formed by simply raising the intonation of your voice. However, the Greek script uses a semicolon in place of a question mark:

Πού πηγαίνετε; Where are you going?

Where? Πού;

Where is it?	Πού είναι; *poo eene*
Where are you going?	Πού πηγαίνετε; *poo peeghenete*
at the meeting place [point]	στο σημείο συνάντησης *sto seemeeo seenandeesees*
here (to here)	εδώ (ως εδώ) *eTHo (os eTHo)*
in the car	μέσα στο αυτοκίνητο *mesa sto aftokeeneeto*
in Greece	στην Ελλάδα *steen elaTHa*
inside	μέσα *mesa*
from the U.S.	από τις Ηνωμένες Πολιτείες *apo tees eenomenes poleetee-es*
near the bank	κοντά στη Τράπεζα *konda steen trapeza*
next to the apples	δίπλα στα μήλα *THeepla sta meela*
opposite the market	απέναντι από την αγορά *apenandee apo teen aghora*
on the left/right	στα αριστερά/δεξιά *sta areestera/THekseea*
over the road	απέναντι *apenandee*
there (to there)	εκεί (ως εκεί) *ekee (os ekee)*
to the hotel	στο ξενοδοχείο *sto ksenoTHokheeo*
towards Athens	προς την Αθήνα *pros teen atheena*
outside the café	έξω από το καφενείο *ekso apo to kafeneeo*
upstairs	επάνω *epano*

When? Πότε;

When does the museum open?	Πότε ανοίγει το μουσείο; *pote aneeyee to mooseeo*
When does the train arrive?	Πότε φτάνει το τραίνο; *pote ftanee to treno*
after lunch	μετά το μεσημεριανό *meta to meseemereeano*
around midnight	γύρω στα μεσάνυχτα *yeero sta mesaneekhta*
at 7 o'clock	στις εφτά *stees efta*
10 minutes ago	πριν από δέκα λεπτά *preen apo тнeka lepta*
before Friday	πριν την Παρασκευή *preen teen paraskevee*
by tomorrow	μέχρι αύριο *mekhree avreeo*
always	πάντα *panda*
daily	καθημερινά *katheemereena*
every week	κάθε εβδομάδα *kathe evтнomaтнa*
for 2 hours	για δύο ώρες *ya тнeeo ores*
frequently	συχνά *seekhna*
from 9 a.m. to 6 p.m.	από τις εννέα π.μ. ως τις έξι μ.μ. *apo tees enea pro meseemvreeas os tees eksee meta meseemvreeas*
immediately	αμέσως *amesos*
in 20 minutes	σε είκοσι λεπτά *se eekosee lepta*
never	ποτέ *pote*
now	τώρα *tora*
often	συχνά *seekhna*
on March 8	στις οχτώ Μαρτίου *stees okhto marteeoo*
on weekdays	τις καθημερινές *tees katheemereenes*
sometimes	μερικές φορές *mereekhes fores*
soon	σύντομα *seendoma*
then	τότε *tote*

What sort of ...? Τι είδους ...;

I'd like something ...	Θα ήθελα κάτι ...	*tha eethela katee*
It's ...	Είναι ...	*eene*
beautiful/ugly	ωραίο/άσχημο	*oreo/askheemo*
better/worse	καλύτερο/χειρότερο	*kaleetero/kheerotero*
big/small	μεγάλο/μικρό	*meghalo/meekro*
cheap/expensive	φτηνό/ακριβό	*fteeno/akreevo*
clean/dirty	καθαρό/βρώμικο	*katharo/vromeeko*
dark/light	σκούρο/ανοιχτό	*skooro/aneekhto*
delicious/revolting	νόστιμο/αηδιαστικό	*nosteemo/aeetheeasteeko*
early/late	νωρίς/αργά	*norees/argha*
easy/difficult	εύκολο/δύσκολο	*efkolo/тнeeskolo*
empty/full	άδειο/γεμάτο	*aтнyo/yemato*
fresh/stale	φρέσκο/μπαγιάτικο	*fresko/bayateeko*
good/bad	καλό/κακό	*kalo/kako*
heavy/light	βαρύ/ελαφρύ	*varee/elafree*
hot/warm/cold	ζεστό/χλιαρό/κρύο	*zesto/khleearo/kreeo*
modern/old-fashioned	μοντέρνο/ντεμοντέ	*monderno/demonde*
narrow/wide	στενό/φαρδύ	*steno/farтнee*
old/new	παλιό/καινούργιο	*paleeo/kenooryo*
open/shut	ανοιχτό/κλειστό	*aneekhto/kleesto*
pleasant, nice/unpleasant	ευχάριστο/δυσάρεστο	*efkhareesto/тнeesaresto*
quick/slow	γρήγορο/αργό	*ghreeghoro/argho*
quiet/noisy	ήσυχο/θορυβώδες	*eeseekho/thoreevoтнes*
right/wrong	σωστό/λάθος	*sosto/lathos*
tall/short	ψηλό/κοντό	*pseelo/kondo*
thick/thin	χοντρό/λεπτό	*khondro/lepto*
vacant/occupied	ελεύθερο/κατειλημμένο	*elefthero/kateeleemeno*
young/old	νέος/γέρος	*neos/yeros*

Nouns in Greek are one of three genders: masculine, feminine, or neuter. (The masculine is used here for general expressions.) Nouns also change their endings according to where they are in a sentence (► 169 for more explanation).

How much/many? Πόσο; /Πόσοι;

How much is that?	Πόσο κάνει αυτό;	_poso kanee afto_
How many are there?	Πόσοι υπάρχουν;	_posee eeparkhoon_
1/2/3	ένας/δύο/τρεις	_enas/THeeo/trees_
4/5	τέσσερις/πέντε	_teserees/pende_
none	κανένας	_kanenas_
about 30 euros	πρίπου 30 ευρώ	_pereepoo treeanda evro_
a little	λίγο	_leegho_
a lot of traffic	πολύ κίνηση	_polee keeneesee_
no more	πια/όχι πια	_pia/okhee_
enough	αρκετό	_arketo_
few/a few of them	λίγα/λίγα απ' αυτά	_leegha/leegha ap afta_
many people	πολύς κόσμος	_polees kozmos_
more than that	περισσότερο απ' αυτό	_pereesotero ap afto_
less than that	λιγότερο απ' αυτό	_leeghotero ap afto_
much more	πολύ περισσότερο	_polee pereesotero_
nothing else	τίποτε άλλο	_teepote alo_
too much	πάρα πολύ	_para polee_

Why? Γιατί;

Why is that?	Για ποιό λόγο;	_ya peeo logho_
Why not?	Γιατί όχι;	_yatee okhee_
because of the weather	λόγω του καιρού	_logho too keroo_
because I'm in a hurry	επειδή βιάζομαι	_epeeTHee veeazome_
I don't know why.	δεν ξέρω γιατί	_THen ksero yatee_

Who? / Which (one)?
Ποιός; / Ποιό (απ' όλα);

Which one do you want?	Ποιό απ' όλα θέλετε; pee_o_ ap ola the_le_te
Who is it for?	Για ποιόν είναι; ya pee_on_ _ee_ne
him/her	αυτόν/αυτήν af_ton_/af_teen_
me	εμένα e_me_na
you (formal)/you (informal)	εσάς/εσένα e_sas_/e_se_na
them	αυτούς af_toos_
none	κανένα ka_ne_na
no one	κανέναν/καμμία/κανένα ka_ne_nan/ka_mee_a/ka_ne_na
one like that	ένα σαν αυτό _e_na san af_to_
that/this one	αυτό/εκείνο af_to_/e_kee_no

Whose? Ποιανού/-ής;

Whose is that?	Ποιανού/-ής είναι αυτό; pee_anoo_/-es _ee_ne af_to_
It's ...	Είναι ... _ee_ne
mine/ours	δικό μου/δικό μας THee_ko_ moo/THee_ko_ mas
yours (formal)/yours (informal)	δικό σας/δικό σου THee_ko_ sas/THee_ko_ soo
his/hers/theirs	δικό του/δικό της/δικό τους THee_ko_ too/THee_ko_ tees/THee_ko_ toos

GRAMMAR

The possessive adjectives are:

my	**moo**	our	**mas**
your	**soo**	your	**sas**
his/its	**too**	their	**toos**
her	**tees**		

They follow the word (with its article) with which they are associated:

my name	to _onoma_ moo	our aunt	ee _thea_ mas
your name	to _onoma_ sou	your aunt	ee _thea_ sas
his name	to _onoma_ too	their house	to _spee_tee toos
her friend	o _feel_os tees		

16

How? Πώς;

How would you like to pay?	Πώς θέλετε να πληρώσετε; *pos thelete na pleerosete*
by credit card	με πιστωτική κάρτα *me peestoteekee karta*
How are you getting here?	Πώς θα έρθετε εδώ; *pos tha erthete etho*
by car	με το αυτοκίνητο *me to aftokeeneeto*
on foot	με τα πόδια *me ta poтнуa*
quickly	γρήγορα *ghreeghora*
slowly	αργά *argha*
too fast	πολύ γρήγορα *polee ghreeghora*
totally	τελείως *teleeos*
by chance	συμπτωματικά *seemptomateeka*
equally	εξίσου *ekseesoo*
extremely	υπερβολικά *eepervoleeka*
very	πολύ *polee*
with a friend	με έναν φίλο *me enan feelo*
without a passport	χωρίς διαβατήριο *khorees тнееavateereeo*

Is it ...? / Is there ...? Είναι ...; /Υπάρχει ...;

Is it free (of charge)?	Είναι δωρεάν; *eene тнorean*
It isn't ready.	Δεν είναι έτοιμο. *тнen eene eteemo*
Is there a bus into town?	Υπάρχει λεωφορείο για την πόλη; *eeparkhee leoforeeo ya teen polee*
There are showers in the rooms.	Υπάρχουν ντουζ στα δωμάτια. *eeparkhoon dooz sta тнomateea*
There isn't any hot water.	Δεν υπάρχει ζεστό νερό. *тнen eeparkhee zesto nero*
Here it is/they are.	Νάτο./Νάτα. *nato/nata*
There it is/they are.	Εκεί είναι. *ekee eene*

Can/May? Μπορώ;

Can I have ...?	Μπορώ να έχω ... ; *boro na ekho*
May we have ...?	Μπορούμε να έχουμε ... ; *boroome na ekhoome*
Can you show me ...?	Μπορείτε να μου δείξετε ... ; *boreete na moo THeeksete*
I can't.	Δεν μπορώ. *THen boro*
Can you tell me ...?	Μπορείτε να μου πείτε ... ; *boreete na moo peete*
Can you help me?	Μπορείτε να με βοηθήσετε; *boreete na me voeetheesete*
Can I help you?	Μπορώ να σας βοηθήσω; *boro na sas voeetheeso*
Can you direct me to ...?	Μπορείτε να με κατευθύνετε προς ... ; *boreete na me kateftheenete pros*

What do you want? Τι θέλετε;

I'd like ...	Θα ήθελα ... *tha eethela*
Could I have ...?	Μπορώ να έχω ... ; *boro na ekho*
We'd like ...	Θα θέλαμε ... *tha thelame*
Give me ...	Δώστε μου ... *THoste moo*
I'm looking for ...	Ψάχνω για ... *psakhno ya*
I need to ...	Χρειάζομαι να... *khreeazome na*
go ...	πάω ... *pao*
find ...	βρω ... *vro*
see ...	δω ... *THo*
speak to ...	μιλήσω με τον/την ... *meeleeso me ton/teen*

– seeghnomee.
– *ne?*
– boro?
– *ne, veveos.*
– efkhareesto.
– *parakalo.*

Other useful words
Άλλες χρήσιμες λέξεις

fortunately	ευτυχώς *efteekhos*
hopefully	ελπίζω να ... *elpeezo na*
of course	βεβαίως *veveos*
perhaps	ίσως *eesos*
unfortunately	δυστυχώς *THeesteekhos*
also	επίσης *epeesees*
and	και *ke*
but	αλλά *ala*
or	ή *ee*

Exclamations Επιφωνήματα

and so on	και λοιπά *ke leepa*
At last!	Επιτέλους! *epeeteloos*
Go on.	Συνεχίστε. *seenekheeste*
Nonsense.	Βλακείες. *vlakee-es*
Really?	Αλήθεια; *aleetheea*
You're joking!	Αστειεύεσαι! *astee-evese*
How are things?	Πώς πάνε τα πράγματα; *pos pane ta praghmata*
great / terrific	θαυμάσια *thavmaseea*
very good	πολύ καλά *polee kala*
fine	μια χαρά *mia khara*
not bad	καλά *kala*
okay	εντάξει *endaksee*
not good	όχι πολύ καλά *okhee polee kala*
pretty bad	μάλλον άσχημα *malon askheema*
terrible	χάλια *khaleea*

Accommodations

If you don't have a place to stay when you arrive in Greece, the tourist police (**tooreesteekee asteenomeea**) or the Greek National Tourist Organisation, EOT (**eleeneekos organeezmos tooreezmoo** or **eot**), will provide you with a list of hotels and telephone numbers. However, they will not book rooms for you. If you would like to make a reservation before you leave, contact the Hellenic Chamber of Hotels in Athens (☏ 01-3310022-6).

The main types of accommodation are:

Ξενοδοχεία *ksenodokheea*

Hotels. Depending on the facilities offered, hotels are classed as deluxe, A´ (**protees kateeghoreeas**), B´ (**THefterees kateeghoreeas**), Γ´ (**treetees**), Δ´ (**tetartees**), and E´ (**pemptees**). Some hotels also have bungalows (**bangalo-oo**). During the summer season (July-August), several hotels rent roof space for sleeping at a nominal price.

Διαμερίσματα *THeeamereezmata*

Furnished self-catering appartments.

Δωμάτια *THomateea*

Furnished rooms, with or without a private bath (**me baneeo/khorees baneeo**). You may be approached by several people offering you THo**mateea**. Haggle for the price, especially during the low season.

Ξενία *kseneea*

Hotels operated by EOT, with strictly controlled standards. They are usually good value.

Παραδοσιακά δωμάτια *paraTHoseeaka THomateea*

Traditional apartments in renovated, traditional old houses. Usually well equipped for self-catering and modernized inside, while retaining some original features. Ask EOT for prices, telephone numbers, and locations.

Ξενώνας νεότητας *ksenonas neoteetas*

Youth hostels. Several operate mainly in Athens and large cities. You can stay for a maximum of three nights, especially during the high season.

Reservations Κρατήσεις

In advance Εμπρός

Can you recommend a hotel in ...?	Μπορείτε να μου συστήσετε ένα ξενοδοχείο στο/στη ...; *boreete na moo seesteesete ena ksenoтноkheeo sto/stee*
Is it near the center of town?	Είναι κοντά στο κέντρο της πόλης; *eene konda sto kendro tees polees*
How much is it per night?	Πόσο κοστίζει τη βραδιά; *poso kosteezee tee vraтнуа*
Is there anything cheaper?	Υπάρχει κάτι φτηνότερο; *eeparkhee katee fteenotero*
Could you reserve me a room there, please?	Μπορείτε να μου κλείσετε ένα δωμάτιο εκεί, παρακαλώ; *boreete na moo kleesete ena тнoмateeo ekee parakalo*
How do I get there?	Πώς πάω εκεί; *pos pao ekee*

At the hotel Στο ξενοδοχείο

Do you have any vacancies?	Έχετε ελεύθερα δωμάτια; *ekhete elefthera тнoмateea*
I'm sorry, we're full.	Λυπάμαι, είμαστε γεμάτοι. *leepame eemaste yematee*
Is there another hotel nearby?	Υπάρχει άλλο ξενοδοχείο εδώ κοντά; *eeparkhee alo ksenoтноkheeo eтнo konda*
I'd like a single/double room.	Θα ήθελα ένα μονό/διπλό δωμάτιο. *tha eethela ena mono/ тнeeplo тнoмateeo*
A room with ...	Ένα δωμάτιο με ... *ena тнoмateeo me*
twin beds	δύο κρεββάτια *тнeeo krevateea*
a double bed	διπλό κρεββάτι *тнeeplo krevatee*
a bath/shower	μπάνιο/ντουζ *baneeo/dooz*

– *ekhete elefthera тнoмateea?*
– *leepame, eemaste yematee.*
– *eeparkhee alo ksenoтноkheeo eтнo konda?*
– *Ne. тнokeemaste to "Ambassador" apenandee.*

Reception Στη ρεσεψιόν

I have a reservation. My name is …	Έχω κλείσει δωμάτιο. Λέγομαι … *ekho kleesee* TH*omateeo. leghome*
We've reserved a double and a single room.	Έχουμε κλείσει ένα διπλό και ένα μονό δωμάτιο. *ekhoome kleesee enah* TH*eeplo ke ena mono* TH*omateeo*
I confirmed my reservation by mail.	Έχω επιβεβαιώσει την κράτησή μου με επιστολή. *ekho epeeveveosee teen krateesee moo me epeestolee*
Could we have adjoining rooms?	Μπορούμε να έχουμε επικοινωνούντα δωμάτια; *boroome na ekhoome epeekeenonoonda* TH*omateea*

Amenities and facilities
Διευκολύνσεις και εξυπηρέτηση

Is there (a) … in the room?	Υπάρχει … στο δωμάτιο; *eeparkhee … sto* TH*omateeo*
air conditioning	κλιματισμός *kleemateezmos*
TV/telephone	τηλεόραση/τηλέφωνο *teeleorasee/teelefono*
Does the hotel have (a) …?	Έχει το ξενοδοχείο …; *ekhee to kseno*TH*okheeo*
fax facilities	υπηρεσία φαξ *eepeereseea "fax"*
laundry service	υπηρεσία πλυντηρίου *eepeereseea pleendeereeoo*
satellite TV	δορυφορική τηλεόραση TH*oreeforeekee teeleorasee*
swimming pool	πισίνα *peeseena*
Could you put … in the room?	Μπορείτε να βάλετε … στο δωμάτιο; *boreete na valete … sto* TH*omateeo*
an extra bed	άλλο ένα κρεββάτι *alo ena krevatee*
a crib [cot]?	ένα παιδικό κρεββάτι *ena pe*TH*eeko krevatee*
Do you have facilities for the disabled?	Έχετε διευκολύνσεις για άτομα με ειδικές ανάγκες; *ekhete* TH*ee-efkoleensees ya atoma me eeTHeekes ananges*
children	παιδιά *peTHya*

How long will you be staying?
Πόσο καιρό θα μείνετε;

We'll be staying ...	Θα μείνουμε ... *tha meenoome*
overnight only	μόνο για ένα βράδυ *mono ya ena vraTHee*
a few days	για λίγες ημέρες *ya leeyes eemeres*
a week (at least)	μια εβδομάδα (τουλάχιστον) *mia evTHomaTHa (toolakheeston)*
I'd like to stay an extra night.	Θα ήθελα να μείνω άλλο ένα βράδυ. *tha eethela na meeno alo ena vraTHee*

> – <u>e</u>kho <u>klee</u>see THo<u>ma</u>teeo. To <u>o</u>noma moo
> <u>ee</u>ne John Newton.
> – A, <u>khe</u>rete <u>kee</u>ree-e Newton. Ya na <u>THoo</u>me?
> <u>Po</u>so tha <u>mee</u>nete?
> – <u>e</u>kho <u>klee</u>see ya <u>THee</u>o <u>vra</u>THya, a<u>la</u> tha
> <u>ee</u>thela na <u>mee</u>no <u>a</u>lo <u>e</u>na <u>vra</u>THee.
> – ne, en<u>dak</u>see. Paraka<u>lo</u> eepo<u>ghra</u>pste e<u>THO</u>.

Μπορώ να δω το διαβατήριό σας, παρακαλώ;	May I see your passport, please?
Παρακαλώ συμπληρώστε αυτό το έντυπο/υπογράψτε εδώ.	Please fill in this form / sign here.
Τι σημαίνει αυτό;	What does this mean?

ΜΕ ΠΡΩΙΝΟ	breakfast included
ΣΕΡΒΙΡΟΝΤΑΙ ΓΕΥΜΑΤΑ	meals available
ΟΝΟΜΑΤΕΠΩΝΥΜΟ/ ΟΝΟΜΑ/ΕΠΩΝΥΜΟ	full name / first name / surname
ΔΙΕΥΘΥΝΣΗ ΚΑΤΟΙΚΙΑΣ/ ΟΔΟΣ/ΑΡΙΘΜΟΣ	home address / street / number
ΥΠΗΚΟΟΤΗΤΑ/ΕΠΑΓΓΕΛΜΑ	nationality / profession
ΗΜΕΡΟΜΗΝΙΑ/ΤΟΠΟΣ ΓΕΝΝΗΣΕΩΣ	date / place of birth
ΑΡΙΘΜΟΣ ΔΙΑΒΑΤΗΡΙΟΥ	passport number
ΑΡΙΘΜΟΣ ΚΥΚΛΟΦΟΡΙΑΣ	car registration number
ΤΟΠΟΣ/ΗΜΕΡΟΜΗΝΙΑ	place / date
ΥΠΟΓΡΑΦΗ	signature

Price Τιμή

How much is it ...?	Πόσο κάνει ...; *poso kanee*
per night/week	τη βραδιά/την εβδομάδα *tee vraTHya/teen evTHomaTHa*
for bed and breakfast	για διαμονή και πρωινό *ya THeeamonee ke proeeno*
excluding meals	χωρίς γεύματα *khorees yevmata*
for full board [American Plan (A.P.)]	με πλήρη διατροφή *me pleeree THeeatrofee*
for half board [Modified American Plan (M.A.P.)]	με ημιδιατροφή *me eemeeTHeeatrofee*
Does the price include ...?	Η τιμή συμπεριλαμβάνει ...; *ee teemee seembereelamvanee*
breakfast	πρωινό *proeeno*
service	το σέρβις *to serves*
sales tax [VAT]	ΦΠΑ *fee-pee-a*
Do I have to pay a deposit?	Πρέπει να πληρώσω προκαταβολή; *prepee na pleeroso prokatavolee*
Is there a reduction for children?	Υπάρχει έκπτωση για τα παιδιά; *eeparkhee ekptosee ya ta peTHya*

Decision Απόφαση

May I see the room?	Μπορώ να δω το δωμάτιο; *boro na THo to THomateeo*
That's fine. I'll take it.	Εντάξει. Θα το πάρω. *endaksee. tha to paro*
It's too ...	Είναι πολύ ... *eene polee*
dark/small	σκοτεινό/μικρό *skoteeno/meekro*
noisy	θορυβώδες *thoreevoTHes*
Do you have anything ...?	Έχετε τίποτα ... ; *ekhete teepota*
bigger/cheaper	μεγαλύτερο/φτηνότερο *meghaleetero/fteenotero*
quieter/warmer	πιό ήσυχο/πιό ζεστό *peeo eeseekho/peeo zesto*
No, I won't take it.	Όχι, δεν θα το πάρω. *okhee, THen tha to paro*

Problems Προβλήματα

The ... doesn't work.	... δεν δουλεύει. THen THoo*levee*
air conditioning	Ο κλιματισμός o kleematee*zmos*
fan	Ο ανεμιστήρας o anemee*steeras*
light	Το φως to fos
radio	Το ραδιόφωνο to raTHee*ofono*
television	Η τηλεόραση ee teele*orasee*
I can't turn the heat [heating] on/off.	Δεν μπορώ να ανάψω/σβήσω τη θέρμανση. THen boro na a*napso*/ sv*eeso* tee *thermansee*
There is no hot water/ toilet paper.	Δεν υπάρχει ζεστό νερό/χαρτί υγείας. THen eepar*khee ze*sto n*ero*/ khar*tee* eey*eeas*
The faucet [tap] is dripping.	Η βρύση στάζει. ee *vreesee* *stazee*
The sink/toilet is blocked.	Έχει βουλώσει ο νιπτήρας/η τουαλέττα. *ekhee* voo*losee* o neep*teeras*/ee tooa*leta*
The window/door is jammed.	Έχει σφηνώσει το παράθυρο/η πόρτα. *ekhee* sfeen*osee* to par*atheero*/ee *porta*
My room has not been made up.	Δεν έχουν καθαρίσει το δωμάτιο μου. THen *ekhoon* kath*areesee* to THom*ateeo* moo
The ... is/are broken.	... έχει/έχουν σπάσει. *ekhee*/*ekhoon* *spasee*
blinds/shutter	Οι περσίδες/Το παραθυρόφυλλο ee per*seeTHes*/to paratheer*ofeelo*
lock	Η κλειδαριά ee kleeTH*arya*

Action Ενέργεια

Could you have that seen to?	Μπορείτε να μας το φτιάξετε; bor*eete* na mas to ftee*aksete*
I'd like to move to another room.	Θα ήθελα να μετακομίσω σε άλλο δωμάτιο. tha *eethela* na metako*meeso* se *alo* THom*ateeo*
I'd like to speak to the manager.	Θα ήθελα να μιλήσω στο διευθυντή. tha *eethela* na meel*eeso* sto THee-eftheen*dee*

Requirements Ανάγκες

In Greece the electricity supply is 220 V, with standard continental 2-pin or 3-pin plugs. A multi-adapter is recommended.

About the hotel Για το ξενοδοχείο

Where's the ...?	Πού είναι ...; _poo eene_
bar	το μπαρ _to bar_
bathroom [toilet]	η τουαλέττα _ee tooaleta_
dining room	η τραπεζαρία _ee trapezareea_
elevator [lift]	το ασανσέρ _to asanser_
parking lot [car park]	το πάρκινγκ _to "parking"_
shower	το ντουζ _to dooz_
swimming pool	η πισίνα _ee peeseena_
Does the hotel have a garage?	Το ξενοδοχείο έχει γκαράζ; _to ksenoᴛʜokheeo ekhee garaz_
Can I use this adapter here?	Μπορώ να χρησιμοποιήσω αυτόν τον προσαρμοστή εδώ; _boro na khreeseemopee-eeso afton ton prosarmostee eᴛʜo_
What time is breakfast served?	Τι ώρα σερβίρεται το πρωινό; _tee ora serveerete to proeeno_
Is there room service?	Υπάρχει υπηρεσία δωματίου; _eeparkhee eepeereseea domateeoo_

ΠΡΙΖΑ ΞΥΡΙΣΜΑΤΟΣ	razors [shavers] only
ΕΞΟΔΟΣ ΚΙΝΔΥΝΟΥ	emergency exit
ΜΗΝ ΕΝΟΧΛΕΙΤΕ	do not disturb
ΑΠΑΓΟΡΕΥΕΤΑΙ ΤΟ ΦΑΓΗΤΟ ΣΤΑ ΔΩΜΑΤΙΑ	no food in the room
ΠΑΡΤΕ ... ΓΙΑ ΕΞΩΤΕΡΙΚΗ ΓΡΑΜΜΗ	dial ... for an outside line
ΠΑΡΤΕ ... ΓΙΑ ΤΗΝ ΡΕΣΕΨΙΟΝ	dial ... for reception

Personal needs Προσωπικές ανάγκες

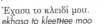

The key to room ..., please.	Το κλειδί για το δωμάτιο ..., παρακαλώ *to kleeTHee ya to THomateeo parakalo*
I've lost my key.	Έχασα το κλειδί μου. *ekhasa to kleeTHee moo*
I've locked myself out of my room.	Κλειδώθηκα έξω από το δωμάτιό μου. *kleeTHotheeka ekso apo to THomateeo moo*
Could you wake me at ...?	Μπορείτε να με ξυπνήσετε στις ...; *boreete na me kseepneesete stees*
I'd like breakfast in my room.	Θα ήθελα πρωινό στο δωμάτιο μου. *tha eethela proeeno sto THomateeo moo*
Can I leave this in the safe?	Μπορώ να αφήσω αυτό στη θυρίδα; *boro na afeeso afto stee theereeTHa*
Could I have my things from the safe?	Μπορώ να έχω τα πράγματά μου από τη θυρίδα; *boro na ekho ta praghmata moo apo tee theereeTHa*
Where can I find a ...?	Πού μπορώ να βρω ...; *poo boro na vro*
maid	μια καμαριέρα *mia kamary-era*
porter	έναν πορτιέρη *enan portee-eree*
May I have a/some ...?	Μπορώ να έχω ...; *boro na ekho*
bath towel	μια πετσέτα του μπάνιου *mia petseta too baneeoo*
blanket	μια κουβέρτα *mia kooverta*
hangers	λίγες κρεμάστρες *leeyes kremastres*
pillow	ένα μαξιλάρι *ena makseelaree*
soap	σαπούνι *sapoonee*
Is there any mail for me?	Υπάρχει αλληλογραφία/γράμμα για μένα; *eeparkhee aleeloghrafeea/ghrama ya mena*
Are there any messages for me?	Υπάρχει κανένα μήνυμα για μένα; *eeparkhee kanena meeneema ya mena*

BREAKFAST ➤ 43; CHANGING MONEY ➤ 138

Renting Ενοικιάζοντας

We've reserved an apartment in the name of ...	Έχουμε κλείσει ένα διαμέρισμα στο όνομα ... *ekhoome kleesee ena THeeameree'ma sto onoma*
Where do we pick up the keys?	Από πού παίρνουμε τα κλειδιά; *apo poo pernoome ta kleeTHya*
Where is the...?	Πού είναι ...; *poo eene*
electricity meter	το ρολόι του ηλεκτρικού ρεύματος *to roloee too eelektreekoo revmatos*
fuse box	το κουτί με τις ασφάλειες *to kootee me tees asfalee-es*
valve [stopcock]	κεντρικός διακόπτης νερού *kendreekos THeeakoptees neroo*
water heater	θερμοσίφωνας *thermoseefonas*
Are there any spare ...?	Υπάρχουν επιπλέον ...; *eeparkhoon epeepleon*
fuses	ασφάλειες *asfalee-es*
sheets	σεντόνια *sendoneea*
Which day does the maid come?	Ποιά ημέρα έρχεται η καθαρίστρια; *pia eemera erkhete ee kathareestreea*
When do I put out the trash [rubbish]?	πότε να βγάλω έξω τα σκουπίδια; *pote na vghalo ekso ta skoopeeTHya*

Problems Προβλήματα

Where can I contact you?	Πώς μπορούμε να επικοινωνήσουμε; *pos boroome na epeekeenoneesoome*
How does the stove [cooker]/ water heater work?	Πώς δουλεύει η κουζίνα/ο θερμοσίφωνας; *pos THoolevee ee koozeena/ o thermoseefonas*
The ... is/are dirty.	Ο/η/το ... είναι βρώμικ-ος/-η/-ο. *o/ee/to ... eene vromeek-os/-ee/-o*
The ... has broken down.	Ο/η/το ... χάλασε. *o/ee/to ... khalase*
We accidentally broke/lost ...	Σπάσαμε/χάσαμε κατά λάθος τον/την/το ... *spasame/khasame kata lathos ton/teen/to*
That was already damaged when we arrived.	Αυτό ήταν ήδη χαλασμένο όταν φτάσαμε. *afto eetan eeTHee khalazmeno otan ftasame*

HOUSEHOLD ARTICLES ➤ 148

Useful terms Χρήσιμοι όροι

boiler	θερμοσίφωνας *thermoseefonas*
crockery	πιατικά *piateeka*
cutlery	μαχαιροπήρουνα *makheropeeroona*
freezer	κατάψυξη *katapseeksee*
frying pan	τηγάνι *teeghanee*
lamp	λάμπα *lamba*
refrigerator	ψυγείο *pseeyeeo*
saucepan	κατσαρόλα *katsarola*
stove [cooker]	κουζίνα *koozeena*
toilet paper	χαρτί υγείας *khartee eeyeeas*
washing machine	πλυντήριο *pleendeereeo*

Room Δωμάτιο

balcony	μπαλκόνι *balkonee*
bathroom	μπάνιο *baneeo*
bedroom	υπνοδωμάτιο *eepnoтнomateeo*
dining room	τραπεζαρία *trapezareea*
kitchen	κουζίνα *koozeena*
living room	σαλόνι *salonee*
toilet	τουαλέττα *tooaleta*

Youth hostel Ξενώνας νεότητας

Is there a youth hostel near here?	Υπάρχει ξενώνας νεότητας εδώ κοντά; *eeparkhee ksenonas neoteetas eтнo konda*
Do you have any places left for tonight?	Έχετε θέση για απόψε; *ekhete thesee ya apopse*
Do you rent out bedding?	Νοικιάζετε σεντόνια; *neekeeazete sendoneea*
What time are the doors locked?	Τί ώρα κλειδώνετε; *tee ora kleeтнonete*
I have an International Student Card.	Έχω διεθνή φοιτητική κάρτα. *ekho тнee-ethnee feeteeteekee karta*

REQUIREMENTS ➤ 26; CAMPING ➤ 30

Camping
Κατασκήνωση/κάμπινγκ

Camping is allowed in designated areas only, and strictly forbidden elsewhere. EOT can provide a list of campsites and facilities. Most campsites have showers, a laundry area, electricity, a bar with snacks and drinks, and an eating area. Arrive early during July and August if you want to find a shady spot to camp.

Reservations Κρατήσεις

Is there a campsite near here?	Υπάρχει χώρος κάμπινγκ εδώ κοντά; eep_arkhee _khoros "camping" eTHo kond_a
What is the charge ...?	Ποιό είναι το κόστος για ...; pee_o _eene to _kostos ya
per day/week	την ημέρα/την εβδομάδα teen eem_era/teen evTHom_aTHa
for a tent/car	μια σκηνή/ένα αυτοκίνητο mia skee_nee/_ena afto_keeneeto
for a trailer [caravan]	ένα τροχόσπιτο _ena trok_hospeeto

Facilities Διευκολύνσεις

Are there cooking facilities on site?	Υπάρχει ειδικός χώρος για μαγείρεμα; eep_arkhee eeTH_eekos _khoros ya may_eerema
Are there any electrical outlets [power points]?	Υπάρχουν πρίζες; eep_arkhoon _preezes
Where is/are the ...?	Πού είναι ...; poo _eene
drinking water	το πόσιμο νερό to p_oseemo ner_o
trashcans [dustbins]	οι τενεκέδες ee tene_keTHes
laundry facilities	ο χώρος για πλύσιμο o _khoros ya pl_eeseemo
showers	τα ντουζ ta dooz
Where can I get some butane gas?	Πού μπορώ να βρω υγραέριο; _poo bor_o na vro eeghra_ereeo

ΑΠΑΓΟΡΕΥΕΤΑΙ Η ΚΑΤΑΣΚΗΝΩΣΗ	no camping
ΠΟΣΙΜΟ ΝΕΡΟ	drinking water
ΜΗΝ ΑΝΑΒΕΤΕ ΦΩΤΙΑ	no fires/barbeques

Complaints Παράπονα

It's too sunny/shady/ crowded here.	Έχει πολύ ήλιο/σκιά/ κόσμο εδώ. *ekhee polee eeleeo/skeea/kozmo* εΤΗΟ
The ground's too hard/uneven.	Το έδαφος είναι πολύ σκληρό/ ανώμαλο. *to* εΤΗafos *eene polee skleero/anomalo*
Do you have a more level spot?	Έχετε μια πιο ομαλή θέση; *ekhete mia peeo omalee thesee*
You can't camp here.	Δεν μπορείτε να κατασκηνώσετε εδώ. ΤΗen *boreete na kataskeenosete* εΤΗΟ

Camping equipment Εξοπλισμός κάμπινγκ

butane gas	το υγραέριο *to eeghraereeo*
campbed	το κρεββάτι εκστρατείας *to krevatee ekstrateeas*
charcoal	το κάρβουνο *to karvoono*
cooler [coolbox]	το φορητό ψυγείο *to foreeto pseeyeeo*
compass	η πυξίδα *ee peekseeΤΗa*
flashlight [torch]	ο φακός *o fakos*
groundcloth [groundsheet]	ο μουσαμάς για το έδαφος *o moosamas ya to* εΤΗafos
guy rope	το σκοινί της τέντας *to skeenee tees tendas*
hammer	το σφυρί *to sfeeree*
kerosene stove	το καμινέτο *to kameeneto*
knapsack	ο σάκκος *o sakos*
mallet	ο κόπανος *o kopanos*
matches	τα σπίρτα *ta speerta*
(air) mattress	το στρώμα (αέρος) *to stroma (aeros)*
paraffin	το παραφινέλαιο *to parafeeneleo*
sleeping bag	ο υπνόσακκος *o eepnosakos*
tent	η σκηνή *ee skeenee*
tent pegs	το παλούκι *to palookee*
tent pole	ο στύλος της σκηνής *o steelos tees skeenees*

Checking out Αναχώρηση

What time do we need to vacate the room?
Τι ώρα πρέπει να αδειάσουμε το δωμάτιο;
tee ora prepee na aTHyasoome to THomateeo

Could we leave our baggage here until ...?
Μπορούμε να αφήσουμε τα πράγματά μας εδώ ως τις ...;
boroome na afeesoome ta praghmata mas eTHo os tees ...

I'm leaving now.
Φεύγω τώρα.
fevgho tora

Could you order me a taxi, please?
Μπορείτε να μου καλέσετε ένα ταξί;
boreete na moo kalesete ena taksee

It's been a very enjoyable stay.
Η διαμονή μου ήταν πολύ ευχάριστη.
ee THeeamonee moo eetan polee efkhareestee

Paying Πληρωμή

Tipping depends largely on what class hotel you are staying at – the higher the class, the more generous the tip. As a guideline, €1 per suitcase to the porter and €1–1.50 per night to the chamber maid (more in a deluxe hotel) are recommended.

May I have my bill, please?
Μπορώ να έχω το λογαριασμό, παρακαλώ;
boro na ekho to logharyazmo parakalo

How much is my telephone bill?
Πόσο είναι ο λογαριασμός τηλεφώνου;
poso eene o logharyazmos teelefonoo

I think there's a mistake in this bill.
Νομίζω ότι έγινε ένα λάθος στο λογαριασμό.
nomeezo otee eyeene ena lathos sto logharyazmo

I've made ... telephone calls.
Έχω κάνει ... τηλεφωνήματα.
ekho kanee ... teelefoneemata

I've taken ... from the mini-bar.
Έχω πάρει ... από το μίνι-μπαρ.
ekho paree ... apo to "mini-bar"

Can I have an itemized bill?
Μπορώ να έχω έναν αναλυτικό λογαριασμό;
boro na ekho enan analeeteeko logharyazmo

Could I have a receipt, please?
Μπορώ να έχω μια απόδειξη, παρακαλώ;
boro na ekho mia apoTHeeksee parakalo

Eating Out

Restaurants Εστιατόρια

Eating out or at home is a social occasion in Greece. Children get used to eating out in restaurants from a very young age, and you will see them with their families even late at night. Restaurants that display tourist menus, or fixed price menus, will usually provide good value meals. But if you wish to sample truly Greek food you should try to seek out more ethnic restaurants. Here you can often select your meal, particularly fish, from a display in the kitchen and even talk to the chef about how you want it cooked.

The following are the most common types of restaurant:

Ταβέρνα *taverna*
The taverna is the most common eating place you will find. Prices are reasonable, and you will find a good selection of **mezeTHes** (appetizers) and **mayeerefta** (baked or stewed snacks), as well as **tees oras** (meat and fish).

Εστιατόριο *esteeatoreeo*
A more general term for restaurant. These tend to be more expensive than tavernas. Most offer a selection of Greek and foreign food.

Ψαροταβέρνα *psarotaverna*
A fish taverna, usually found on the islands and in coastal areas. These specialize in fish (**psaree**) and seafood (**thalaseena**). If you can't decide what to eat, ask to see the fish in the kitchen (sometimes still alive!). Point to the one you want – and you will soon be enjoying it cooked on your plate!

Ψησταριά *pseestareea*

Like a taverna but specializes in grilled meat (always cooked **sta karvoona**, charcoal grilled), which gives it a very distinctive flavor. Apart from meat, the usual choice of salads and **meze**THes can be found, but no **mayeerefta** or a very limited choice.

Μεζεδοπωλείο *meze*THo*poleeo*

Specializes in **meze**THes, which can be incredibly substantial and filling. These are served with wine, beer, or **oozo** (ouzo, an anise-flavored aperitif).

Ουζερί *oozeree*

A traditional establishment, nowadays popular with young people, where you can enjoy an ouzo with a few **meze**THes – traditionally, **khtapo**THee (octopus), **elee-es** (olives), **antzooyes** (anchovies), and **feta** (feta cheese).

Σουβλατζίδικο *soovlatzee*THeeko

The Greek answer to fast food, these shops, often mere stalls, serve grilled skewered meat (**soovlakee**) or **yeeros** (gyros) in pita bread (**peeta**) with tomatoes, onions, and **tzatzeekee** (tzatziki).

Those who prefer something more familiar will feel at home in a McDonald's or Wendy's, or their Greek equivalents, Goodies and Hambo.

Meal times Τα φαγητά

Breakfast Πρωινό *proeeno*

Greeks rarely eat breakfast. They usually have a strong sweet cup of coffee (**varee ghleeko**) in the morning, followed by another one at work between 10 and 11 a.m., maybe with a pastry. At summer resorts, however, you will typically have a wider choice of English or continental breakfast ➤ 43.

Lunch μεσημεριανό *meseemeryano*

The main meal, although because of the summer heat some Greeks eat lighter at lunchtime and have their main meal in the evening. Lunch is usually eaten from 2 to 3 p.m., but most restaurants will serve it until 4 p.m.

Dinner βραδινό *vra*THeeno

This is often eaten late – normally at 9 or 10 p.m., and it is not unusual to find restaurants serving food until midnight or later. Snacks can be bought at **soovlatzee**THeeka (souvlaki stalls) or **snak bar** (snack bars) until the early hours of the morning.

Greek cuisine η Ελληνική κουζίνα

Greek cuisine has a tradition almost as long as Greek history itself. The emphasis is on fresh meat, fish, vegetables, and fruit, flavored with a delicate combination of herbs and spices found in abundance in the Greek mountains. Some of the food you can taste today in the Greek islands probably does not differ much from what the ancient Greeks enjoyed 2,500 years ago, albeit with Turkish and Italian influences .

A table for ..., please.	Ένα τραπέζι για ..., παρακαλώ. *ena trapezee ya ..., parakalo*
1/2/3/4	έναν (μια)/δύο/τρεις/τέσσερις *enan/тнeeo/trees/teserees*
Thank you.	Ευχαριστώ. *efkhareesto*
I'd like to pay.	Θα ήθελα να πληρώσω. *tha eethela na pleeroso*

Finding a place to eat
Βρίσκοντας ένα μέρος για φαγητό

Can you recommend a good restaurant?	Μπορείτε να μας συστήσετε ένα καλό εστιατόριο; *boreete na mas seesteesete ena kalo esteeatoreeo*
Is there a(n) ... near here?	Υπάρχει ... εδώ κοντά; *eeparkhee...eтнo konda*
traditional local restaurant	ένα τοπικό παραδοσιακό εστιατόριο *ena topeeko paraтнoseeako esteeatoreeo*
fish restaurant	μια ψαροταβέρνα *mia psarotaverna*
Greek restaurant	ένα ελληνικό εστιατόριο *ena eleeneeko esteeatoreeo*
Italian restaurant	ένα ιταλικό εστιατόριο *ena eetaleeko esteeatoreeo*
inexpensive restaurant	ένα φτηνό εστιατόριο *ena fteeno esteeatoreeo*
Where can I find a(n) ...?	Πού μπορώ να βρω ...; *poo boro na vro*
souvlaki / gyros stand	ένα σουβλατζίδικο *ena soovlatzeeтнeeko*
café	μια καφετέρια *mia kafeteria*
fast food restaurant	ένα φαστ φουντ *ena "fast food"*
pizzeria	πιτσαρία *peetsareea*
pastry shop	ένα ζαχαροπλαστείο *ena zakharoplasteeo*

DIRECTIONS ➤ 94

Reservations Κρατήσεις

I'd like to reserve a table for 2 this evening at ...	Θα ήθελα να κλείσω ένα τραπέζι για δύο απόψε στις ... *tha eethela na kleeso ena trapezee ya THeeo apopse stees*
We'll come at 11:00.	Θα έρθουμε στις έντεκα. *tha erthoome stees endeka*
A table for 2, please.	Ένα τραπέζι για δύο, παρακαλώ. *ena trapezee ya THeeo, parakalo*
We have a reservation.	Έχουμε κλείσει τραπέζι. *ekhoome kleesee trapezee*

Τό όνομα, παρακαλώ;	What's the name, please?
Λυπάμαι, είμαστε γεμάτοι.	I'm sorry. We're very busy / full up.
Θα έχουμε ένα ελεύθερο τραπέζι σε ... λεπτά.	We'll have a free table in ... minutes.
Ελάτε σε ... λεπτά.	You'll have to come back in ... minutes.

Where to sit Πού να καθήσετε

Could we sit ...?	Μπορούμε να καθήσουμε ...; *boroome na katheesoome*
over there / outside	εκεί/έξω *ekee/ekso*
in a non-smoking area	σε μια περιοχή για μη καπνίζοντες *se mia pereeokhee ya mee kapneezondes*
by the window	κοντά στο παράθυρο *konda sto paratheero*
Smoking or non-smoking?	Καπνίζοντες ή μη καπνίζοντες; *kapneezondes ee mee kapneezondes*

- tha *eethela* na *klee*so ena trapezee ya a*po*pse.
- *ya posa atoma?*
- *ya tesera.*
- *tee ora tha erthete?*
- tha *erthoome* stees okh*to*.
- *ke to onoma, parakalo?*
- Smith.
- *endaksee*. Tha sas *THoome* stees okh*to*.

Ordering Παραγγέλνοντας

Waiter! / Waitress!	Γκαρσόν!/Δεσποινίς! *garson/THespeenees*
May I see the wine list, please?	Μπορώ να δω τον κατάλογο κρασιών, παρακαλώ; *boro na THo ton katalogho kraseeon, parakalo*
Do you have a set menu?	Υπάρχει μενού α λα κάρτ; *eeparkhee menoo a la kart*
Can you recommend some typical local dishes?	Μπορείτε να μας συστήσετε τυπικά παραδοσιακά πιάτα; *boreete na mas seesteesete teepeeka paraTHoseeaka piata*
Could you tell me what ... is?	Μπορείτε να μου πείτε τι είναι το ...; *boreete na moo peete tee eene to*
What's in it?	Τι έχει μέσα; *tee ekhee mesa*
What kind of ... do you have?	Τι είδους ... έχετε; *tee eeTHoos ... ekhete*
I'll have ...	Θα πάρω ... *tha paro*
a bottle / glass / carafe of ...	ένα μπουκάλι/ένα ποτήρι/μια καράφα ... *ena bookalee/ena poteeree/ mia karafa*

Είσαστε έτοιμοι να παραγγείλετε;	Are you ready to order?
Τι θα πάρετε;	What would you like?
Σας συστήνω ...	I recommend ...
Δεν έχουμε ...	We don't have ...
Θα πάρει ... λεπτά.	That will take ... minutes.
Καλή όρεξη.	Enjoy your meal.

- *eeste eteemee na parangeelete?*
- *boreete na seesteesete katee teepeeka eeleeneeko?*
- *ne. sas seesteeno* ...
- *endaksee, tha paro afto ke mia salata, parakalo.*
- *veveos. Ke tee tha thelate na pee-eete?*
- *mia karafa kokeeno krasee.*

DRINKS ➤ 50; MENU READER ➤ 52

Accompaniments Συνοδεία φαγητού

Could I have ... without ...?	Μπορώ να έχω ... χωρίς ...; *boro na ekho ... khorees*
Could I have a salad instead of vegetables, please?	Μπορώ να πάρω σαλάτα αντί λαχανικά, παρακαλώ; *boro na paro salata andee lakhaneeka, parakalo*
Does the meal come with vegetables/potatoes?	Το φαγητό σερβίρεται με λαχανικά/πατάτες; *to fayeeto serveerete me lakhaneeka/patates*
Do you have any sauces?	Έχετε σάλτσες; *ekhete saltses*
Would you like ... with that?	Θέλετε ... με αυτό; *thelete ... me afto*
vegetables/a salad	λαχανικά/σαλάτα *lakhaneeka/salata*
potatoes/fries	πατάτες/πατάτες τηγανητές *patates/patates teeghaneetes*
sauce	σάλτσα *saltsa*
ice	πάγο *pagho*
May I have some ...?	Μπορώ να έχω λίγο ...; *boro na ekho leegho*
bread	ψωμί *psomee*
butter	βούτυρο *vooteero*
lemon	λεμόνι *lemonee*
mustard	μουστάρδα *moostarтнa*
pepper	πιπέρι *peeperee*
salt	αλάτι *alatee*
seasoning	αλατοπίπερο *alatopeepero*
sugar	ζάχαρη *zakharee*
artificial sweetener	ζακχαρίνη *zak-khareenee*
vinaigrette [French dressing]	λαδόξιδο *laтнokseeтнo*
olive oil	ελαιόλαδο *eleolaтнo*

General questions Γενικές ερωτήσεις

Could I / we have a(n) (clean) ..., please?	Μπορώ να έχω/μπορούμε να έχουμε ένα/μια (καθαρό/καθαρή) ... παρακαλώ; *boro na ekho/boroome na ekhoome ena/mia (katharo/ katharee) ... parakalo*
ashtray	σταχτοδοχείο *stakhtoTHokheeo*
cup / glass	φλυτζάνι/ποτήρι *fleetzanee/poteeree*
fork / knife	πηρούνι/μαχαίρι *peeroonee/makheree*
napkin [serviette]	πετσέτα *petseta*
plate / spoon	πιάτο/ένα κουτάλι *piato/kootalee*
I'd like some more ..., please.	Θα ήθελα λίγο ακόμη ..., παρακαλώ. *tha eethela leegho akomee ..., parakalo*
Nothing more, thanks.	Τίποτε άλλο, ευχαριστώ. *teepote alo, efkhareesto*

Special requirements Ειδικές ανάγκες

I mustn't eat food containing ...	Δεν πρέπει να φάω φαγητό που περιέχει ... *THen prepee na fao fayeeto poo peree-ekhee*
flour / fat	αλεύρι/λίπος *alevree/leepos*
salt / sugar	αλάτι/ζάχαρη *alatee/zakharee*
Do you have meals for diabetics?	Έχετε φαγητά/ποτά για διαβητικούς; *ekhete fayeeta ya THeeaveeteekoos*
Do you have vegetarian meals?	Έχετε φαγητά για χορτοφάγους; *ekhete fayeeta ya khortofaghoos*

For the children Για τα παιδιά

Could we have a child's seat, please?	Μπορούμε να έχουμε ένα παιδικό κάθισμα; *boroome na ekhoome ena peTHeeko katheezma*
Where can I feed / change the baby?	Πού μπορώ να ταΐσω/αλλάξω το μωρό; *poo boro na taeeso/alakso to moro*

CHILDREN ➤ 113

Café/Fast food
Καφετέρια/Φαστ φουντ

Something to drink Κάτι να πιείτε

I'd like ...	Θα ήθελα ... *tha eethela ...*
beer	μια μπύρα *mia beera*
(hot) chocolate	μια ζεστή σοκολάτα *mia zestee sokolata*
coffee/tea	ένα καφέ/ένα τσάι *ena kafe/ena tsaee*
black/with milk	σκέτο/με γάλα *sketo/me ghala*
fruit juice	ένα χυμό φρούτων *ena kheemo frooton*
mineral water	ένα εμφιαλωμένο νερό *ena emfeealomeno nero*
red/white wine	άσπρο/κόκκινο κρασί *aspro/ kokeeno krasee*

And to eat Και να φάτε

A piece of ..., please.	Ένα κομμάτι ..., παρακαλώ. *ena komatee ..., parakalo*
I'd like two of those.	Θα ήθελα δύο από αυτά. *tha eethela THeeo apo afta*
burger/cake	το χάμπουργκερ/το κέηκ *to khamboorger/to "cake"*
fries/omelet	οι τηγανητές πατάτες/η ομελέττα *ee teeghaneetes patates/ee omeleta*
sandwich/sausage	το σάντουιτς/το λουκάνικο *to "sandwich"/to lookaneeko*
A ... ice cream, please.	Ένα παγωτό ..., παρακαλώ. *ena paghoto ..., parakalo*
vanilla/chocolate	βανίλλια/σοκολάτα *vaneeleea/sokolata*
A ... portion, please.	Μια ... μερίδα, παρακαλώ. *mia ... mereeTHa, parakalo*
small/medium/large	μικρή/κανονική/μεγάλη *meekree/kanoneekee/meghalee*
It's to go [take away].	Είναι για να το πάρω (σπίτι). *eene ya na to paro (speetee)*

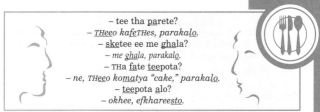

- tee tha _parete_?
- _THee_o kaf_eTH_es, paraka_lo_.
- _ske_tee ee me g_ha_la?
- _me g_hala, paraka_lo_.
- _THa_ _fate_ _tee_pota?
- ne, _THee_o kom_a_tya "cake," paraka_lo_.
- _tee_pota a_lo_?
- _o_khee, efkhar_ee_sto.

Complaints Παράπονα

I have no knife / fork / spoon.	Δεν έχω μαχαίρι/πηρούνι/κουτάλι. _THen _ekho mak_her_ee/ peer_oo_nee/koo_ta_lee
There must be some mistake.	Πρέπει να έγινε κάποιο λάθος. _prepee na _eyeene kap_ee_o _la_thos
That's not what I ordered.	Δεν παρήγγειλα αυτό. _THen par_een_geela af_to
I asked for ...	Ζήτησα ... _zee_teesa
The meat is ...	Το κρέας είναι ... to _kreas _eene ...
overdone	πολύ ψημένο _polee psee_meno
underdone	όχι καλά ψημένο _okhee ka_la psee_meno
too tough	πολύ σκληρό _polee skle_ero
This is too ...	Αυτό είναι πολύ ... af_to _eene polee ...
bitter / sour / salty	πικρό/ξυνό/αλμυρό peek_ro_/ksee_no_/al_meero
The food is cold.	Το φαγητό είναι κρύο. to fayee_to _eene _kreo
This isn't fresh.	Αυτό δεν είναι φρέσκο. af_to _THen _eene _fresko
How much longer will our food be?	Πόση ώρα ακόμη θα κάνει το φαγητό; _posee ora ak_omee tha _kanee to fayee_to
Have you forgotten our drinks?	Ξεχάσατε τα ποτά μας; kse_kha_sate ta po_ta mas
This isn't clean.	Αυτό δεν είναι καθαρό. af_to _THen _eene katha_ro
I'd like to speak to the head waiter / manager.	Θα ήθελα να μιλήσω στον αρχισερβιτόρο/μάνατζερ. tha _eethela na mee_leeso ston ar_kheeserveet_oro/ "manager"

Paying Πληρωμή

In Greek restaurants the service charge is included in the price. However, it is still customary to leave a little extra if you are satisfied with the service.

I'd like to pay.	Θα ήθελα να πληρώσω. *tha eethela na pleeroso*
We'd like to pay separately.	Θα πληρώσουμε ξεχωριστά. *tha pleerosoome ksekhoreesta*
It's all together.	Όλοι μαζί. *olee mazee*
I think there's a mistake in this bill.	Νομίζω ότι έχει γίνει λάθος στο λογαριασμό. *nomeezo otee ekhee yeenee lathos sto logharyazmo*
What is this amount for?	Τι είναι αυτό το ποσό; *tee eene afto to poso*
I didn't have that. I had ...	Δεν πήρα αυτό. Πήρα ... *тнen peera afto. peera*
Is service included?	Συμπεριλαμβάνεται και η υπηρεσία; *seembereelamvanete ke ee eepeereseea*
Can I pay with this credit card?	Μπορώ να πληρώσω με αυτήν την πιστωτική κάρτα; *boro na pleeroso me afteen teen peestoteekee karta*
I've forgotten my wallet.	Ξέχασα το πορτοφόλι μου. *ksekhasa to portofolee moo*
I don't have enough money.	Δεν έχω αρκετά χρήματα. *тнen ekho arketa khreemata*
Could I have a tax [VAT] receipt, please?	Μπορώ να έχω απόδειξη με ΦΠΑ, παρακαλώ; *boro na ekho apoтнeeksee me fee-pee-a, parakalo*
That was a delicious meal.	Ήταν ένα πολύ νόστιμο γεύμα. *eetan ena polee nosteemo yevma*

- garson! to logharyazmo, parakalo.
- *veveos. oreeste.*
- seembereelamvanete ee eepeereseea?
- *ne.*
- boro na pleeroso me afteen teen peestoteekee karta?
- *veveos.*
- efkhareesto. eetan ena polee nosteemo yevma.

Course by course Κατά πιάτο

Breakfast Πρωινό

Breakfast is not an important meal in Greece (➤ 34). Hotels that cater for tourists will probably offer a contintental style breakfast, and maybe also eggs (➤ 44).

I'd like …	Θα ήθελα … *tha eethela*
fruit juice	ένα χυμό φρούτων *ena kheemo frooton*
jam	μαρμελάδα *marmelaтнa*
yogurt (with honey)	γιαούρτι (με μέλι) *yaoortee (me melee)*
bread	ψωμί *psomee*
butter	βούτυρο *vooteero*
milk	γάλα *ghala*
rolls	ψωμάκια *psomakeea*

Appetizers [Starters] Ορεκτικά

ελιές (γεμιστές)	*elee-es (yemeestes)*	(stuffed) olives
κρύο κρέας	*kreeo kreas*	cold meat
πατέ	*pate*	pâté
πεπόνι	*peponee*	melon
ποικιλία ορεκτικών	*peekeeleea orekteekon*	assorted appetizers
ρέγγα (καπνιστή)	*renga (kapneestee)*	(smoked) herring
καλαμαράκια	*kalamarakeea*	baby squid fried in batter
μαρίδα τηγανητή	*mareeтнa teeghaneetee*	whitebait fried in batter

Ντολμαδάκια *dolmaтнakeea*
Vine leaves stuffed with rice and onions and flavored with dill.

Ταραμοσαλάτα *taramosalata*
Dip made from fish roe blended with bread, olive oil, lemons, and onions.

Τζατζίκι *tzatzeekee*
A dip of yogurt, garlic, cucumber and olive oil.

Σπανακόπιττα *spanakopeeta*
Filo pastry pies filled with spinach, feta cheese, and eggs.

Κεφτεδάκια *kefteтнakeea*
Fried mincemeat balls containing onions, bread crumbs, and herbs.

Soups Σούπες

κοτόσουπα	*kotosoopa*	clear chicken soup
ρεβύθια	*reveetheea*	chickpea soup
σούπα αυγολέμονο	*soopa avgholemono*	soup with rice, eggs, and lemon juice
πατσάς	*patsas*	tripe soup
σούπα φακές	*soopa fakes*	lentil soup
τοματόσουπα	*tomatosoopa*	tomato soup
ταχινόσουπα	*takheenosoopa*	"tahini" (sesame seed) soup
φασολάδα	*fasolaTHa*	bean soup with tomatoes and parsley
χορτόσουπα	*khortosoopa*	vegetable soup
κακαβιά	*kakavya*	fish stew with tomatoes

Κρεατόσουπα *kreatosoopa*
Meat soup, sometimes thickened with egg and lemon.

Ψαρόσουπα *psarosoopa*
Fish soup thickened with egg and lemon, and often also with white rice.

Τραχανάς *trakhanas*
Cracked wheat soup. Varies by region. Eaten plain for breakfast (like porridge) in winter, or with chopped tomatoes and grated cheese as a more substantial meal. Typically eaten without the cheese during fasting periods.

Egg dishes/Omelets Πιάτα αυγών/Ομελέτες

I'd like an omelet.	Θα ήθελα μια ομελέττα. *tha eethela mia omeleta*
eggs	αυγά *avgha*
soft-boiled	μελάτα *melata*
hard-boiled	σφικτά *sfeekhta*
fried	τηγανητά (μάτια) *teeghaneeta (mateea)*
poached	ποσέ *pose*
cheese omelet	ομελέττα με τυρί *omeleta me teeree*
ham omelet	ομελέττα με ζαμπόν *omeleta me zambon*

Fish and seafood Ψάρι και θαλασσινά

Fresh fish and seafood are always available in Greece, and fish products are widely consumed. Don't miss the boiled fish (scorpion fish, grouper, and blackfish are the best). A soup made from fish broth and thickened with egg and lemon (**afgholemono**) is eaten first, followed by the fish itself and vegetables with mayonnaise. Smaller fish are eaten fried in olive oil (**teeghaneeta**) or grilled over charcoal (**pseeta**).

αντζούγιες	*antzooyes*	anchovies
αστακός	*astakos*	lobster
γαρίδες	*ghareeтнes*	shrimp [prawns]
γλώσσα	*ghlosa*	sole
καβούρι	*kavooree*	crab
καλαμάρι	*kalamaree*	squid
κέφαλος	*kefalos*	mullet
μπακαλιάρος	*bakalee-aros*	fresh cod
μπακαλιάρος παστός	*bakaleearos pastos*	salted cod
μπαρμπούνι	*barboonee*	red mullet
μύδια	*meeтнya*	mussels
ξιφίας	*kseefeeas*	swordfish
σαρδέλλα	*sarтнela*	sardines
σουπιά	*soopia*	cuttlefish
στρείδια	*streeтнya*	oysters
σφυρίδα	*sfeereeтнa*	grouper
τόννος	*tonos*	tuna
χέλι	*khelee*	eel
χταπόδι	*khtapoтнee*	octopus

Αστακός astakos
Lobster, often served with oil and lemon sauce or garlic mayonnaise.

Γαρίδες με φέτα/σαγανάκι ghareeтнes me feta/saghanakee
Shrimp [prawns] with onions, tomatoes, and seasonings, baked with feta.

Χταπόδι κρασάτο khtapoтнee krasato
Octopus stewed in wine sauce.

Ψάρι μαρινάτο psaree mareenato
Mullet, sole, or mackerel, fried and served with a wine sauce.

Meat and poultry Κρέας και πουλερικά

βοδινό	*vоTHeeno*	beef
χοιρινό	*kheereeno*	pork
μοσχάρι	*moskharee*	veal
αρνί	*arnee*	lamb
ζαμπόν	*zambon*	ham
κατσικάκι	*katseekakee*	goat
κοτολέτες	*kotoletes*	cutlets
λουκάνικα	*lookaneeka*	sausages
μπριζόλα βοδινή/χοιρινή	*breezola voTHeenee/heereenee*	beef/pork steak
μυαλό	*mialo*	brains
νεφρά	*nefra*	kidneys
συκώτι	*seekotee*	liver
φιλέτο	*feeleto*	fillet
γαλοπούλα	*ghalopoola*	turkey
κοτόπουλο	*kotopoolo*	chicken
κουνέλι	*koonelee*	rabbit
πάπια	*papia*	duck
φασιανός	*faseeanos*	pheasant
χήνα	*kheena*	goose

Αρνάκι εξοχικό *arnakee eksokheeko*
Spiced lamb and potatoes baked in parchment (sometimes in filo pastry).

Γιουβέτσι *yoovetsee*
Meat (usually lamb) with Greek pasta baked in the oven with tomatoes.

Κοντοσούβλι *kondosoovlee*
Skewered pork or lamb, well seasoned and cooked over charcoal.

Μελιτζανάτο *meleetzanato*
Beef or veal stewed with tomatoes and eggplant [aubergine].

Μουσακάς *moosakas*
Layers of eggplant [aubergine] and minced meat topped with bechamel sauce.

Μπιφτέκι *beeftekee*
A Greek "beefburger" – mincemeat burger with breadcrumbs, onions, and herbs grilled over charcoal, sometimes topped with grilled cheese or egg.

Vegetables and pulses
Λαχανικά και όσπρια

Vegetables (**lakhaneeka**) and beans (**ospreea**) often tend to be mixed or cooked with meat or fish. Vegetarians should ask for **ena fayeeto poo na meen ekhee kre-as** ("a dish that has no meat").

αγγούρι	*angooree*	cucumber
αγκινάρες	*angeenares*	artichokes
αρακάς	*arakas*	peas
καρότα	*karota*	carrots
κολοκύθια	*kolokeetheea*	zucchini [courgettes]
κουνουπίδι	*koonoopeeтнee*	cauliflower
κουκιά	*kookeea*	broad beans
κρεμμύδια	*kremeeтнya*	onions
λάχανο	*lakhano*	cabbage
κόκκινο λάχανο	*kokeeno lakhano*	red cabbage
μανιτάρια	*maneetarya*	mushrooms
μαρούλι	*maroolee*	(cos) lettuce
μελιτζάνες	*meleetzanes*	eggplant [aubergine]
μπάμιες	*bamee-es*	okra
ντομάτες	*domates*	tomatoes
πατάτες	*patates*	potatoes
πιπεριές	*peeperyes*	peppers
πιπεριές πράσινες	*peeperyes praseenes*	green peppers
πράσα	*prasa*	leeks
ρύζι	*reezee*	rice
σέλινο	*seleeno*	celery
σπαράγγια	*sparangeea*	asparagus
σπανάκι	*spanakee*	spinach
φασολάκια φρέσκα	*fasolakeea freska*	green beans
ρεβύθια	*reveetheea*	chickpeas
φακές	*fakes*	lentils
φασόλια γίγαντες	*fasoleea yeeghandes*	butter beans

Herbs and spices Βότανα και μπαχαρικά

Greek	Pronunciation	English
άνηθος	_aneethos_	dill
βασιλικός	_vaseeleekos_	basil
δάφνη	_THafnee_	bay leaf
δεντρολίβανο	_THendroleevano_	rosemary
δυόσμος	_THeeozmos_	mint
θυμάρι	_theemaree_	thyme
κανέλλα	_kanela_	cinnamon
μαϊντανός	_maeeTHanos_	parsley
μαστίχα	_masteekha_	mastic
ρίγανη	_reeghanee_	oregano
σκόρδο	_skorTHo_	garlic
φασκόμηλο	_faskomeelo_	sage

Fruit Φρούτα

Greek	Pronunciation	English
ανανάς	_ananas_	pineapple
αχλάδι	_akhlaTHee_	pear
βερύκοκο	_vereekoko_	apricot
δαμάσκηνο	_THamaskeeno_	plum
γκρέιπφρουτ	_"grapefruit"_	grapefruit
καρπούζι	_karpoozee_	watermelon
κεράσι	_kerasee_	cherry
λεμόνι	_lemonee_	lemon
μήλο	_meelo_	apple
μπανάνα	_banana_	banana
πεπόνι	_peponee_	melon
πορτοκάλι	_portokalee_	orange
μανταρίνι	_mantareenee_	tangerine
ροδάκινο	_roTHakeeno_	peach
σταφύλι	_stafeelee_	grape
σύκο	_seeko_	fig
χουρμάς	_khoormas_	date

Cheese Τυρί

Cheese is eaten by itself and also frequently used in cooking.
These are some of the wide variety of white and hard cheeses:

φέτα _feta_
Crumbly salted white cheese made from goat's milk. This is the
most popular cheese and varies in texture and saltiness by region.

γραβιέρα _ghravy-era_
A Swiss-style cheese. The best varieties are made in Crete and Dodoni (Ipiros).

κασέρι _kaseree_
Light, yellow cheese, rich in cream with a soft texture.

κασκαβάλι _kaskavalee_
Yellow cheese, very creamy and rich.

μανούρι _manooree_
Similar to cottage cheese; makes a tasty dessert when mixed with honey.

Desserts/Pastries Επιδόρπια/Γλυκά

Greeks rarely eat dessert after their meal. Sweets are usually eaten after
the afternoon siesta and accompanied by a strong cup of coffee.

γρανίτα	_ghraneeta_	sherbet [water-ice]
καραμέλες	_karameles_	candy [sweets]
καρυδόπιτα	_kareeтΗopeeta_	walnut cake
κρέμα καραμελέ	_krema karamele_	caramel custard
μηλόπιτα	_meelopeeta_	apple pie
παγωτό	_paghoto_	ice cream
ρυζόγαλο	_reezoghalo_	rice pudding
φρουτοσαλάτα	_frootosalata_	fruit salad
λουκούμι	_lookoomee_	Turkish delight

γαλακτομπούρεκο _ghalaktobooreko_
Flaky pastry filled with custard and steeped in syrup.

καταΐφι _kata-eefee_
Shredded pastry roll filled with nuts and steeped in syrup.

κοπεγχάγη _kopenkhaghee_
Filo pastry filled with a mixture of almonds, orange juice, and cinnamon.

μπακλαβάς _baklavas_
Baklava; a flaky pastry with a nut filling.

χαλβάς _khalvas_
Halva; sesame seed paste and sugar.

Alcoholic drinks Οινοπνευματώδη

Aperitifs Απεριτίφ

The usual aperitif is ouzo (**oozo**), a fairly strong anise-flavored drink served either neat (**sketo**) or with water. As Greeks rarely drink alcohol without food, your drink will be served with a few savory **mezeTHes**, such as octopus, pieces of cheese, and olives.

I'd like an ouzo.	Θα ήθελα ένα ούζο.	tha _eethela_ _ena_ _oozo_

Beer Μπύρα

The Greeks used to make their own Bavarian-style lager, but this is no longer the case. However, you will find a range of imported beers.

Do you have ... beer?	Έχετε ... μπύρα;	ekhete ... _beera_
bottled	εμφιαλωμένη	emfee-alomenee
draft	βαρελίσια	vareleeseea
light/dark	ξανθή/μαύρη	ksan_thee_/_mavree_

Wine Κρασί

The quality of wine that you will encounter is likely to vary. Greece produces some wines good enough to rival some of the French names, but unfortunately in tiny quantities not sufficient for export. Among the top rated are the red wines from the Averof vineyards and the Athos Peninsula. Porto Carras in Chalkidiki and Achaea Clauss in northwest Peloponnisos produce excellent wines at affordable prices. Also well known is the sweet muscat from Samos and Mavrodaphni. A type of typically Greek wine that takes some getting used to is retsina, essentially a white wine containing pine resin.

Wine is usually produced very locally: it is often the case that a restaurant owner will bring you a carafe of his very own wine, made from grapes from his few square meters of vineyard, if you ask for house wine (**krasee vareleeseeo**).

I'd like a a bottle of red/ blush [rosé]/white wine.	Θα ήθελα ένα μπουκάλι κόκκινο/ροζέ/ άσπρο κρασί.	tha _eethela_ _ena_ bookalee kokeeno/roze/aspro krasee
a carafe	μια καράφα	mia ka_rafa_
a liter	ένα λίτρο	ena _leetro_
dry/sweet	ξηρό/γλυκό	ksee_ro_/ghlee_ko_
light/full-bodied	ελαφρύ/δυνατό	elafree/тнеenato
chilled	παγωμένο	pagho_me_no

Other alcoholic drinks
Ἄλλα οινοπνευματώδη ποτά

Bars serve a variety of cocktails and the usual range of spirits . Note that brandy is **koneeak** and rum is **roomee** – other spirits are known by their English names (whisky, vodka, gin, etc.).

straight [neat]	σκέτο *sketo*
on the rocks	με πάγο *me pagho*
and soda	και σόδα *ke soтна*
glass	ένα ποτήρι *ena poteree*
bottle	ένα μπουκάλι *ena bookalee*

κίτρο *keetro*
A sweet liqueur, with a citrus flavor; found on the island of Naxos.

Μεταξά *metaksa*
A Greek brandy (from two to seven stars, indicating quality).

κουμ-κουάτ *koom-kooat*
Orange-colored brandy made from tiny oranges (*Corfu*).

Nonalcoholic drinks
Μη οινοπνευματώδη ποτά

The most popular drink in the summer is **frape** – iced coffee shaken with or without milk and sugar – found at most coffee shops and bars. Freshly squeezed juices are also widely consumed. Tap water is drinkable almost everywhere, but if you prefer you can get bottled water (**emfeealomeno**).

coffee	ένα καφέ *ena kafe*
instant	ένα Νεσκαφέ *ena neskafe*
Greek	ελληνικό *eleeneeko*
black	σκέτο *sketo*
with cream / milk	με κρέμα/γάλα *me krema/ghala*
tea	ένα τσάι *ena tsaee*
with milk / lemon	με γάλα/με λεμόνι *me ghala/me lemonee*
iced tea	ένα παγωμένο τσάι *ena paghomeno tsaee*
fruit juice	ένα χυμό φρούτων *ena kheemo frooton*
mineral water	ένα μεταλλικό νερό *ena metaleeko nero*
cabonated [fizzy] / still	αεριούχο/χωρίς ανθρακικό *aereeookho/khorees anthrakeeko*

Menu Reader

This Menu Reader gives listings of common food types and dishes. The Greek words are shown in large type to help you identify the basic ingredients making up a dish from a menu that has no English. Note that tavernas rarely have menus, but you could ask the waiter to write down the dish if you don't understand what's on offer.

Meat and poultry

κρέας	kreas	meat (general)
βοδινό	voтнeeno	beef
χοιρινό	kheereeno	pork
κουνέλι	koonelee	rabbit
αρνί	arnee	lamb
κοτόπουλο	kotopoolo	chicken
πάπια	papia	duck
κιμάς	keemas	minced meat
αρνάκι γάλακτος	arnakee ghalaktos	baby lamb
περιστέρι	pereesteree	pigeon
μυαλό	mialo	brains
κατσικάκι	katseekakee	goat
χήνα	kheena	goose

Fish

ψάρι	_ps_aree	fish (general)
θαλασσινά	_thalaseena_	seafood (general)
αντζούγιες	_antzooyes_	anchovies
μπακαλιάρος	_bakaleearos_	cod
καβούρι	_kavooree_	crab
αστακός	_astakos_	lobster
κέφαλος	_kefalos_	mullet
λιθρίνι	_leethreenee_	gray mullet
μύδια	_meeTHya_	mussels
χταπόδι	_khtapoTHee_	octopus
στρείδια	_streeTHya_	oysters
γαρίδες	_ghareeTHes_	shrimp [prawns]
σαρδέλλα	_sarTHela_	sardine
καλαμάρι	_kalamaree_	squid
τόννος	_tonos_	tuna

λαχανικά	lakhaneeka	vegetables (general)
αγκινάρες	ageenares	artichokes
μελιτζάνες	meleetzanes	eggplant [aubergine]
λάχανο	lakhano	cabbage
αγγούρι	agooree	cucumber
χωριάτικη σαλάτα	khoryateekee salata	Greek salad *made of olives, tomatoes, cucumber, onions, green peppers, and feta*
καρότα	karota	carrots
σέλινο	seleeno	celery
κολοκύθι	kolokeethee	zucchini [courgette]
μπάμιες	bamee-es	okra
κρεμμύδια	kremeeтнya	onions
αρακάς	arakas	peas
πατάτες	patates	potatoes
σαλάτα	salata	salad
σπανάκι	spanakee	spinach
ντομάτα	domata	tomato

Fruit

φρούτα	_froota_	fruit (general)
μήλο	_meelo_	apple
βερύκοκο	_vereekoko_	apricot
μπανάνα	_banana_	banana
χουρμάς	_khoormas_	date
σύκο	_seeko_	fig
σταφύλι	_stafeelee_	grape
γκρέιπφρουτ	_"grapefruit"_	grapefruit
λεμόνι	_lemonee_	lemon
πεπόνι	_peponee_	melon
πορτοκάλι	_portokalee_	orange
ροδάκινο	_roτΗakeeno_	peach
αχλάδι	_akhlaτΗee_	pear
ανανάς	_ananas_	pineapple
δαμάσκηνο	_τΗamaskeeno_	plum
φράουλα	_fraoola_	strawberry

ψωμί	*psomee*	bread
ρεβύθια	*reveetheea*	chickpeas
φακές	*fakes*	lentils
ζυμαρικά	*zeemareeka*	pasta
ρύζι	*reezee*	rice
ψωμάκι	*psomakee*	bread roll
ζάχαρη	*zakharee*	sugar
ταχινόσουπα	*takheenosoopa*	tahini (sesame seed) soup
ψωμί φρυγανιά	*psomee freeghaneea*	toast
λαγάνα	*laghana*	unleavened bread

Cooking methods

του φούρνου	too foornoo	baked
της σχάρας	tees skharas	barbecued, grilled
βραστός	vrastos	boiled
λαδερό	laтнero	cooked in olive oil
τηγανητός	teeghaneetos	fried
μαρινάτος	mareenatos	marinated
ποσέ	pose	poached
ψητό	pseeto	roasted, baked
παστός	pastos	salted
μαγειρευτό	mayeerefto	stewed
γιαχνί	yakhnee	stewed in tomato sauce
κρασάτο	krasato	stewed in wine
γεμιστό	yemeesto	stuffed

Classic dishes

μελιτζανοσαλάτα	meleetzanosalata	a dip of baked eggplant mashed with garlic, lemon, and olive oil
τζατζίκι	tzatzeekee	tzatziki a dip of yogurt, garlic, cucumber, and olive oil
ταραμοσαλάτα	taramosalata	taramasalata cod roe dip
κεφτεδάκια	kefteTHakeea	fried mincemeat balls containing onions, bread crumbs, and herbs
σπανακόπιτα	spanakopeeta	filo pastry pies filled with spinach, feta cheese, and eggs
μουσακάς	moosakas	moussaka oven-baked layers of sliced eggplant and minced meat (lamb or beef) topped with bechamel sauce
ντολμαδάκια	dolmaTHakeea	vine leaves stuffed with rice and onions and flavored with herbs (sometimes also contain mince-meat)

νερό	*ne<u>ro</u>*	water
μεταλλικό νερό	*metalee<u>ko</u> ne<u>ro</u>*	mineral water
τσάι	*<u>tsa</u>ee*	tea
καφέ	*ka<u>fe</u>*	coffee (instant)
Ελληνικό καφέ	*eleenee<u>ko</u> ka<u>fe</u>*	Greek coffee
Μεταξά	*meta<u>ksa</u>*	Metaxa *a Greek brandy (from two to seven stars* ➤ 51*)*
μπύρα	*<u>bee</u>ra*	beer
ούζο	*<u>oo</u>zo*	ouzo
κρασί	*kra<u>see</u>*	wine
χυμό φρούτων	*khee<u>mo</u> <u>froo</u>ton*	fruit juice
χυμό πορτοκάλι	*khee<u>mo</u> porto<u>ka</u>lee*	orange juice
χυμό λεμόνι	*khee<u>mo</u> lemonee*	lemon juice
λεμονάδα	*lemo<u>na</u>THa*	lemonade

σάντουιτς	"sandwich"	sandwich
ελιές (γεμιστές)	elee-es (yemeestes)	(stuffed) olives
μπιφτέκι	beeftekee	a Greek "beefburger": minced meat burger with breadcrumbs, onions, and herbs grilled over charcoal, sometimes topped with cheese or egg
τσιπς	"chips"	chips [crisps]
πατάτες τηγανητές	patates teeghaneetes	french fries [chips]
λουκάνικα	lookaneeka	sausages
μπισκότα	beeskota	cookies [biscuits]
κέικ	"cake"	cake
τυροπιττάκια	teeropeetakia	baked triangular pastries containing feta and another hard cheese

Dairy products

αυγά	*avgha*	eggs
γιαούρτι	*yaoortee*	yogurt
κρέμα	*krema*	cream
βούτυρο	*vooteero*	butter
γάλα	*ghala*	milk
τυρί	*teeree*	cheese
φέτα	*feta*	feta *crumbly salted white cheese made from goat's milk. Varies regionally in texture and saltiness.*
μυζήθρα	*meezeethra*	*salted white soft cheese made from ewe's milk*
μανούρι	*manooree*	*similar to cottage cheese, makes a tasty dessert when mixed with honey*

Herbs and spices

βασιλικός	*vaseelee<u>kos</u>*	basil
κανέλλα	*ka<u>ne</u>la*	cinnamon
γαρύφαλλο	*gha<u>ree</u>falo*	cloves
άνηθος	*<u>a</u>neethos*	dill
σκόρδο	*<u>skor</u>тно*	garlic
δυόσμος	*тнее<u>oz</u>mos*	mint
μουστάρδα	*moo<u>star</u>тнa*	mustard
ρίγανη	*<u>ree</u>ghanee*	oregano
μαϊντανός	*maeeтн<u>a</u>nos*	parsley
πιπέρι	*<u>pee</u>peree*	pepper
δεντρολίβανο	*тнendrol<u>ee</u>vano*	rosemary
σαφράνη	*sa<u>fra</u>nee*	saffron
αλάτι	*a<u>la</u>tee*	salt
θυμάρι	*thee<u>ma</u>ree*	thyme

Desserts

τούρτα αμυγδάλου	_toor_ta ameegh_THa_loo	almond cake
ρεβανί	reva_nee_	*almond sponge cake with syrup*
μπακλαβάς	bakla_vas_	baklava *a flaky pastry with a nut filling*
κρέμα καραμελέ	_kre_ma karame_le_	caramel custard
δίπλες	_THee_ples	*crispy fried dough sprinkled with nuts and sweetened with honey*
φρουτοσαλάτα	frootosa_la_ta	fruit salad
χαλβάς	khal_vas_	halva *sesame seed paste and sugar, sometimes flavored with pistachio nuts*
μέλι	_me_lee	honey

μαντολάτο	mandolato	nougat *best on the island of Zakinthos*
παγωτό	paghoto	ice cream
ρυζόγαλο	reezoghalo	rice pudding
πάστα	pasta	cake (general)
τάρτα	tarta	fruit tart
πίτα	peeta	pie
λουκουμάδες	lookoomaтнes	fritters *round fritters, served with honey and cinnamon*
μελομακάρονα	melomakarona	*traditional small Christmas cakes, containing walnuts and cinnamon*
τσουρέκι	tsoorekee	*similar to the Italian Panattone. Traditionally made at Easter but now eaten all year.*

Travel

ESSENTIAL

A ticket to …	Ένα εισιτήριο για … *ena eeseeteereeo ya*
How much …?	Πόσο κάνει …; *poso kanee*
When?	Πότε; *pote*
When will … arrive/leave?	Πότε θα φτάσει/φύγει ο/η/το …; *pote tha ftasee/feeyee o/ee/to*

How you get around will depend mainly on which part of Greece you would like to visit. If you plan on visiting the islands there are regular ferry links from Piraeus, Athens' main port.

The most efficient way of traveling on the mainland, unless you have your own car, is by bus. The train offers a picturesque view but takes longer.

Safety Ασφάλεια

Would you accompany me to the bus stop?	Μπορείτε να με συνοδεύσετε ως τη στάση του λεωφορείου; *boreete na me seenoTHefsete os tee stasee too leoforeeoo*
I don't want to … on my own.	Δεν θέλω να … μόνος (μόνη) μου. *THen thelo na … monos (monee) moo*
stay here	μείνω εδώ *meeno eTHo*
walk home	περπατήσω σπίτι *perpateeso speetee*
I don't feel safe here.	Δεν αισθάνομαι ασφαλής εδώ. *THen esthanome asfalees eTHo*

Arrival Άφιξη

If you are an EU citizen, there are minimal arrival formalities – either a valid passport, a visitor's passport, or an ID card are acceptable. A visa is not required for nationals of the U.S., Canada, Australia, and New Zealand for a three-month stay. If you are coming from an EU country and have nothing to declare, go through the blue channel (**ble eksoτhos**); from a non-EU country with nothing to declare go through the green channel (**praseenee eksoτhos**); otherwise through the red channel (**kokeenee eksoτhos**). Be advised: some random checks are carried out in both green and blue channels, mainly for drugs.

Passport control Έλεγχος διαβατηρίων

Μπορώ να δω το διαβατήριό σας, παρακαλώ;	May I see your passport, please?
Ποιός είναι ο σκοπός του ταξιδιού σας;	What's the purpose of your visit?
Με ποιόν είστε εδώ;	Who are you here with?

We have a joint passport.	Έχουμε κοινό διαβατήριο. *ekhoome kee<u>no</u> τheeavat<u>ee</u>reeo*
The children are on this passport.	Τα παιδιά είναι σε αυτό το διαβατήριο. *ta pe<u>τη</u>ya <u>ee</u>ne se a<u>ftο</u> to τheeavat<u>ee</u>reeo*
I'm here on vacation [holiday]/business.	Είμαι εδώ για διακοπές/δουλειά. *<u>ee</u>me eτ<u>ho</u> ya τheeak<u>ope</u>s/τhool<u>ee</u>a*
I'm just passing through.	Απλώς περνώ από εδώ. *a<u>plos</u> per<u>no</u> a<u>po</u> eτ<u>ho</u>*
I'm going to …	Θα … *tha*
I won't be working here.	Δεν θα δουλέψω εδώ. *τhen tha τhool<u>e</u>pso eτ<u>ho</u>.*
I'm …	Είμαι … *<u>ee</u>me*
on my own	μόνος (μόνη) μου *monos (monee) moo*
with my family	με την οικογένειά μου *me teen eekoy<u>e</u>neea moo*
with a group	με γκρουπ *me "group"*

WHO ARE YOU WITH? ➤ 120

Customs Τελωνείο

I have only the normal allowances.	Έχω μόνο τα επιτρεπόμενα όρια. *ekho mono ta epeetrepomena oreea*
It's a gift/for my personal use.	Είναι για δώρο/για προσωπική μου χρήση. *eene ya THoro/ya prosopeekee moo khreesee*

Έχετε τίποτα να δηλώσετε;	Do you have anything to declare?
Πρέπει να πληρώσετε φόρο γι αυτό.	You must pay duty on this.
Από πού το αγοράσατε;	Where did you buy this?
Παρακαλώ ανοίξτε αυτή τη τσάντα.	Please open this bag.
Έχετε άλλες αποσκευές;	Do you have any more baggage?

I would like to declare ...	Θα ήθελα να δηλώσω ... *tha eethela na THeeloso*
I don't understand.	Δεν καταλαβαίνω. *THen katalaveno*
Does anyone here speak English?	Μιλάει κανείς εδώ Αγγλικά; *meelaee kanees eTHo angleeka*

ΕΛΕΓΧΟΣ ΔΙΑΒΑΤΗΡΙΩΝ	passport control
ΣΥΝΟΡΑ	border crossing
ΤΕΛΩΝΕΙΑ	customs
ΤΙΠΟΤΑ ΓΙΑ ΔΗΛΩΣΗ	nothing to declare
ΕΙΔΗ ΓΙΑ ΔΗΛΩΣΗ	goods to declare
ΑΣΤΥΝΟΜΙΑ	police
ΑΦΟΡΟΛΟΓΗΤΑ ΕΙΔΗ	duty-free goods

Duty-free shopping Αγορά αφορολόγητων ειδών

What currency is this in?	Σε ποιό νόμισμα είναι αυτό; *se peeo nomeezma eene afto*
Can I pay in ...	Μπορώ να πληρώσω σε ...; *boro na pleeroso se*
dollars/euros/pounds	δολλάρια/ευρώ/λίρες Αγγλίας *THolareea/evro/leeres angleeas*

Plane Αεροπλάνο

The national airline of Greece is Olympic Airways (**oleembeeakee aeroporeea**) and it offers both international and domestic flights. Airports exist in all main towns and most of the larger islands.

A bus connects the airport to downtown Athens – Sintagma square and Omonia. Domestic flights get very full during July and August, and you might not find a seat unless you have reserved in advance.

Tickets and reservations Εισιτήρια και κρατήσεις

When is the … flight to Athens?	Πότε είναι η … πτήση για Αθήνα; *pote eene ee … pteesee ya athena*
first/next/last	πρώτη/επόμενη/τελευταία *protee/epomenee/teleftea*
I'd like 2 … tickets to …	Θα ήθελα δύο … εισιτήρια για … *tha eethela THeeo …* *eeseeteereea ya*
one-way [single]	απλό *aplo*
round-trip [return]	με επιστροφή *me epeestrofee*
first class	πρώτη θέση *protee thesee*
business class	μπίζνες *"busines"*
economy class	τουριστική *tooreesteekee*
How much is a flight to …?	Πόσο κάνει η πτήση για …; *poso kanee ee pteesee ya*
I'd like to … my reservation for flight number …	Θα ήθελα να … την κράτησή μου για τον αριθμό πτήσεως … *tha eethela na …* *teen krateesee moo ya ton areethmo* *pteeseos*
cancel	ακυρώσω *akeeroso*
change	αλλάξω *alakso*
confirm	επιβεβαιώσω *epeeveveoso*

Inquiries about the flight Πληροφορίες για την πτήση

How long is the flight?	Πόσο διαρκεί η πτήση; *poso THeearkee ee pteesee*
What time does the plane leave?	Τι ώρα φεύγει το αεροπλάνο; *tee ora fevyee to aeroplano*
What time will we arrive?	Τι ώρα θα φτάσουμε; *tee ora tha ftasoome*

Checking in Έλεγχος αποσκευών

Where is the check-in desk for flight …?	Πού είναι το γραφείο ελέγχου αποσκευών για την πτήση …; _poo eene to ghrafeeo elenkhoo aposkevon ya teen pteesee_
I have …	Έχω … _ekho_
3 cases to check in	τρεις βαλίτσες να ελέγξω _trees valeetses na elenkso_
2 pieces of hand baggage	δύο τεμάχια αποσκευών χειρός _THeeo temakheea aposkevon kheeros_
How much baggage is allowed free?	Πόσο είναι το επιτρεπόμενο βάρος; _poso eene to epeetrepomeno varos_

Το εισιτήριο/διαβατήριο σας, παρακαλώ.	Your ticket/passport, please.
Θέλετε παράθυρο ή διάδρομο;	Would you like a window or an aisle seat?
Καπνίζοντες ή μη καπνίζοντες;	Smoking or non-smoking?
Παρακαλώ, προχωρήστε στην αίθουσα αναχωρήσεων.	Please go through to the departure lounge.
Πόσες αποσκευές έχετε;	How many pieces of baggage do you have?
Έχετε υπέρβαρο.	You have excess baggage.
Θα πρέπει να πληρώσετε … ευρώ για κάθε κιλό υπέρβαρου.	You'll have to pay a supplement of … euros per kilo of excess baggage.
Αυτό είναι πολύ βαρύ/μεγάλο για αποσκευή χειρός.	That's too heavy/large for hand baggage.
Φτιάξατε τις βαλίτσες σας μόνος σας/μόνη σας;	Did you pack these bags yourself?
Περιέχουν αιχμηρά ή ηλεκτρικά αντικείμενα;	Do they contain any sharp or electronic items?

ΑΦΙΞΕΙΣ	arrivals
ΑΝΑΧΩΡΗΣΕΙΣ	departures
ΕΛΕΓΧΟΣ ΑΣΦΑΛΕΙΑΣ	security check
ΜΗΝ ΑΦΗΝΕΤΕ ΤΙΣ ΑΠΟΣΚΕΥΕΣ ΣΑΣ ΑΣΥΝΟΔΕΥΤΕΣ.	Do not leave bags unattended.

BAGGAGE ➤ 71

Information Πληροφορίες

Is flight … delayed?	Υπάρχει καθυστέρηση στην πτήση …; *eeparkhee katheestereesee steen pteesee*
How late will it be?	Πόσο θα αργήσει; *poso tha argheesee*
Has the flight from … landed?	Προσγειώθηκε η πτήση από … *prozyeeotheeke ee pteesee apo*
Which gate does flight … leave from?	Από ποιά έξοδο φεύγει η πτήση …; *apo pia eksotho fevyee ee pteesee*

Boarding/In-flight Επιβίβαση/Στην πτήση

Your boarding card, please.	Το δελτίο επιβιβάσεως, παρακαλώ. *teen karta epeeveevaseos, parakalo*
Could I have a drink/ something to eat, please?	Μπορώ να έχω ένα ποτό/κάτι να φάω; *boro na ekho ena poto/katee na fao*
Please wake me for the meal.	Παρακαλώ, ξυπνήστε με για το γεύμα. *parakalo, kseepneeste me ya to yevma*
What time will we arrive?	Τί ώρα θα φτάσουμε; *tee ora tha ftasoome*
An air sickness bag, please.	Μια σακούλα ναυτίας, παρακαλώ. *mia sakoola nafteeas, parakalo*

Arrival Άφιξη

Where is/are the …?	Πού είναι …; *poo eene*
currency exchange	συναλλάγματος *seenalaghmatos*
buses	τα λεωφορεία *ta leoforeea*
car rental [hire]	το γραφείο ενοικιάσεως αυτοκινήτων *to ghrafeeo eneekeeaseos aftokeeneeton*
exit	η έξοδος *ee eksothos*
taxis	τα ταξί *ta taksee*
telephone	το τηλέφωνο *to teelefono*
Is there a bus into town?	Υπάρχει λεωφορείο για το κέντρο της πόλης; *eeparkhee leoforeeo ya to kendro tees polees*
How do I get to the … Hotel?	Πώς πάω στο ξενοδοχείο …; *pos pao sto ksenotHokheeo*

BAGGAGE➤ 71; CUSTOMS ➤ 67

Baggage Αποσκευές

Porter! Excuse me! — Αχθοφόρε! Παρακαλώ!
akhthofore! parakalo!

Could you take my baggage to …? — Μπορείτε να πάτε τις αποσκευές μου …; *boreete na pate tees aposkeves moo …*

a taxi/bus — στο ταξί/στο λεωφορείο *sto taksee/sto leoforeeo*

Where is/are …? — Πού είναι …; *poo eene …*

baggage carts [trolleys] — τα καροτσάκια αποσκευών *ta karotsakeea aposkevon*

baggage lockers — οι θυρίδες *ee theereeTHes*

baggage check [left-luggage office] — η φύλαξη αποσκευών *ee feelaksee aposkevon*

Where is the baggage from flight …? — Πού είναι οι αποσκευές από την πτήση …; *poo eene ee aposkeves apo teen pteesee*

Loss, damage, and theft Απώλεια, ζημιά και κλοπή

My baggage has been lost/stolen. — Οι αποσκευές μου χάθηκαν/κλάπηκαν. *ee aposkeves moo khatheekan/klapeekan*

My suitcase was damaged in transit. — Η βαλίτσα μου χάλασε στη μεταφορά. *ee valeetsa moo khalase stee metafora*

Our baggage has not arrived. — Οι αποσκευές μας δεν έφτασαν. *ee aposkeves mas THen eftasan*

Do you have a claim form in English? — Έχετε αίτηση αποζημίωσης στα Αγγλικά; *ekhete eteesee apozeemeeosees sta angleeka*

Πώς είναι οι αποσκευές σας;	What does your baggage look like?
Έχετε την ετικέττα παραλαβής αποσκευών;	Do you have the claim check [reclaim tag]?
Οι αποσκευές σας …	Your baggage …
ίσως στάλθηκαν στο/στη …	may have been sent to …
ίσως φτάσουν αργότερα σήμερα	may arrive later today
Παρακαλώ, ελάτε πάλι αύριο.	Please come back tomorrow.
Καλέστε αυτόν τον αριθμό για να δείτε αν έφτασαν οι αποσκευές σας.	Call this number to check if your baggage has arrived.

POLICE ➤ 152; COLORS ➤ 143

Train Τραίνο

The Greek rail system is operated by OSE (ΟΣΕ, **osse** or **orghaneezmos** seeTHeeroTHromon elaTHos). The network is quite limited: a main line connects Athens with Kalamata via Patras; Athens with Tripolis; and Athens with Thessaloniki, stopping at the main towns in between. There are connections to Kalavrita, Trikkala, Volos, and Kalampaka within Greece; and Sofia and Istanbul via Thessaloniki.

The train journey is usually quite slow but scenic, and is cheaper than the bus. It is not recommended if you are short of time.

The Intercity (**eepertakheea**, abbreviated I/C) makes fewer stops, but you have to pay an extra charge of around €3–4 each way on this train. Interail and Eurorail passes are accepted on all trains but you have to reserve in advance.

All trains have bars and a sleeping car for longer journeys.

There are cheap rates for children under 12 (50% off) and groups over 10 people (30% off), but there are no season tickets available.

In summer, reservations are recommended at least three days in advance. However, there will not be a ticket on the seat to show it has been reserved, so you may have to fight for your right to sit in your reserved place!

Tourist season tickets are available and are valid for a defined period for an unlimited number of trips on all routes.

You can normally leave your baggage in a locker at larger stations, or at the baggage check [left-luggage office] – look for the sign ΦΥΛΑΞΗ ΑΠΟΣΚΕΥΩΝ **fee**laksee aposke**von**.

ΕΙΣΟΔΟΣ	entrance
ΕΞΟΔΟΣ	exit
ΠΡΟΣ ΑΠΟΒΑΘΡΕΣ	to the platforms
ΠΛΗΡΟΦΟΡΙΕΣ	information
ΚΡΑΤΗΣΕΙΣ	reservations
ΑΦΙΞΕΙΣ	arrivals
ΑΝΑΧΩΡΗΣΕΙΣ	departures

To the station Προς το σταθμό

How do I get to the (main) train station?	Πώς πάνε στον (κεντρικό) σιδηροδρομικό σταθμό; *pos pane ston (kendreeko) seeTHeeroTHromeeko stathmo*
Do trains to ... leave from ... Station?	Αναχωρούν τραίνα για ... από το σταθμό ...; *anakhoroon trena ya ... apo to stathmo*
How far is it?	Πόσο απέχει; *poso apekhee*
Can I leave my car there?	Μπορώ να αφήσω το αυτοκίνητό μου εδώ; *boro na afeeso to aftokeeneeto moo eTHo*

At the station Στο σταθμό

Where is/are the ...?	Πού είναι ...; *poo eene*
information desk	το γραφείο πληροφοριών *to ghrafeeo pleeroforeeon*
baggage check [left-luggage office]	η φύλαξη αποσκευών *ee feelaksee aposkevon*
lost and found [lost property office]	το γραφείο απωλεσθέντων αντικειμένων *to ghrafeeo apolesthendon andeekeemenon*
platform	η αποβάθρα *ee apovathra*
snack bar	το κυλικείο *to keeleekeeo*
telephones	τα τηλέφωνα *ta teelefona*
ticket office	το γραφείο εισιτηρίων *to ghrafeeo eeseeteereeon*
toilets	οι τουαλέττες *ee tooaletes*
waiting room	η αίθουσα αναμονής *ee ethoosa anamonees*

DIRECTIONS ➤ 94

Tickets Εισιτήρια

I'd like a ...
Θα ήθελα ένα ...
tha eethela ena

one-way [single] ticket
απλό εισιτήριο *aplo eeseeteereeo*

round-trip [return] ticket
εισιτήριο με επιστροφή
eeseeteereeo me epeestrofee

first/second class
πρώτη/δεύτερη θέση
protee/THefteree thesee

concessionary
μειωμένο *meeomeno*

I'd like to reserve a seat.
Θα ήθελα να κλείσω μια θέση.
tha eethela na kleeso mia thesee

aisle seat
μια θέση στο διάδρομο
mia thesee sto THeeaTHromo

window seat
μια θέση στο παράθυρο
mia thesee sto paratheero

berth
μια κουκέτα *mia kooketa*

Is there a sleeper?
Υπάρχει βαγόνι με κουκέτες;
eeparkhee vaghonee me kooketes

I'd like a ... berth.
Θα ήθελα μια ... κουκέτα.
tha eethela mia ... kooketa

upper/lower
πάνω/κάτω *pano/kato*

Can I buy a ticket on board?
Μπορώ να αγοράσω εισιτήριο μέσα στο τραίνο; *boro na aghoraso eeseeteereeo sto treno*

Price Τιμή

How much is that?
Πόσο κάνει αυτό; *poso kanee afto*

Is there a discount for ...?
Υπάρχει μειωμένο εισιτήριο για ...
eeparkhee meeomeno eeseeteereeo ya

children/families
παιδιά/οικογένειες *peTHya/eekoyenee-es*

senior citizens
συνταξιούχους *seendakseeookhoos*

students
φοιτητές *feeteetes*

Do you offer a cheap same-day round-trip [return] fare?
Υπάρχει έκπτωση για επιστροφή αυθημερόν; *eeparkhee ekptosee ya epeestrofee aftheemeron*

There is a supplement of ...
Υπάρχει επιβάρυνση των ...
eeparkhee epeevareensee ton

Queries Ερωτήσεις

Do I have to change trains?
Χρειάζεται να αλλάξω
τραίνο; *khreeazete na
alakso treno*

It's a direct train.
Είναι κατευθείαν τραίνο.
eene kateftheean treno

You have to change at …
Πρέπει να αλλάξετε στο/στη …
prepee na alaksete sto/stee

How long is this ticket
valid for?
Για πόσο ισχύει αυτό το εισιτήριο …
*ya poso eeskhee-ee afto to
eeseeteereeo*

Can I return on the same ticket?
Μπορώ να επιστρέψω με το ίδιο εισιτήριο;
*boro na epeestrepso me to eeTHyo
eeseeteereeo*

In which car [coach] is my seat?
Σε ποιά αμαξοστοιχία είναι η κουκέτα
μου; *se pia amaksosteekheea eene
ee kooketa moo*

Is there a dining car on
the train?
Υπάρχει εστιατόριο στο τραίνο;
eeparkhee esteeatoreeo sto treno

> – tha eethela ena eeseeteereeo ya teen Kavala, parakalo.
> – aplo ee me epeestrofee?
> – me epeestrofee.
> – kanee 13 evro ke 20 lepta (THekatreea evro ke
> eekosee lepta).
> – khreeazete na alakso treno?
> – ne, prepee na alaksete stee Thessaloneekee.
> – efkhareesto. kherete.

Train times Δρομολόγιο τραίνου

Could I have a timetable,
please?
Μπορώ να έχω ένα δρομολόγιο,
παρακαλώ; *boro na ekho ena
THromoloyeeo, parakalo*

When is the … train to …?
Πότε είναι το … τραίνο για …;
pote eene to … treno ya

first/next/last
πρώτο/επόμενο/τελευταίο
proto/epomeno/telefteo

There's a train to … at …
Υπάρχει τραίνο για … στις …
eeparkhee treno ya … stees

How frequent are the trains to …?	Πόσο συχνά είναι τα τραίνα για …; _poso seekhna eene ta trena ya_
once/twice a day	μια φορά/δύο φορές την ημέρα _mia fora/THeeo fores teen eemera_
5 times a day	πέντε φορές την ημέρα _pende fores teen eemera_
every hour	μια φορά την ώρα _mia fora teen ora_
What time do they leave?	Τι ώρα φεύγουν; _tee ora fevghoon_
on the hour	στην ώρα _steen ora_
20 minutes past the hour	20 λεπτά μετά την ώρα _eekosee lepta meta teen ora_
What time does the train stop/arrive in …?	Τι ώρα σταματάει/φτάνει το τραίνο στο/στη …; _tee ora stamataee/ftanee to treno sto/stee_
How long is the trip [journey]?	Πόση ώρα διαρκεί το ταξίδι; _posee ora THeearkee to takseeTHee_
Is the train on time?	Είναι το τραίνο στην ώρα του; _eene to treno steen ora too_

Departures Αναχώρηση

Which platform does the train to … leave from?	Από ποιά αποβάθρα φεύγει το τραίνο για …; _apo pia apovathra fevyee to treno ya_
Where is platform 4?	Πού είναι η αποβάθρα τέσσερα; _poo eene ee apovathra tesera_
over there	εκεί _ekee_
on the left/right	στα αριστερά/δεξιά _sta areestera/THekseea_
through the underpass	κάτω από την υπόγεια διάβαση _kato apo teen eepoyeea THeeavasee_
over the bridge	από την άλλη μεριά της γέφυρας _apo teen alee merya tees yefeeras_
Where do I change for …?	Πού αλλάζω για …; _poo alazo ya_
How long will I have to wait for a connection?	Πόση ώρα πρέπει να περιμένω για ανταπόκριση; _posee ora prepee na pereemeno ya andapokreesee_

TIME ➤ 220; DIRECTIONS ➤ 94

Boarding Εμβίβαση

Is this the right platform for the train to …?	Αυτή είναι η σωστή αποβάθρα για το τραίνο για …; *aftee eene ee sostee apovathra ya to treno ya*
Is this the train to …?	Αυτό είναι το τραίνο για …; *afto eene to treno ya*
Is this seat taken?	Αυτή η θέση είναι πιασμένη; *aftee ee thesee eene piazmenee*
I think that's my seat.	Νομίζω αυτή είναι η θέση μου. *nomeezo aftee eene ee thesee moo*
Here's my reservation.	Αυτή είναι η κράτησή μου. *aftee eene ee krateesee moo*
Are there any seats/ berths available?	Υπάρχουν ελεύθερες θέσεις/κουκέτες; *eeparkhoon eleftheres thesees/kooketes*
Do you mind …?	Σας πειράζει …; *sas peerazee*
if I sit here	να καθήσω εδώ *na katheeso etho*
if I open the window	να ανοίξω το παράθυρο *na aneekso to paratheero*

On the journey Στο ταξίδι

How long are we stopping here for?	Για πόσο θα σταματήσουμε εδώ; *ya poso tha stamateesoome etho*
When do we get to …?	Πότε θα φτάσουμε στο/στη …; *pote tha ftasoome sto/stee*
Have we passed …?	Έχουμε περάσει τον/την/το … ; *ekhoome perasee ton/teen/to*
Where is the dining/ sleeping car?	Πού είναι το εστιατόριο/το βαγκόν-λι; *poo eene to esteeatoreeo/to vagon-lee*
Where is my berth?	Πού είναι η κουκέτα μου; *poo eene ee kooketa moo*
I've lost my ticket.	Έχασα το εισιτήριό μου. *ekhasa to eeseeteereeo moo*

ΦΡΕΝΟ ΚΙΝΔΥΝΟΥ	emergency brake
ΑΥΤΟΜΑΤΕΣ ΠΟΡΤΕΣ	automatic doors

TIME ➤ 220

Long-distance bus [Coach]
Υπεραστικό λεωφορείο

KTEL (ΚΤΕΛ) runs a very efficient and reliable service linking most major towns. Reserving a seat is advisable. The main bus station in Athens is at Kifissos. To find your seat look for the number after the word θέση (**thesee**) on your ticket. There is no food or beverage service on long-distance buses, but the driver will stop every three hours or so at a café.

Where is the bus [coach] station?	Πού είναι ο σταθμός ΚΤΕΛ;
	poo eene o stathmos ktel
When's the next bus [coach] to …?	Πότε είναι το επόμενο λεωφορείο για …;
	pote eene to epomeno leforeeo ya·
Where does it leave from?	Από πού φεύγει; _apo poo fevyee_
Does the bus [coach] stop at …?	Το λεωφορείο σταματάει στο/στη …;
	to leforeeo stamatae sto/stee
How long does the trip [journey] take?	Πόση ώρα διαρκεί το ταξίδι;
	posee ora theearkee to takseethee

Bus/Trolley [Tram]   Λεωφορείο-Τρόλλεϋ

Before boarding a bus you need to buy a ticket at the special kiosks marked ΕΙΣΙΤΗΡΙΑ (**eeseeteereea**). There's only one fare whatever the distance. You validate your ticket by placing it in the special orange machine on the bus. You can also get around Athens by trolley [tram] (**trole-ee**). Blue and yellow signs mark bus and trolley [tram] stops respectively, and tickets are interchangeable.

Where can I get a bus/trolley [tram] to …?	Από πού μπορώ να πάρω ένα λεωφορείο/τρόλλεϋ για τον/την/το …;
	apo poo boro na paro ena leforeeo/trole-ee ya ton/teen/to
What time is the next bus to …?	Τί ώρα είναι το επόμενο λεωφορείο για τον/την/το …; _tee ora eene to epomeno leforeeo ya ton/teen/ton …_

| Θέλετε το λεωφορείο αριθμός … | You want bus number … |
| Πρέπει να αλλάξετε λεωφορείο στο/στη … | You must change buses at … |

| ΣΤΑΣΗ ΛΕΩΦΟΡΕΙΩΝ | bus stop |
| ΕΞΟΔΟΣ (ΚΙΝΔΥΝΟΥ) | (emergency) exit |

78

DIRECTIONS ➤ 94; TIME ➤ 220

Buying tickets Αγοράζοντας εισιτήρια

Where can I buy tickets?	Από πού μπορώ να αγοράσω εισιτήρια; *apo poo boro na aghoraso eeseeteereea*
A ... ticket to ..., please.	Ένα ... εισιτήριο για τον/τη/το ..., παρακαλώ. *ena ... eeseeteereeo ya ton/teen/to ..., parakalo*
one-way [single]	απλό εισιτήριο *aplo eeseeteereeo*
round-trip [return]	εισιτήριο με επιστροφή *eeseeteereeo me epeestrofee*
multi-trip	εισιτήριο πολλαπλών διαδρομών *eeseeteereeo polaplon тнeeaтнromon*
A booklet of tickets, please.	Μια δεσμίδα εισιτηρίων, παρακαλώ. *mia тнezmeeтна eeseeteereeon, parakalo*
How much is the fare to ...?	Πόσο κάνει το εισιτήριο για τον/την/το ...; *poso kanee to eeseeteereeo ya ton/teen/to*

Traveling Ταξιδεύοντας

Is this the right bus / trolley [tram] to ...?	Αυτό είναι το σωστό λεωφορείο/τρόλλεϋ για ...; *afto eene to sosto leoforeeo/ trole-ee ya*
Could you tell me when to get off?	Μπορείτε να μου πείτε πού να κατεβώ; *boreete na moo peete poo na katevo*
Do I have to change buses?	Χρειάζεται να αλλάξω λεωφορείο; *khreeazete na alakso leoforeeo*
Next stop, please!	Η επόμενη στάση, παρακαλώ. *ee epomenee stasee, parakalo*

⊘ ΑΚΥΡΩΣΤΕ ΤΟ ΕΙΣΙΤΗΡΙΟ ΣΑΣ   validate your ticket ⊘

– *seeghnomee. afto eene to sosto leoforeeo ya to leemanee?*
– *okhee. thelete to okto. nato, ekee eene.*
– *ena eeseeteereeo ya to leemanee, parakalo.*
– *kanee 45 (sarandapende) lepta.*
– *boreete na moo peete poo na katevo?*
– *se teserees stasees apo eтно.*

NUMBERS ➤ 216; *DIRECTIONS* ➤ 94

Subway [Metro] Μετρό

Athens is the only Greek city currently served by a subway, or underground, system, known as **eepoyeeos** or **eelektreekos**. The word "metro" refers to a new subway system, currently under construction. Fenced-off, dug-up squares and road junctions with the sign ΕΡΓΑ ΜΕΤΡΟ all around Athens mark these stations-to-be, which will not be unveiled before the year 2000. The existing system runs from Piraeus to Kifissia. Subway [metro] tickets are different from bus tickets and can be purchased at the ticket desk at each station. Tickets must be validated by punching then in the special machines by the platform.

General inquiries Γενικές πληροφορίες

Where's the nearest subway [metro] station?	Πού είναι ο κοντινότερος σταθμός μετρό; *poo eene o kondeenoteros stathmos metro*
Where do I buy a ticket?	Από πού αγοράζω εισιτήριο; *apo poo aghorazo eeseeteereeo*
Could I have a map of the subway [metro]?	Μπορώ να έχω ένα χάρτη του μετρό; *boro na ekho ena khartee too metro*

Traveling Ταξιδεύοντας

Which line should I take for …?	Ποιά γραμμή πρέπει να πάρω για το …; *pia ghramee prepee na paro ya to*
Is this the right train for …?	Αυτό είναι το σωστό τραίνο για …; *afto eene to sosto treno ya*
Which stop is it for …?	Ποιά στάση είναι για …; *pia stasee eene ya*
How many stops is it to …?	Πόσες στάσεις είναι για …; *poses stasees eene ya*
Is the next stop …?	Η επόμενη στάση είναι ο/η/το …; *ee epomenee stasee eene o/ee/to*
Where are we?	Πού είμαστε; *poo eemaste*
Where do I change for …?	Πού αλλάζω για τον/την/το …; *poo alazo ya ton/teen/to*
What time is the last train to …?	Πότε είναι το τελευταίο τραίνο για τον/την/το …; *pote eene to telelfteo treno ya ton/teen/to*

ΑΝΤΑΠΟΚΡΙΣΗ ΜΕ ΑΛΛΕΣ ΓΡΑΜΜΕΣ	to other lines/transfer

NUMBERS ➤ 216; *BUYING TICKETS* ➤ 74, 79

Ferry / Boat Φέρρυ-μπωτ/Πλοίο

It is likely that after your arrival in Athens, you will be
heading straight for the port of Piraeus to catch a ferry. The
harborfront is lined with ticket agents – and ferry prices are
fixed. So as long as you go to an approved agent the price is
the same everywhere. Each agent tends to sell tickets for one company
serving a particular route. A window display (usually in Greek and English) will tell you exactly what islands that ferry goes to. Eurorail and
Interail ticket holders can travel deck class for free on the Brindisi-Patras
route on Adriatica and HNL liners. Sleeping on the deck is allowed, but
take a sleeping bag and wear warm clothes, even in July!

Once on an island you may decide to go on an island tour. Several con-
verted fishing boats run daily trips and stop at the nicer spots for a quick
dive in the sea. However, throwing anything into the sea off a boat deck is
an offense in Greece, and you will be fined if caught.

When is the … car ferry to …?	Πότε είναι το … φέρρυ-μπωτ για …; *pote eene to feree-bot ya*
first / next / last	πρώτο/επόμενο/τελευταίο *proto/epomeno/telefteo*
A round-trip [return] ticket for …	Ένα εισιτήριο με επιστροφή για … *ena eeseeteereeo me epeestrofee ya*
1 car and 1 trailer [caravan]	ένα αυτοκίνητο και ένα τροχόσπιτο *ena aftokeeneeto ke ena trokhospeeto*
2 adults and 3 children	δύο ενήλικες και τρία παιδιά *THeeo eneeleekes ke treea peTHya*
I want to reserve a … cabin.	Θέλω να κλείσω μια … καμπίνα. *thelo na kleeso mia … kambeena*
single / double	μονή/διπλή *monee/THeeplee*

ΣΩΣΙΒΙΟ	life preserver [life belt]
ΝΑΥΑΓΟΣΩΣΤΙΚΗ ΛΕΜΒΟΣ	life boat
ΑΠΑΓΟΡΕΥΕΤΑΙ Η ΠΡΟΣΒΑΣΗ ΣΤΑ ΓΚΑΡΑΖ	no access to car decks

Boat trips Ταξίδια με το βαπόρι

Is there a boat trip?	Υπάρχει ένα ταξίδι με πλοίο; *eeparkhee ena takseeTHee me pleeo*
What time does it leave / return?	Τι ώρα ξεκινάει/επιστρέφει; *tee ora ksekeenaee/epeestrefee*

TIME ➤ 220; BUYING TICKETS ➤ 74, 79

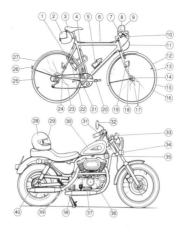

1 brake pad το τακάκι φρένου *to takakee frenoo*
2 bicycle bag το σακκίδιο *to sakeetheeo*
3 saddle η σέλα *ee sela*
4 pump η αεραντλία *ee aerandleea*
5 water bottle η φιάλη νερού *ee feealee neroo*
6 frame το πλαίσιο *to pleseeo*
7 handlebars οι χειρολαβές *ee kheerolaves*
8 bell το κουδούνι *to kootHoonee*
9 brake cable το σύρμα φρένων *to seerma frenon*
10 gear shift [lever] ο μοχλός ταχυτήτων *o mokhlos takheeteeton*
11 gear/control cable το σύρμα ταχυτήτων *to seerma takheeteeton*
12 inner tube η σαμπρέλλα *ee sambrela*
13 front/back wheel ο μπροστινός/πίσω τροχός *o brosteenos/peeso trokhos*
14 axle ο άξονας τροχού *o aksonas trokhoo*
15 tire [tyre] το λάστιχο *to lasteekho*
16 wheel η ρόδα *ee rotHa*
17 spokes οι ακτίνες τροχού *ee akteenes trokhoo*
18 bulb ο λαμπτήρας *o lambteeras*
19 headlight το μπροστινό φως *to brosteeno fos*
20 pedal το πετάλι *to petalee*

21 lock η κλειδαριά *ee kleetHarya*
22 generator [dynamo] το δυναμό *to tHeenamo*
23 chain η αλυσίδα *ee aleeseetHa*
24 rear light το πίσω φως *to peeso fos*
25 rim η στεφάνη τροχού *ee stefanee trokhoo*
26 reflector οι ανταυγαστήρες *ee andafghasteeres*
27 fender [mudguard] ο λασπωτήρας *o laspoteeras*
28 helmet το κράνος *to kranos*
29 visor το γυαλί του κρανίου *to yalee too kraneeoo*
30 fuel tank το ντεπόζιτο καυσίμων *to depozeeto kafseemon*
31 clutch lever ο μοχλός συμπλέκτη *o mokhlos seemblektee*
32 mirror ο καθρέπτης *o kathreptees*
33 ignition switch η ανάφλεξη *ee anafleksee*
34 turn signal [indicator] το φλας *to flas*
35 horn η κόρνα *ee korna*
36 engine η μηχανή *ee meekhanee*
37 gear shift [stick] ο μοχλός ταχυτήτων *o mokhlos takheeteeton*
38 kick [main] stand το σταντ *to stand*
39 exhaust pipe η εξάτμιση *ee eksatmeesee*
40 chain guard ο εκτροχιαστής αλυσίδας *o ektrokheeastees aleeseetHas*

Bicycle/Motorbike
Ποδήλατο/μοτοσυκλέτα

Motorbikes, or usually mopeds, and bicycles are widely available for hire on the islands, but not so common on the mainland.
Despite what you might see, crash helmets are compulsory and rid-
ing a motorbike is forbidden during the siesta hours (2–5 p.m.) and after midnight, although the latter rule is rarely enforced in most tourist resorts.

I'd like to rent [hire] a …	Θα ήθελα να νοικιάσω ένα … *tha eethela na neekeeaso ena*
3-/10-speed bicycle	ποδήλατο τριών/δέκα ταχυτήτων *poTHeelato treeon/THeka takheeteeton*
moped	μοτοποδήλατο *motopoTHeelato*
motorbike	μοτοσυκλέτα *motoseekleta*
How much does it cost per day/week?	Πόσο κοστίζει την ημέρα/την εβδομάδα *poso kosteezee teen eemera/teen evTHomaTHa*
The brakes don't work.	Τα φρένα δεν δουλεύουν. *ta frena THen THoolevoon*
There is/are no …	Δεν υπάρχει/υπάρχουν … *THen eeparkhee/eeparkhoon …*
lights	φώτα *fota*
pump	τρόμπα/αεραντλία *trompa/aerandleea*
The front/rear tire [tyre] has a flat [puncture].	Μού τρύπησε το μπροστινό/πίσω λάστιχο. *moo treepeese to brosteeno/peeso lasteekho*

Hitchhiking Ώτο-στοπ

Hitchhiking is reasonably wide-spread and usually safe, but it's better for
women to travel together. If you decide to hitchhike, toll booth areas on
roads are a good spot to wait for a ride.

Where are you heading?	Προς τα πού πηγαίνετε; *pros ta poo peeyenete*
Can you give me/us a lift?	Μπορείτε να μας πάρετε; *boreete na mas parete*
Could you drop me off here?	Μπορείτε να με αφήσετε εδώ; *boreete na me afeesete eTHo*
Thanks for the lift.	Σας ευχαριστώ για το ταξίδι. *sas efkhareesto ya to takseeTHee*

DIRECTIONS ➤ 94; NUMBERS ➤ 216

Taxi Ταξί

Licensed taxis are yellow with a blue stripe in Athens, although private companies and radio cabs may have their own colors. Within Athens and in all major cities, fares are fixed. For longer distances you should agree to a fare before the trip. Tipping is not compulsory, but it is common to round the amount to the nearest hundred.

Where can I get a taxi?	Πού μπορώ να βρω ταξί; _poo boro na vro taksee_
Do you have the number for a taxi?	Έχετε το τηλέφωνο κάποιου ταξί; _ekhete to teelefono kapeeoo taksee_
I'd like a taxi …	Θα ήθελα ένα ταξί … _tha eethela ena taksee …_
now	τώρα _tora_
in an hour	σε μια ώρα _se mia ora_
for tomorrow at 9 a.m.	για αύριο στις εννέα _ya avreeo stees enea_

ΕΛΕΥΘΕΡΟΣ	for hire

Please take me to …	Παρακαλώ πηγαίνετέ με … _parakalo peeyenete me …_
the airport	στο αεροδρόμιο _sto aeroTHromeeo_
the train station	στο σιδηροδρομικό σταθμό _sto seeTHeeroTHromeeko stathmo_
this address	σε αυτή τη διεύθυνση _se aftee tee THee-eftheensee_
How much will it cost?	Πόσο θα κοστίσει; _poso tha kosteesee_
Is it far?	Είναι μακριά; _eene makreea_
You said … euros.	Είπατε … ευρώ. _eepate … evro_
Keep the change.	Κρατήστε τα ρέστα. _krateeste ta resta_

> – bo_ree_te na me _pa_te sto stath_mo_, paraka_lo_?
> – ve_ve_os.
> – po_see_ _o_ra tha mas pa_ree_?
> – THeka lep_ta_ …
> – _fta_same.
> – efkha_ree_sto. poso _ka_nee?
> – e_na_meesee ev_ro_, paraka_lo_.
> – kra_tee_ste ta _re_sta.

NUMBERS ➤ 216; DIRECTIONS ➤ 94

Car/Automobile Αυτοκίνητο

In Greece you drive on the right, but in Cyprus you drive on
the left. Seat belts are officially compulsory, although you
will see many people without them. There are car ferries to
and from most Mediterranean ports or you can drive overland
(depending on the prevailing conditions in neighboring countries).
Make sure you have an international license and comprehensive
insurance. Greece is part of the EU and so the *Green Card* is valid.

While in Greece you will need to adapt to the more forceful style of
driving. Flashing headlights and horns are more often a signal or greeting
than a rebuke and could mean anything from "I'm about to pass you," to
"The police are speed-checking just ahead of us."

Conversion chart

km	1	10	20	30	40	50	60	70	80	90	100	110	120	130
miles	0.62	6	12	19	25	31	37	44	50	56	62	68	74	81

Road network

A highway links Thessaloniki to Athens, although in the more mountain-
ous areas this is limited to one lane per side plus a narrow lane for passing. Another highway links Athens to Patras, and this is being extended.
Most highways are tolled although some are free. Other roads linking
main towns tend to be one lane each way, with perhaps a passing lane in
the middle. Roads linking smaller towns and villages range from asphalt
to mud-track. Cars are not allowed on a few of the islands, so check before
you go.

Road signs giving directions, town and street names are usually in both Greek
and English characters, so you will have little problem reading them.
However, names may vary a little from what you have on your map, for
example Piraeus could be written as "Pireas" or "Pireefs," Athens as "Athine"
or "Athina."

Cars are now restricted in central Athens. No car can enter without a catalytic
converter, and Greek-registered cars can only enter on even or odd days of
the month, depending on the last number of the car registration. Much of his-
toric Athens and the main shopping area are closed completely to traffic.

Honking your horn during siesta hours (2–5 p.m.) and between 12–7 a.m.
is prohibited in residential areas.

Gas [petrol] stations are widespread, apart from the more remote areas and
smaller islands. In villages they can be part of the local coffee shop. Lead-
free and diesel fuel, as well as regular leaded, are widely available. Most
stations are not self-service, and it is customary to tip the attendant, who
will probably also clean your windshield [windscreen].

Car rental Ενοικίαση αυτοκινήτου

Most international car rental companies have branches in Greece. However, renting a car can be expensive, and there is usually a large deposit required and additional charges for mileage above 100km/day or for delivering the car to a different office. Fire and third-party insurance is included in the cost but not collision damage, which is extra. A special permit is needed for taking rental cars outside of Greece or on a ferry.

Where can I rent a car?	Πού μπορώ να νοικιάσω ένα αυτοκίνητο; _poo boro na neekeeaso ena aftokeeneeto_
I'd like to rent a car.	Θα ήθελα να νοικιάσω ένα αυτοκίνητο. _tha eethela na neekeeaso ena aftokeeneeto_
2-/4-door car	δίπορτο/τετράπορτο _THeeporto/tetraporto_
an automatic	αυτόματο _aftomato_
with 4-wheel drive	τετρακινητήριο _tetrakeeneeteereeo_
with air conditioning	με κλιματισμό _me kleemateezmo_
with a child seat	με παιδικό κάθισμα _me peTHeeko katheezma_
I'd like it for a day/week.	Θα το ήθελα για μια μέρα/μια εβδομάδα _tha to eethela ya mia mera/ mia evTHomaTHa_
How much does it cost per day/week?	Πόσο κάνει την ημέρα/εβδομάδα; _poso kanee teen eemera/teen evTHomaTHa_
Is mileage/insurance included?	Συμπεριλαμβάνονται τα χιλιόμετρα/ συμπεριλαμβάνεται η ασφάλεια; _sembereelamvanonde ta kheeleeometra/ seembereelamvanete ee asfaleea_
Can I leave the car at your office in …?	Μπορώ να αφήσω το αυτοκίνητό στο γραφείο σας στο/στη …; _boro na afeeso to aftokeeneeto sto ghrafeeo sas sto/stee_
What sort of fuel does it take?	Τί είδους καύσιμα παίρνει; _tee eeTHoos kafseema pernee_
Where's the high [full]/low [dipped] beam?	Πού είναι τα φώτα πόλεως/φώτα πορείας; _poo eene ta fota poleos/fota poreeas_
Could I have full insurance, please?	Μπορώ να έχω ολική ασφάλεια, παρακαλώ; _boro na ekho oleekee asfaleea, parakalo_

Gas [Petrol] station Βενζινάδικο

Where's the next gas [petrol] station, please?	Πού είναι το επόμενο βενζινάδικο, παρακαλώ; _poo_ _eene_ to _epomeno_ _venzeena_THeeko, parakalo
Is it self-service?	Είναι σελφ-σέρβις; _eene_ "self-service"
Fill it up, please.	Γεμίστε το, παρακαλώ. _yemeeste_ to, parakalo
… liters of gasoline [petrol], please.	… λίτρα βενζίνη, παρακαλώ. _leetra_ _venzenee, parakalo_
regular	απλή _aplee_
lead-free	αμόλυβδη _amoleev_THee_
diesel	ντήζελ "diesel"
Where is the air pump/water?	Πού είναι η αντλία αέρος/νερού …; _poo_ _eene_ ee and_leea_ a_eroos/neroo_

Φ	ΤΙΜΗ ΑΝΑ ΛΙΤΡΟ	price per liter	Θ

Parking Πάρκινγκ

Parking in large cities, particularly Athens, can be a problem as parking spaces are limited. Often you will need to buy a parking ticket from a roadside machine and attach it to your car. If you break a parking rule you will get a ticket which you'll need to take to the traffic police station to pay. More serious offenses (causing an obstruction, parking on a double-yellow line, etc.) can lead to the removal of your registration plates, which you will have to pay to reclaim at the traffic police station.

Is there a parking lot [car park] nearby?	Υπάρχει χώρος στάθμευσης εδώ κοντά; ee_parkhee_ khoros sta_th_mefsees e_THo_ konda
What's the charge per hour/day?	Πόσο κοστίζει την ώρα/ημέρα; _poso_ ko_steezee_ teen _ora/eemera_
Do you have some change for the parking meter?	Έχετε ψιλά για το παρκόμετρο; _ekhete_ psee_la_ ya to par_kometro_
They have taken my registration plates. Who do I call?	Μου πήραν τις πινακίδες. Ποιόν να καλέσω; moo _peeran_ tees peena_keeTHes._ pee_on_ na ka_leso_

NUMBERS ➤ 216; DIRECTIONS ➤ 94

Breakdown Βλάβη

There are a number of automobile rescue organizations in Greece. The most well known is ELPA (☎ 104), but Express Service, Hellas Service, and SOS Service are also fine. These organizations often have links with other international services. Additionally, there are regular emergency phones, marked SOS on most highways.

Where is the nearest garage?	Πού είναι το κοντινότερο συνεργείο; _poo_ _eene_ to kondee_notero_ seener_yeeo_
My car broke down.	Έπαθα βλάβη. _epatha_ _vlavee_
Can you send a mechanic/ tow [breakdown] truck?	Μπορείτε να στείλετε ένα μηχανικό/οδικό συνεργείο; _boreete_ na _steelete_ _ena_ meekhanee_ko_/о_Ηeeko_ seener_yeeo_
I belong to … recovery service.	Ανήκω στην εταιρία … οδικής βοήθειας. _aneeko_ steen eter_eea_ … о_Ηeekees_ voee_theeas_
My registration number is …	Ο αριθμός κυκλοφορίας μου είναι … o areeth_mos_ keeklofor_eeas_ moo _eene_
The car is …	Το αυτοκίνητο είναι … to af_tokeeneeto_ _eene_
on the highway [motorway]	στον αυτοκινητόδρομο ston aftokeeneetо_Ηromo_
2 km from …	δύο χιλιόμετρα από … _Ηeeo_ kheelee_ometra_ _apo_
How long will you be?	Πόση ώρα θα κάνετε; _posee_ _ora_ tha _kanete_

What is wrong? Τί πρόβλημα έχει;

I don't know what's wrong.	Δεν ξέρω τί πρόβλημα έχει. Ηen _ksero_ _tee_ _provleema_ _ekhee_
My car won't start.	Η μηχανή δεν παίρνει μπρος. ee meekha_nee_ Ηen _pernee_ bros
I've run out of gas [petrol].	Έχω μείνει από βενζίνη. _ekho_ _meenee_ _apo_ ven_zeenee_
I have a flat [puncture].	Μου έσκασε το λάστιχο. moo _eskase_ to _lasteekho_
There is something wrong with …	Υπάρχει κάποιο πρόβλημα με … ee_parkhee_ _kapeeo_ _provleema_ me
I've locked the keys in the car.	Κλείδωσα τα κλειδιά στο αυτοκίνητο. _kleeΗosa_ ta kleeΗ_ya_ sto af_tokeeneeto_

TELEPHONING ➤ 127; CAR PARTS ➤ 90–91

Repairs Επισκευές

Do you do repairs?	Κάνετε επισκευές; _kanete epeeskeves_
Could you take a look at my car?	Μπορείτε να ρίξετε μια ματιά στο αυτοκίνητό μου; _boreete na reekete mia mateea sto aftokeeneeto moo_
Can you repair it (temporarily)?	Μπορείτε να το διορθώσετε (προσωρινά); _boreete na to theeorthosete (prosoreena)_
Please make only essential repairs.	Παρακαλώ κάνετε μόνο τις αναγκαίες επισκευές. _parakalo kanete mono tees anange-es epeeskeves_
Can I wait for it?	Μπορώ να περιμένω; _boro na pereemeno_
Can you repair it today?	Μπορείτε να το επισκευάσετε σήμερα; _boreete na to epeeskevasete seemera_
When will it be ready?	Πότε θα είναι έτοιμο; _pote tha eene eteemo_
How much will it cost?	Πόσο θα κοστίσει; _poso tha kosteesee_
That's outrageous!	Αυτό είναι εξωφρενικό ποσό! _afto eene eksofreneeko poso_
Can I have a receipt for my insurance?	Μπορώ να έχω μια απόδειξη για την ασφάλεια; _boro na ekho mia apotheeksee ya teen asfaleea_

Ο/η/το … δεν δουλεύει.	The … isn't working.
Δεν έχω τα απαραίτητα ανταλλακτικά.	I don't have the necessary parts.
Πρέπει να παραγγείλω τα ανταλλακτικά.	I will have to order the parts.
Μπορώ να το επισκευάσω μόνο προσωρινά.	I can only repair it temporarily.
Δεν μπορεί να επισκευαστεί.	It can't be repaired.
Θα είναι έτοιμο …	It will be ready …
αργότερα σήμερα	later today
αύριο	tomorrow
σε … ημέρες	in … days

DAYS OF THE WEEK ➤ 218; _NUMBERS_ ➤ 216

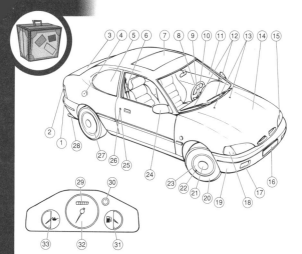

1   tail lights [back lights] πίσω φῶτα πορείας *peeso fota poreeas*

2   brakelights τα φῶτα φρένων *to fota frenon*

3   trunk [boot] το πόρτ-μπαγκάζ *to port-bagaz*

4   gas tank door [petrol cap] η τάπα βενζίνης *ee tapa venzeenees*

5   window το παράθυρο *to paratheero*

6   seat belt η ζώνη ασφαλείας *ee zonee asfaleeas*

7   sunroof η ηλιοροφή *ee eeleeorofee*

8   steering wheel το τιμόνι *to teemonee*

9   ignition η ανάφλεξη *ee anafleksee*

10   ignition key κλειδί ανάφλεξης *kleeTHee anafleksees*

11   windshield [windscreen] το παρμπρίζ *to parbreez*

12   windshield [windscreen] wipers οι υαλοκαθαριστήρες *ee eealokathareesteeres*

13   windshield [windscreen] washer ο καθαριστήρας παρμπρίζ *o katha-reesteeras parbreez*

14   hood [bonnet] το καπό *to kapo*

15   headlights τα φῶτα πορείας *ta fota poreeas*

16   licence [number] plates οι πινακίδες κυκλοφορίας *ee peenakeeTHes keekloforeeas*

17   fog lamp τα φῶτα ομίχλης *ta fota omeekhlees*

18   turn signals [indicators] το φλας *to flas*

19   bumper ο προφυλακτήρας *o profeelakteeras*

20   tires [tyres] τα λάστιχα *ta lasteekha*

21   hubcap το τάσι *to tasee*

22   valve η βαλβίδα *ee valveeTHa*

23   wheels οι ρόδες *ee roTHes*

24   outside [wing] mirror ο εξωτερικός καθρέπτης *o eksotereekos kathreptees*

25   central locking το κεντρικό κλείδωμα *to kendreeko kleeTHoma*

26   lock η κλειδαριά *ee kleeTHarya*

27   wheel rim η ζάντα *ee zanda*

28   exhaust pipe η εξάτμιση *ee eksatmeesee*

29   odometer [milometer] ο χιλιομετρυτης *o kheeleeometreetees*

30   warning light τα προειδοποιητικά φῶτα *ta proeeTHopee-eeteeka fota*

31   fuel gauge ο δείκτης καυσίμων *o THeektees kafseemon*

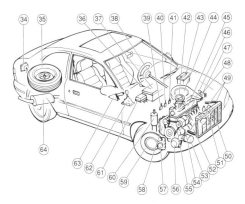

32	speedometer το κοντέρ *to konder*
33	oil gauge ο δείκτης λαδιού **ο THeektees laTHyoo**
34	backup [reversing] lights φώτα όπισθεν *fota opeesthen*
35	spare tire η ρεζέρβα *ee rezerva*
36	choke το τσοκ *to tsok*
37	heater το καλοριφέρ *to kaloreefer*
38	steering column η βάση τιμονιού *ee vasee teemoneeoo*
39	accelerator το γκάζι *to gazee*
40	pedal το πετάλι *to petalee*
41	clutch ο συμπλέκτης *ο seemblektees*
42	carburetor το καρμπυρατέρ *to karbeerater*
43	battery η μπαταρία *ee batareea*
44	alternator ο εναλλακτής *ο enalaktees*
45	camshaft ο (εκκεντροφόρος) άξονας *ο (ekendroforos) aksonas*
46	air filter το φίλτρο αέρα *to feeltro aera*
47	distributor ο διανομέας *ο THeeanomeas*
48	points οι πλατίνες *ee plateenes*

49	radiator hose (top/bottom) ο αγωγός θέρμανσης *ο aghoghos thermansees*
50	radiator το καλοριφέρ *to kaloreefer*
51	fan ο ανεμιστήρας *ο anemeesteeras*
52	engine η μηχανή *ee meekhanee*
53	oil filter το φίλτρο λαδιού *to feeltro laTHyoo*
54	starter η μίζα *ee meeza*
55	fan belt ο ιμάντας ανεμιστήρα *ο eemandas anemeesteera*
56	horn η κόρνα *ee korna*
57	brake pads τα τακάκια φρένων *ta takakeea frenon*
58	transmission [gearbox] το κιβώτιο ταχυτήτων *to keevoteeo takheeteeton*
59	brakes τα φρένα *ta frena*
60	shock absorbers τα αμορτισέρ *ta amorteeser*
61	fuses οι ασφάλειες *ee asfalee-es*
62	shift [gear lever] ο μοχλός ταχυτήτων *ο mokhlos takheeteeton*
63	handbrake το χειρόφρενο *to kheerofreno*
64	muffler [silencer] ο σιγαστήρας *ο seeghasteeras*

Accidents Ατυχήματα

The emergency number in Greece is 100, and it links directly with the police. If you think you will need an interpreter, call the tourist police (☎ 171) who will also help you fill in Greek forms.

There has been an accident.	Έγινε ένα ατύχημα. *eyeene ena ateekheema*
It's …	Είναι … *eene*
2 km from …	δύο χιλιόμετρα από εδώ. *THeeo kheeleeometra apo eTHo*
on the highway [motorway]	στον εθνικό δρόμο *ston ethneeko THromo*
near …	κοντά … *konda*
Where's the nearest telephone?	Πού είναι το κοντινότερο τηλέφωνο; *poo eene to kondeenotero teelefono*
Call …	Καλέστε … *kaleste*
the police	την αστυνομία *teen asteenomeea*
an ambulance	ένα ασθενοφόρο *ena asthenoforo*
a doctor	ένα γιατρό *ena yatro*
the fire department [brigade]	την πυροσβεστική *teen peerozvesteekee*
Can you help me please?	Μπορείτε να με βοηθήσετε; *boreete na me voeetheesete*

Injuries Τραυματισμοί

There are people injured.	Υπάρχουν τραυματίες. *eeparkhoon travmatee-es*
No one is hurt.	Δεν υπάρχουν τραυματίες. *THen eeparkhoon travmatee-es*
He is seriously injured/bleeding.	Είναι σοβαρά τραυματισμένος/αιμορραγεί. *eene sovara travmateezmenos/emorayee*
She's unconscious.	Είναι αναίσθητη. *eene anestheetee*
He can't breathe/move.	Δεν μπορεί να αναπνεύσει/κινηθεί. *THen boree na anapnefsee/keeneethee*
Don't move him.	Μην τον μετακινήσετε. *meen ton metakeeneesete*

INJURIES ➤ 162; DIRECTIONS ➤ 94

Legal matters Νομικά θέματα

What's your insurance company?	Ποιά είναι η ασφαλιστική εταιρία σας; *pia eene ee asfaleesteekee etereea sas*
What's your name and address?	Ποιό είναι το όνομα και η διεύθυνσή σας; *peeo eene to onoma ke ee THee-eftheensee sas*
He ran into me.	Με χτύπησε. *me khteepeese*
She was driving too fast / close.	Οδηγούσε πολύ γρήγορα/πολύ κοντά. *oTHeeghoose polee ghreeghora/ konda*
I had the right of way.	Είχα προτεραιότητα. *eekha protereoteeta*
I was (only) driving at … km/h.	Έτρεχα μόνο … χιλιόμετρα την ώρα. *etrekha mono me … kheeleeometra teen ora*
I'd like an interpreter.	Θα ήθελα έναν/μια διερμηνέα. *tha eethela enan/mia THee-ermeenea*
I didn't see the sign.	Δεν είδα την πινακίδα. *THen eeTHa teen peenakeeTHa*
He/She saw it happen.	Αυτός/αυτή είδε τι συνέβη. *aftos/aftee eeTHe tee seenevee*
The registration number was …	Ο αριθμός κυκλοφορίας ήταν … *o areethmos keekloforeeas eetan*

Μπορώ να δω …, παρακαλώ;	Can I see your …, please?
την άδεια οδήγησης.	driver's license
το πιστοποιητικό της ασφάλειας	insurance card
την άδεια κυκλοφορίας	vehicle registration
Τί ώρα συνέβηκε;	What time did it happen?
Πού συνέβηκε;	Where did it happen?
Ήταν κανείς άλλος αναμεμειγμένος;	Was anyone else involved?
Υπάρχουν μάρτυρες;	Are there any witnesses?
Τρέχατε.	You were speeding.
Δεν δουλεύουν τα φώτα σας.	Your lights aren't working.
Πρέπει να πληρώσετε πρόστιμο.	You'll have to pay a fine (on the spot).
Πρέπει να κάνετε δήλωση στο τμήμα.	We need you to make a statement at the station.

Asking directions
Ρωτώντας το δρόμο

Excuse me, please!	Παρακαλώ! *parakalo*
How do I get to …?	Πώς πάνε στο/στη …; *pos pane sto/stee*
Where is …?	Πού είναι …; *poo eene*
Can you show me on the map where I am?	Μπορείτε να μου δείξετε στο χάρτη πού είμαι; *boreete na moo THeeksete sto khartee poo eeme*
I've lost my way.	Έχασα το δρόμο μου. *ekhasa to THromo moo*
Can you repeat that please?	Μπορείτε να το επαναλάβετε; *boreete na to epanalavete*
More slowly, please.	Πιο αργά, παρακαλώ. *peeo argha, parakalo*
Thanks for your help.	Ευχαριστώ για τη βοήθεια σας. *efkhareesto ya tee voeetheea sas*

Traveling by car Ταξιδεύοντας με το αυτοκίνητο

Is this the right road for …?	Αυτός είναι ο σωστός δρόμος για …; *aftos eene o sostos THromos ya*
How far is it to … from here?	Πόσο απέχει ο/η/το … από εδώ; *poso apekhee o/ee/to … apo eTHO*
Where does this road lead?	Πού πάει αυτός ο δρόμος; *poo paee aftos o THromos*
How do I get onto the highway [motorway]?	Πώς πάω στην Εθνική οδό; *pos pao steen ethrieekee oTHO*
What's the next town called?	Πώς λέγεται η επόμενη πόλη; *pos leyete ee epomenee polee*
How long does it take by car?	Πόση ώρα είναι με το αυτοκίνητο; *posee ora eene me to aftokeeneeto*

> – seeghnomee, parakalo. pos pane
> sto seeTHeeroTHromeeko stathmo?
> – parte to treeto steno sta areestera ke eene eftheea.
> – treeto sta areestera. eene makreea?
> – eene pende lepta me ta poTHya.
> – efkhareesto ya teen voeetheea sas.
> – parakalo.

Location Θέση

Είναι ...	It's ...
ευθεία	straight ahead
στα αριστερά	on the left
στα δεξιά	on the right
από την άλλη μεριά του δρόμου	on the other side of the street
στη γωνία	on the corner
στη γωνία λίγο πιο κάτω	around the corner
στην κατεύθυνση προς ...	in the direction of ...
απέναντι .../πίσω ...	opposite .../behind ...
δίπλα στο/στη .../μετά ...	next to .../after ...
Πάρτε ...	Go down the .../Take the ...
τον παράδρομο/τον κεντρικό δρόμο	side street/main street
το τρίτο στενό στα δεξιά	third right
Περάστε ...	Cross the ...
την πλατεία/την γέφυρα	square/bridge
Στρίψτε αριστερά ...	Turn left ...
μετά τα πρώτα φώτα	after the first traffic lights
στο δεύτερο σταυροδρόμι	at the second intersection [crossroad]

By car Με το αυτοκίνητο

Είναι ... από δω.	It's ... of here.
βόρεια/νότια	north/south
ανατολικά/δυτικά	east/west
Πάρτε το δρόμο για ...	Take the road for ...
Είστε σε λάθος δρόμο.	You're on the wrong road.
Πρέπει να πάτε πίσω στο ...	You'll have to go back to ...
Ακολουθήστε τα σήματα για ...	Follow the signs for ...

How far? Πόσο απέχει;

Είναι ...	It's ...
κοντά/όχι πολύ μακριά/μακριά	close/not far/a long way
πέντε λεπτά με τα πόδια	5 minutes on foot
δέκα λεπτά με το αυτοκίνητο	10 minutes by car
περίπου εκατό μέτρα πιο κάτω	about 100 meters down the road

TIME ➤ 220; NUMBERS ➤ 216

Road signs Σήματα

ΜΟΝΟ ΓΙΑ ΠΡΟΣΒΑΣΗ	access only
ΠΑΡΑΚΑΜΨΗ	detour [diversion]
ΔΩΣΤΕ ΠΡΟΤΕΡΑΙΟΤΗΤΑ	yield [give way]
ΧΑΜΗΛΗ ΓΕΦΥΡΑ	low bridge
ΜΟΝΟΔΡΟΜΟΣ	one-way street
ΟΔΟΣ ... ΚΛΕΙΣΤΗ	road closed
ΣΧΟΛΕΙΟ	school
ΑΝΑΨΤΕ ΤΑ ΦΩΤΑ ΠΟΡΕΙΑΣ	use headlights

Town plan Χάρτης της πόλης

αεροδρόμιο	*aeroTHromeeo*	airport
αθλητικό στάδιο	*athleeteeko staTHeeo*	playing field [sports ground]
αστυνομικό τμήμα	*asteenomeeko tmeema*	police station
βρισκόσαστε εδώ	*vreeskosaste eTHo*	you are here
γραφείο πληροφοριών	*ghrafeeo pleeroforeeon*	information office
δημόσιο κτίριο	*THeemoseeo kteereeo*	public building
διάβαση πεζών	*THeeavasee pezon*	pedestrian crossing
διαδρομή λεωφορείων	*THeeaTHromee leoforeeon*	bus route
εκκλησία	*ekleeseea*	church
θέατρο	*theatro*	theater
κινηματογράφος	*keeneematoghrafos*	movie theater [cinema]
παλιά πόλη	*paleÂa polee*	old town
πάρκο	*parko*	park
πεζόδρομος	*pezoTHromos*	pedestrian precinct
πιάτσα ταξί	*peeatsa taksee*	taxi stand [rank]
προκυμαία	*prokeemea*	harborfront
στάδιο	*staTHeeo*	stadium
σταθμός	*stathmos*	station
σταθμός μετρό	*stathmos metro*	subway [metro] station
στάση λεωφορείων	*stasee leoforeeon*	bus stop
ταχυδρομείο	*takheeTHromeeo*	post office
τουαλέττες	*tooaletes*	toilets
υπόγεια διάβαση	*eepoyeea THeeavasee*	underpass
χώρος στάθμευσης	*khoros stathmefsees*	parking lot [car park]

DICTIONARY ➤ 169; SIGHTSEEING ➤ 97–107

Sightseeing

Tourist information office EOT/KOT

Tourist information offices are known as EOT (**eleeneekos orghaneesmos tooreesmoo** or **eot**) in Greece, and KOT (**keepreeakos orghaneesmos tooreesmoo** or **kot**) in Cyprus. They can be found in most tourist resorts and major towns. The principal tourist attractions are the ancient sites.

Where's the tourist office?	Πού είναι το γραφείο τουρισμού; _poo_ _eene_ to ghra_feeo_ tooree_zmoo_
What are the main points of interest?	Ποιά είναι τα κυριότερα αξιοθέατα; _pia_ _eene_ ta keeree_otera_ akseeo_theata_
We're here for …	Είμαστε εδώ για … _eemaste_ e_тно_ ya
only a few hours	λίγες ώρες μόνο _leeyes_ ores _mono_
a day	μια ημέρα _mia_ _eemera_
a week	μια εβδομάδα _mia_ ev_тнoma_тнa
Can you recommend …?	Μπορείτε να συστήσετε …; bo_reete_ na sees_teesete_
a sightseeing tour	μια ξενάγηση στα αξιοθέατα _mia_ ksen_ayeesee_ sta akseeo_theata_
an excursion	μια εκδρομή _mia_ ek_тнromee_
a boat trip	μια εκδρομή με βάρκα _mia_ ek_тнromee_ me _varka_
Are these leaflets free?	Αυτά τα φυλλάδια είναι δωρεάν; _afta_ ta feel_a_тнeea _eene_ тно_rean_
Do you have any information on …?	Έχετε πληροφορίες για …; _ekhete_ pleerofor_oree_-es ya
Are there any trips to …?	Υπάρχουν ταξίδια για …; _eeparkhoon_ tak_see_тнya ya

DAYS OF THE WEEK ➤ 218; _DIRECTIONS_ ➤ 94

Excursions Εκδρομές

How much does the tour cost?	Πόσο κοστίζει η περιήγηση; *poso kosteezee ee peree-eeyeesee*
Is lunch included?	Συμπεριλαμβάνεται το μεσημεριανό; *seembereelamvanete to meseemeryano*
Where do we leave from?	Από πού φεύγουμε; *apo poo fevghoome*
What time does the tour start?	Τι ώρα αρχίζει η εκδρομή; *tee ora arkheezee ee ekTHromee*
What time do we get back?	Τι ώρα θα επιστρέψουμε; *tee ora tha epeestrepsoome*
Do we have free time in …?	Έχουμε ελεύθερο χρόνο στο …; *ekhoome elefthero khrono sto*
Is there an English-speaking guide?	Υπάρχει Αγγλόφωνος ξεναγός; *eeparkhee anglofonos ksenaghos*

On tour Στην ξενάγηση

Are we going to see …?	Θα δούμε …; *tha THOOme*
We'd like to have a look at the …	Θα θέλαμε να ρίξουμε μια ματιά … *tha thelame na reeksoome mia mateea*
Can we stop here …?	Μπορούμε να σταματήσουμε εδώ …; *boroome na stamateesoome eTHO*
to take photographs	για να πάρουμε φωτογραφίες *ya na paroome fotohrafee-es*
to buy souvenirs	για να αγοράσουμε σουβενίρ *ya na aghorasoome sooveneer*
to use the bathroom [toilet]	για την τουαλέττα *ya teen tooaleta*
Would you take a photo of us, please?	Μπορείτε να μας πάρετε μια φωτογραφία, παρακαλώ; *boreete na mas parete mia fotohrafeea parakalo*
How long do we have here/ in …?	Πόση ώρα έχουμε εδώ/στο …; *posee ora ekhoome eTHO/sto*
Wait! … isn't back yet.	Περιμένετε! … δεν έχει γυρίσει ακόμη. *pereemenete! … THen ekhee yeereesee akomee*
Stop the bus! My child is feeling sick.	Σταματήστε το λεωφορείο! το παιδί μου δεν αισθάνεται καλά. *stamateeste to leoforeeo! to peTHee moo THen esthanete kala*

98

Sights Τα αξιοθέατα

Where is the …	Πού είναι …; *poo eene*
art gallery	η γκαλερί τέχνης *ee galeree tekhnees*
botanical garden	ο βοτανικός κήπος *o votaneekos keepos*
castle	το κάστρο *to kastro*
cathedral	ο καθεδρικός ναός *o katheтнreekos naos*
chapel	το παρεκκλήσι *to parekleesee*
church	η εκκλησία *ee ekleeseea*
city wall	το τείχος *to teekhos*
downtown area	το κέντρο της πόλης *to kendro tees polees*
fountain	το συντριβάνι *to seendreevanee*
harbor	το λιμάνι *to leemanee*
market	η αγορά *ee aghora*
memorial/monument	το μνημείο *to mneemeeo*
monastery	το μοναστήρι/η μονή (on road signs) *to monasteeree/ee monee*
museum	το μουσείο *to mooseeo*
old town	η παλιά πόλη *ee paleea polee*
opera house	η όπερα *ee opera*
palace	τα ανάκτορα *ta anaktora*
park	το πάρκο *to parko*
parliament building	η Βουλή *ee voolee*
shopping area	η εμπορική περιοχή *ee emboreekee pereeokhee*
statue	το άγαλμα *to aghalma*
temple	ναός *naos*
(ancient) theater	το (αρχαίο) θέατρο *to arkheo theatro*
tower	ο πύργος *o peerghos*
town hall	το Δημαρχείο *to тнeemarkheeo*
viewpoint	το πανόραμα *to panorama*
Can you show me on the map?	Μπορείτε να μου δείξετε στο χάρτη; *boreete na moo тнeeksete sto khartee*

DIRECTIONS ➤ 94

Admission Είσοδος

Most sites and museums are closed at least once a week – usually Monday. Admission is often free on Sunday.

If you want to visit a monastery it is best to avoid religious service times (early morning, sunset) and lunchtime. The tourist office or tourist police will have more detailed local opening hours.

Is the … open to the public?	Είναι το … ανοιχτό στο κοινό; *eene to … aneekhto sto keeno*
What are the opening hours?	Ποιές είναι οι ώρες λειτουργίας; *pee-es eene ee ores leetooryeeas*
When does it close?	Τί ώρα κλείνει; *tee ora kleenee*
Is … open on Sundays?	Είναι το … ανοιχτό τις Κυριακές; *eene to … aneekhto tees keereeakes*
When's the next guided tour?	Πότε είναι η επόμενη ξενάγηση; *pote eene ee epomenee ksenayeesee*
Do you have a guidebook (in English)?	Έχετε ένα ταξιδιωτικό οδηγό (στα Αγγλικά); *ekhete ena takseeтнeeoteeko отнeegho (sta angleeka)*
Can I take photos?	Μπορώ να πάρω φωτογραφίες; *boro na paro fotoghrafee-es*
Is there access for the disabled?	Υπάρχει πρόσβαση για άτομα με ειδικές ανάγκες; *eeparkhee prozvasee ya atoma me eeтнeekes ananges*
Is there an audioguide in English?	Υπάρχει ξενάγηση με κασέτα στα Αγγλικά; *eeparkhee ksenayeesee me kaseta sta angleeka*

Paying/Tickets Πληρωμή/Εισιτήρια

How much is the entrance fee?	Πόσο κάνει η είσοδος; *poso kanee ee eesoтнos*
Are there discounts for …?	Υπάρχει μειωμένο εισιτήριο για …; *eeparkhee meeomeno eeseeteereeo ya*
children/students	παιδιά/φοιτητές *peтнya/feeteetes*
senior citizens	συνταξιούχους *seendakseeookhoos*
1 adult and 2 children, please.	Ένας ενήλικας και δύο παιδιά, παρακαλώ. *enas eneeleekas ke тнeeo peтнya parakalo*

– <u>pen</u>de eeseet<u>tee</u>reea, paraka<u>lo</u>.
eep<u>ar</u>khee mee<u>o</u>meno eeseet<u>tee</u>reeo?
– *ne. ya* peTH<u>ya</u> *ke seendaksee<u>oo</u>khoos*
eene TH<u>ee</u>o *evro.*
– THeeo e<u>nee</u>leekes ke <u>tree</u>a peTH<u>ya</u>, paraka<u>lo</u>.
– <u>kan</u>ee <u>te</u>serees kheelee<u>a</u>THes
okhta<u>ko</u>see-es, paraka<u>lo</u>.

ΕΛΕΥΘΕΡΗ ΕΙΣΟΔΟΣ	free admission
ΑΝΟΙΧΤΟ	open
ΚΛΕΙΣΤΟ	closed
ΣΟΥΒΕΝΙΡ	gift shop
ΤΕΛΕΥΤΑΙΑ ΕΙΣΟΔΟΣ ΣΤΙΣ 5 μμ	last entry at 5 p.m.
Η ΕΠΟΜΕΝΗ ΞΕΝΑΓΗΣΗ ΣΤΙΣ ...	next tour at ...
ΑΠΑΓΟΡΕΥΕΤΑΙ Η ΕΙΣΟΔΟΣ	no entry
ΑΠΑΓΟΡΕΥΕΤΑΙ Η ΦΩΤΟΓΡΑΦΗΣΗ ΜΕ ΦΛΑΣ	no flash photography
ΩΡΕΣ ΛΕΙΤΟΥΡΓΙΑΣ	visiting hours

Impressions Εντυπώσεις

It's ...	Είναι ... *eene*
amazing	καταπληκτικό *katapleekteeko*
beautiful	όμορφο *omorfo*
boring	βαρετό *vareto*
breathtaking	φαντασμαγορικό *fandazmaghoreeko*
impressive	εντυπωσιακό *endeeposeeako*
incredible	απίστευτο *apeestefto*
interesting	ενδιαφέρον *enTHeeaferon*
magnificent	μεγαλοπρεπές *meghaloprepes*
romantic	ρομαντικό *romandeeko*
strange	παράξενο *parakseno*
superb	έξοχο *eksokho*
terrible	φοβερό *fovero*
ugly	άσχημο *askheemo*
It's good value	Είναι καλή τιμή. *eene kalee teemee*
It's a rip-off.	Είναι κλεψιά. *eene klepseea*
I like it.	Μου αρέσει. *moo aresee*
I don't like it.	Δεν μου αρέσει. *THen moo aresee*

λουτρά	lootra	baths
αμφιθέατρο(ν)	amfeetheatro(n)	amphitheater
εκκλησία	ekleeseea	church
μονή	monee	monastery
τάφος	tafos	grave, tomb
το μουσείο	to mooseeo	museum
εικόνα	eekona	icon
ακρόπολις	akropolees	fortified city
ανάκτορα	anaktora	palace
κίονας	keeonas	column
ναός	naos	temple
άγαλμα	aghalma	statue

αρχαιολογία	*arkheolo<u>yee</u>a*	archaeology
αρχαία	*ar<u>khea</u>*	antiquities
αρχιτεκτονική	*arkheetektonee<u>kee</u>*	architecture
(βυζαντινή) τέχνη	*(veezandee<u>nee</u>) <u>te</u>khnee*	(Byzantine) art
αγγειοπλαστική	*angeeoplastee<u>kee</u>*	ceramics / pottery
διάζωμα	*THee<u>a</u>zoma*	frieze
κοσμήματα	*koz<u>mee</u>mata*	jewelry
ψηφιδωτό	*pseefeeTHo<u>to</u>*	mosaic
πίνακας	*<u>pee</u>nakas*	painting
γλυπτό	*ghleep<u>to</u>*	sculpture
ταπετσαρία	*tapetsa<u>ree</u>a*	tapestry

Who/What/When? Ποιός/Τί/Πότε;

What's that building? Τι είναι αυτό το κτίριο;
tee eene afto to kteereeo

Who was the …? Ποιός ήταν ο/η …; *peeos eetan o/ee*

architect αρχιτέκτονας *arkheetektonas*

artist καλλιτέχνης *kaleetekhnees*

painter ζωγράφος *zoghrafos*

When was it built / painted? Πότε κτίστηκε/ζωγραφίστηκε;
pote kteesteeke/zoghrafeesteeke

Temple architectural styles

Δωρικός ρυθμός *THoreekos reethmos*
Doric style – famous for its simplicity and perfect symmetry. The best example is the Parthenon, on the Acropolis of Athens.

Ιωνικός ρυθμός *eeoneekos reethmos*
Ionic style – The column capital is in the form of a spiral, sometimes with intricate decorations. Example: the Temple of Athena Nike on the Acropolis.

Κορινθιακός ρυθμός *koreentheeakos reethmos*
Corinthian style – Columns are similar to Ionic, but the capital is decorated with thistle leaves. The Temple of Olympian Zeus in Athens is of this style.

Αττικός ρυθμός *ateekos reethmos*
Attic style – generally refers to the style of art in Athens (Attica).

Church styles

Βασιλική *vaseeleekee*
Basilica – early form of Christian church. Rectangular in shape, later ones have a single dome.

Βυζαντινός ρυθμός *veezandeenos reethmos*
Byzantine style – churches built in the shape of a cross, with a main central dome and four smaller ones at each point of the cross. More elaborate churches are made in the shape of a double cross (8 points) with a dome at each point. The Hagia Sophia built in A.D. 537 (in Istanbul, Turkey) became the prototype.

History

What period is that? Ποιάς περιόδου είναι αυτό;
pias pereeoTHoo eene afto

Κυκλαδικός πολιτισμός *keeklaTHeekos poleeteezmos* 3200–1100 B.C.
Cycladic civilization; ruins can be found on the island of Thira or Santorini.

Μινωικός πολιτισμός *meenoeekos poleeteezmos* c.2500–c.1500 B.C.
Minoan civilization; ruins at Knossos and Phaestos on Crete.

Μυκηναϊκός πολιτισμός
meekeenaeekos poleeteezmos 1600–1100 B.C.
Mycenaean civilization, centered on Mycenae.

Ελληνοπερσικοί πόλεμοι
eleenoperseekee polemee c. 500 B.C.
Greco-Persian wars; battles of Marathon and Salamis.

Κλασσική εποχή *klaseekee epokhee* 500–400 B.C.
Classical period. Flourishing of all art. Building of the Acropolis and the temples of Olympian Zeus in Athens and Artemis at Ephesus.

Ελληνιστικοί χρόνοι *eleeneesteekee khronee*
late 4th–1st century B.C.
Hellenistic period. Rise of Macedonia under Philip and later his son Alexander the Great. Expansion of "Hellas" to Afghanistan.

Ρωμαϊκοί χρόνοι *romaeekee khronee* 27 B.C.–A.D. 330
Roman period. Greece becomes a Roman province.

Βυζαντινή Αυτοκρατορία
veezandeenee aftokratoreea 330–1453
Foundation of Eastern Roman Empire in 330 A.D., also known as the Byzantine Empire. Capital moves from Rome to Constantinople.

Τουρκοκρατία *toorkokrateea* 1453–1821
Turkish occupation ended by the Greek War of Independence (1821–1829).

Νεοελληνική εποχή *neoeleeneekee epokhee* 1829–present
Modern Greek period

Religious services Θρησκευτικές λειτουργίες

The prevalent religion in Greece is Greek Orthodox. As a tourist, you will find the religious service fascinating, the ritual having barely changed since the early Byzantine years (see above). The head of the Eastern Orthodox Church is the patriarch, who is based in Istanbul. The main churches stay open all day. You will not be allowed into a church or a monastery if you are wearing shorts, a mini skirt, or a sleeveless top/dress.

(Greek) Orthodox Church	(Ελληνική) Ορθόδοξος εκκλησία *eleeneekee orthoтнoksos ekleeseea*
Catholic/Protestant Church	Καθολική/Διαμαρτυρόμενη εκκλησία *katholeekee/тнeeamarteeromenee ekleesseea*
mosque	τζαμί *tzamee*
synagogue	συναγωγή *seenaghoyee*
What time is …?	Τί ώρα είναι …; *tee ora eene*
mass/the service	η λειτουργία *ee leetooryeea*

In the countryside Στην εξοχή

I'd like a map of …	Θα ήθελα ένα χάρτη … *tha eethela ena khartee*
this region	αυτής της περιοχής *aftees tees pereeokhees*
walking routes	διαδρομών περιήγησης *THeeaTHromon peree-eeyeesees*
cycle routes	ποδηλατόδρομων *poTHeelatoTHromon*
How far is it to …?	Πόσο μακριά είναι για …; *poso makreea eene ya*
Is there a right of way?	Υπάρχει προτεραιότητα; *eeparkhee protereoteeta*
Is there a scenic route to …?	Υπάρχει μονοπάτι/γραφικός δρόμος για …; *eeparkhee monopatee/ghrafeekos THromos ya*
Can you show me on the map?	Μπορείτε να μου δείξετε στο χάρτη; *boreete na moo THeeksete sto khartee*
I'm lost.	Έχω χαθεί. *eho khathee*

Organized walks Οργανωμένοι περίπατοι

When does the guided walk/hike set out?	Πότε ξεκινάει ο περίπατος/η πεζοπορία με τον ξεναγό; *pote ksekeenaee o pereepatos/ee pezoporeea me ton ksenagho*
When will we return?	Πότε θα επιστρέψουμε; *pote tha epeestrepsoome*
What is the walk/hike like?	Πώς είναι ο περίπατος/η πεζοπορία; *pos eene o pereepatos/ee pezoporeea*
gentle/medium/tough	ομαλός/μέτριος/δύσκολος *omalos/metreeos/THeeskolos*
Where do we meet?	Πού θα συναντηθούμε; *poo tha seenandeethoome*
I'm exhausted.	Είμαι ξεθεωμένος/-η. *eeme ksetheomenos/-ee*
What kind of … is that?	Τι είδους … είναι αυτό; *tee eeTHoos … eene afto*
animal/bird	ζώο/πουλί *zoo/poolee*
flower/tree	λουλούδι/δέντρο *loolooTHee/THendro*

HIKING GEAR ➤ 145

Geographic features
Γεωγραφικά χαρακτηριστικά

bridge	η γέφυρα *ee yefeera*
cave	το σπήλαιο *to speeleo*
cliff	ο γκρεμός *o gremos*
farm	η φάρμα *ee farma*
field	το χωράφι *to khorafee*
forest	το δάσος *to THasos*
hill	ο λόφος *o lofos*
lake	η λίμνη *ee leemnee*
mountain	το βουνό, το όρος (on maps) *to voono, to oros*
mountain pass	το ορεινό πέρασμα *to oreeno perazma*
nature reserve	ο εθνικός δρυμός *o ethneekos THreemos*
panorama	το πανόραμα *to panorama*
park	ο κήπος/το πάρκο *o keepos/to parko*
path	το μονοπάτι *to monopatee*
peak	η κορυφή *ee koreefee*
picnic area	η περιοχή για πικ-νικ *ee pereeokhee ya "picnic"*
pond	η λιμνούλα *ee leemnoola*
rapids	το ρεύμα ποταμού *to revma potamoo*
ravine	η ρεματιά *ee remateea*
river	ο ποταμός *o potamos*
sea	η θάλασσα *ee thalasa*
spa	τα ιαματικά λουτρά *ta eeamateeka lootra*
stream	το ρυάκι *to reeakee*
valley	η κοιλάδα *ee keelaTHa*
viewing point	η πανοραμική θέση *ee panorameekee thesee*
village	το χωριό *to khoryo*
vineyard / winery	ο αμπελώνας/η οινοποιεία *o ambelonas/ee eenopee-eea*
waterfall	ο καταρράχτης *o katarakhtees*
wood	το δάσος *to THasos*

Leisure

Events Εκδηλώσεις

The tourist police and EOT can provide a list of cultural events in the area. For Athens the EOT publication *Athina* and the English newspaper *Athens News* give a comprehensive guide of what's on, where to eat, current exhibits etc. A separate magazine *Music Hall*, giving a diary of events, is published by **megharo mooseekees**.

Do you have a program of events?	Έχετε έναν οδηγό θεαμάτων; *ekhete enan oτHeegho theamaton*
Can you recommend a …?	Μπορείτε να συστήσετε ένα … *boreete na seesteesete ena*
ballet / concert	μπαλέτο/συναυλία *baleto/seenavleea*
movie [film]	ταινία *teneea*
opera	όπερα *opera*
ancient tragedy / comedy	αρχαία τραγωδία/κωμωδία *arkhea traghoτHeea/ komoτHeea*
When does it start / end?	Τί ώρα αρχίζει/τελειώνει; *tee ora arkheezee/teleeonee*

Availability Διαθεσιμότητα

During the Athens festival (**festeeval atheenon**) in the summer (June–September), information and tickets for performances at the Theater of Herodeion Attikon and Epidaros can be obtained from the ticket office at Stadiou 4 St. Tickets for other performances can be bought directly from the theater box office.

Where can I get tickets?	Πού μπορώ να βρω εισιτήρια; *poo boro na vro eeseeteereea*
Are there any seats for tonight?	Υπάρχουν θέσεις για απόψε; *eeparkhoon thesees ya apopse*
There are … of us.	Είμαστε … *eemaste*

Tickets Εισιτήρια

How much are the seats?	Πόσο κοστίζουν οι θέσεις; *poso kosteezoon ee thesees*
Do you have anything cheaper?	Έχετε τίποτα φτηνότερο; *ekhete teepota fteenotero*
I'd like to reserve …	Θα ήθελα να κλείσω … *tha eethela na kleeso*
3 for Sunday matinée/evening	τρία για την απογευματινή/βραδινή της Κυριακή *treea ya tee apoyevmateenee/ vratHeenee tees keereeakees*

Ποιός/-ά/-ό είναι … της πιστωτικής σας κάρτας;	What's your credit card …?
ο αριθμός/το είδος	number/type
η ημερομηνία λήξεως	expiration [expiry] date
Παρακαλώ, να παραλάβετε τα εισιτήρια …	Please pick up the tickets …
μέχρι τις … μ.μ.	by … p.m.
στο γραφείο κρατήσεων	at the reservations desk

(May I have) a program, please?	(Μπορώ να έχω) ένα πρόγραμμα, παρακαλώ; *(boro na ekho) ena proghrama parakalo*
Where's the coatcheck [cloakroom]?	Πού είναι η γκαρνταρόμπα; *poo eene ee gardaromba*

ΚΡΑΤΗΣΕΙΣ ΘΕΣΕΩΝ	advance reservations
ΕΙΣΙΤΗΡΙΑ ΓΙΑ ΑΠΟΨΕ	tickets for today

– *boro na sas voeetheeso?*
– tha *eethela treea eeseeteereea ya teen
apopseenee seenavleea.*
– *veveos.*
– *boro na pleeroso me peestoteekee karta?*
– *maleesta, keeree-e.*
– *tote tha khreeseemopee-eeso VISA.*
– *efkhareesto … eepoghrapste eтно, parakalo..*

NUMBERS ➤ 216

Movies [Cinema] Κινηματογράφος

After a sharp decline in the 1980s, movie theaters are experiencing a revival in Greece. There is at least one movie theater in most resorts. And if you are there in the summer, it is worth going to an open air theater – watching a film on a warm summer evening with the rising moon and a star-studded sky as a backdrop is a unique experience.

Foreign films are always subtitled, so you should have no problem finding English-language films.

What's playing at the movies [cinema] tonight?	Τί παίζει ο κινηματογράφος αμόψε; *tee pezee o keeneematoghrafos ·apopse*
Is the film dubbed/subtitled?	Η ταινία είναι μεταγλωττισμένη/με υπότιτλους; *ee teneea eene metaghloteezmenee/me eepoteetloos*
Is the film in the original English?	Η ταινία είναι στα Αγγλικά; *ee teneea eene sta angleeka*
Who's the main actor/actress?	Ποιός είναι ο πρωταγωνιστής; *peeos eene o protaghoneestees*
A ..., please.	... , παρακαλώ. *... parakalo*
box of popcorn	ένα πακέτο ποπ-κορν *ena paketo "popcorn"*
chocolate ice cream	ένα παγωτό σοκολάτα *ena paghoto sokolata*
hot dog	ένα χοτ-ντογκ *ena "hot dog"*
soft drink/soda	ένα αναψυκτικό *ena anapseekteeko*
small/regular/large	μικρό/μέτριο/μεγάλο *meekro/metreeo/meghalo*

Theater Θέατρο

What's playing at the ... Theater?	Τί παίζεται στο Θέατρο ...; *tee pezete sto theatro*
Who's the playwright?	Ποιός είναι ο δραματουργός; *peeos eene o THramatoorghos*
Do you think I'd enjoy it? I don't know much Greek.	Νομίζετε ότι θα το ευχαριστηθώ; Δεν μιλώ πολλά Ελληνικά. *nomeezete otee tha to efkhareesteetho? THen meelo pola eleeneeka*

Opera/Ballet/Dance
Όπερα/Μπαλέτο/Χορός

Who's the composer/soloist?	Ποιός είναι ο συνθέτης/ο σολίστας; *peeos eene o seenthetees/o soleestas*
Is formal evening dress required?	Χρειάζεται βραδυνό ένδυμα; *khreeazete vraTHeeno enTHeema*
Where's the opera house?	Πού είναι η Όπερα; *poo eene ee opera*
Who's dancing?	Ποιός χορεύει; *peeos khorevee*
I'm interested in contemporary/folk dance.	Με ενδιαφέρει ο μοντέρνος χορός/οι παραδοσιακοί χοροί. *me enTHeeaferee o modernos khoros/ee paraTHoseeakee khoree*

Music/Concerts Μουσική/Συναυλίες

Where's the concert hall?	Πού είναι η αίθουσα συναυλιών; *poo eene ee ethoosa seenavleeon*
Which orchestra/band is playing?	Ποιά ορχήστρα/ποιό συγκρότημα παίζει; *peea orkheestra/peeo seegroteema pezee*
What are they playing?	Τί παίζουν; *tee pezoon*
Who's the conductor?	Ποιός είναι ο διευθυντής ορχήστρας; *peeos eene o THeeeftheendees orkheestras*
Who's the support band?	Ποιό είναι το βοηθητικό συγκρότημα; *peeo eene to voeetheeteeko seengroteema*
I really like …	Με ενδιαφέρει … *me enTHeeaferee*
folk music	η δημοτική μουσική *ee THeemoteekee mooseekee*
jazz	η τζαζ *ee "jazz"*
pop	η ποπ *ee "pop"*
rock music	η μουσική ροκ *ee mooseekee "rock"*
soul music	η σόουλ *ee so-ool*
rembetika (traditional Greek music)	τα ρεμπέτικα *ta rembeteeka*
Have you ever heard of her/him?	Τον/Την έχετε ακουστά; *ton/teen ekhete akoosta*

Nightlife Νυχτερινή ζωή

What is there to do in the evenings?	Τι μπορώ να κάνω τα βράδυα; *tee boro na kano ta vraTHya*
Can you recommend a good …?	Μπορείτε να συστήσετε ένα καλό …; *boreete na seesteesete ena kalo*
Is there a … in town?	Υπάρχει … στην πόλη; *eeparkhee … steen polee*
(music) bar	μπαρ (με μουσική) *"bar" (me mooseekee)*
casino	καζίνο *"casino"*
discotheque	ντισκοτέκ *deeskotek*
gay club	κλαμπ για ομοφυλόφιλους *"club" ya omofeelofeeloos*
nightclub	νυχτερινό κέντρο *neekhtereeno kendro*
restaurant (with live Greek music)	εστιατόριο (με ζωντανή ελληνική μουσική) *esteeatoreeo (me zondanee eleeneekee mooseekee)*
Is there a floor show/cabaret?	Υπάρχει ζωντανό σώου/καμπαρέ; *eeparkhee zondano "show"/"cabaret"*
How do I get there?	Πώς πάω εκεί; *pos pao ekee*

Admission Είσοδος

What time does the show start?	Τι ώρα αρχίζει το σώου; *tee ora arkheezee to "show"*
Is evening dress required?	Χρειάζεται βραδυνό ένδυμα; *khreeazete vraTHeeno enTHeema*
Is a reservation necessary?	Είναι απαραίτητη η κράτηση; *eene apareteetee ee krateesee*
Do we need to be members?	Χρειάζεται να είμαστε μέλη; *khreeazete na eemaste melee*
How long will we have to stand in line [queue]?	Πόση ώρα πρέπει να περιμένουμε στην ουρά; *posee ora prepee na pereemenoome steen oora*
I'd like a good table.	Θα ήθελα ένα καλό τραπέζι. *tha eethela ena kalo trapezee*

Children Παιδιά

Can you recommend something for the children?	Μπορείτε να μας συστήσετε κάτι για τα παιδιά; _boreete na mas seesteesete katee ya ta peтнeea_
Where can I change the baby's diaper [nappy]?	Που μπορώ να αλλάξω την πάνα του μωρού; _poo boro na alakso teen pana too moroo_
Where are the bathrooms [toilets]?	Πού είναι οι τουαλέττες; _poo eene ee tooaletes_
amusement arcade	αίθουσα ψυχαγωγίας _ethoosa pseekhaghoyeeas_
fairground	λούνα-παρκ _loona-park_
kiddie [paddling] pool	ρηχή πισίνα _reekhee peeseena_
playground	παιδική χαρά _peтнeekee khara_
play group	παιδικός σταθμός _peтнeekos stathmos_
zoo	ζωολογικός κήπος _zooloyeekos keepos_

Baby-sitting Φύλαξη παιδιών

Can you recommend a reliable baby-sitter?	Μπορείτε να συστήσετε μια υπεύθυνη μπέιμπυ-σίτερ; _boreete na seesteesete mia eepeftheenee "babysitter/dada_
Is there constant supervision?	Υπάρχει συνεχής επίβλεψη; _eeparkhee seenekhees epeevlepsee_
Is the staff properly trained?	Οι βοηθοί είναι καλά εκπαιδευμένοι; _ee voeethee eene kala ekpeтнevmenee_
When can I drop them off?	Πότε μπορώ να τα αφήσω; _pote boro na ta afeeso_
I'll pick them up at ...	Θα τα πάρω στις ... _tha ta paro stees_
We'll be back by ...	Θα είμαστε πίσω στις ... _tha eemaste peeso stees_
What age is he/she?	Τι ηλικίας είναι; _tee eeleekeeas eene_
She's 3 and he's 18 months.	Αυτή είναι τριών χρονών και αυτός δεκαοχτώ μηνών. _aftee eene treeon khronon ke aftos тнekaokhto meenon_

Sports Αθλητισμός

The most popular sports in Greece are basketball (**kalathosfe-reesee**) – even the smallest towns have their own basketball team – followed closely by soccer (**poτHosfero**). Soccer matches are usually played on Sunday. The main stadiums are **panatheena-eeko staτHeeo** in Athens and **staτHeeo kara-eeskakee** in Piraeus.

Water sports are very popular on the islands and in coastal areas. However, you need a special permit to dive with oxygen tanks.

Winter skiing has gained popularity in the last few years – and there are 16 ski resorts on the mainland. Ask EOT for details on locations and snow conditions.

Spectating Ως θεατής

Is there a soccer [football] game [match] this Sunday?	Υπάρχει αγώνας ποδοσφαίρου αυτή τη Κυριακή; *eeparkhee aghonas poτHosferoo aftee teen keereeakee*
Which teams are playing?	Ποιές ομάδες παίζουν; *pee-es omaτHes pezoon*
Can you get me a ticket?	Μπορείτε να μου βρείτε ένα εισιτήριο; *boreete na moo vreete ena eeseeteereeo*
What's the admission charge?	Πόσο κάνει η είσοδος; *poso kanee ee eesoτHos*
Where's the racetrack [racecourse]?	Πού είναι το ιπποδρόμιο; *poo eene to eepoτHromeeo*
Where can I place a bet?	Πού μπορώ να βάλω στοίχημα; *poo boro na valo steekheema*
athletics	τα αθλήματα στίβου *ta athleemata steevoo*
basketball	η καλαθοσφαίρηση, το μπάσκετ *ee kalathosfereesee, to "basket"*
cycling	η ποδηλασία *ee poτHeelaseea*
golf	το γκόλφ *to "golf"*
horse racing	οι ιπποδρομίες *ee eepoτHromee-es*
sailing	η ιστιοπλοΐα *ee eesteeoploeea*
soccer [football]	το ποδόσφαιρο *to poτHosfero*
swimming	η κολύμβηση *ee koleemveesee*
tennis	το τέννις *to "tennis"*
volleyball	το βόλεϋ *to "volley"*
water-skiing	το θαλάσσιο σκι *to thalaseeo "ski"*

114

Playing Το παιχνίδι

Where's the nearest …?	Πού είναι ο/το κοντινότερος/-ο …; _poo eene o/to kondeenoteros/-o_
golf course	γήπεδο γκόλφ _yeepeтно "golf"_
sports club	αθλητικός όμιλος _athleeteekos omeelos_
Where are the tennis courts?	Πού είναι τα γήπεδα τέννις; _poo eene ta yeepeтна "tennis"_
What's the charge per …?	Ποιό είναι το κόστος για … _peeo eene to kostos ya_
day/round/hour	την ημέρα/το παιχνίδι/την ώρα _teen eemera/to pekhneeтнee/teen ora_
Do I need to be a member?	Πρέπει να είμαι μέλος; _prepee na eeme melos_
Where can I rent …?	Πού μπορώ να νοικιάσω …; _poo boro na neekeeaso_
boots	μπότες _botes_
clubs	μπαστούνια _bastooneea_
equipment	εξοπλισμό _eksopleezmo_
a racket	μια ρακέτα _mia raketa_
Can I get lessons?	Μπορώ να πάρω μαθήματα; _boro na paro matheemata_
Do you have a fitness room?	Έχετε δωμάτιο γυμναστικής; _ekhete тнomateeo yeemnasteekees_
Can I join in?	Μπορώ να συμμετάσχω; _boro na seemetaskho_

Λυπάμαι. Είναι όλα κλεισμένα.	I'm sorry, we're booked up.
Υπάρχει μια προκαταβολή των …	There is a deposit of …
Τί μέγεθος είστε;	What size are you?
Χρειαζόσαστε μια φωτογραφία διαβατηρίου.	You need a passport size photo.

ΑΠΑΓΟΡΕΥΕΤΑΙ ΤΟ ΨΑΡΕΜΑ	no fishing
ΑΠΟΔΥΤΗΡΙΑ	changing

At the beach Στην παραλία

Greek beaches are mostly free and often offer a range of water sports. The beaches run by EOT require an entrance fee, but they tend to have more facilities. The use of jet-skis is restricted to a few beaches only, at a certain distance from the land, and at specific hours (ask at your resort). In most island and mainland resorts, it is acceptable to lie on the beach topless, but ask for information on nudist beaches. If in doubt, don't go topless unless you see others first. Greeks rarely go topless, and you may cause offense if you sunbathe topless on a beach frequented by locals.

Is the beach …?	Είναι η παραλία …; *eene ee paraleea*
pebbly / sandy	με χαλίκια/με άμμο *me khaleekeea/me amo*
Is there a … here?	Υπάρχει … εδώ *eeparkhee … eTHO*
children's pool	παιδική πισίνα *peTHeekee peeseena*
swimming pool	πισίνα *peeseena*
indoor / open-air	κλειστή/ανοιχτή *kleestee/aneekhtee*
Is it safe to swim / dive here?	Είναι ασφαλές εδώ για κολύμπι/κατάδυση; *eene asfales eTHO ya koleembee/kataTHeesee*
Is it safe for children?	Είναι ασφαλές για παιδιά; *eene asfales ya ta peTHya*
Is there a lifeguard?	Υπάρχει ναυαγοσώστης; *eeparkhee navaghosostees*
Is this a nudist beach?	Αυτή είναι παραλία για γυμνιστές; *aftee eene paraleea ya yeemneestes*
I want to rent a / some …	Θέλω να νοικιάσω … *thelo na neekeeaso*
deck chair	μια σεζ-λονγκ *mia sez-long*
diving equipment	εξοπλισμό για υποβρύχιο κολύμπι *eksopleezmo ya eepovreekheeo koleembee*
jet-ski	ένα τζετ-σκι *ena "jet-ski"*
motorboat	μια εξωλέμβιο *mia eksolemveeo*
sailing boat	ένα ιστιοπλοϊκό *ena eesteeoploeeko*
umbrella [sunshade]	μια ομπρέλα *mia ombrela*
water skis	θαλάσσια σκι *thalaseea "ski"*
windsurfer	ένα γουίντσερφ *ena "windsurfer"*

Skiing Χειμερινό σκι

Skiing has become very popular in the last few years – with 16 ski resorts on all the main summits on the mainland. Ask EOT for details on locations and snow conditions.

I'd like to rent ...	Θα ήθελα να νοικιάσω ... *tha eethela na neekeeaso*
poles	μπαστούνια του σκι *bastooneea too "ski"*
skates	παγοπέδιλα *paghopeтнeela*
ski boots/skis	μπότες του σκι/σκι *botes too "ski"/"ski"*
These are too ...	Αυτά είναι πολυ ... *afta eene polee*
big/small	μεγάλα/μικρά *meghala/meekra*
loose/tight	φαρδιά/στενά *farтнeea/stena*
A lift pass for a day/ 5 days.	Μια άδεια για μια ημέρα/πέντε ημέρες. *mia aтнea ya mia eemera/pende eemeres*
I'd like to join the ski school.	Θα ήθελα να γραφτώ στη σχολή σκι. *tha eethela na ghrafto stee skholee "ski"*.
I'm a beginner.	Είμαι αρχάριος/αρχάρια. *eeme arkhareeos/arkhareea*
I'm experienced.	Είμαι έμπειρος/έμπειρη. *eeme embeeros/embeeree*

ΤΕΛΕΣΕΖ	cable car/gondola
ΤΕΛΕΦΕΡΙΚ	chair lift

On the slopes Στην πίστα σκι

Is this slope suitable for ...?	Αυτή η πλαγιά είναι κατάλληλη για ...; *aftee ee playa eene kataleelee ya*
beginners	αρχάριους *arkhareeoos*
average skiers	μέτριους σκιερ *metreeoos skee-er*
good skiers	καλούς σκιέρ *kaloos skee-er*
Where does the ski school meet?	Πού συγκεντρώνεται η σχολή σκι; *poo seegendronete ee skholee "ski"*
Are the chair lifts in operation?	Λειτουργούν οι τελεσέζ; *leetoorghoon ee telesez*

Making Friends

Introductions Συστάσεις

Greeks always shake hands when they meet for the first time, and also on subsequent meetings. With close friends, it is customary to exchange kisses on both cheeks when meeting and parting.

When you meet people for the first time, it is more polite to address them by their surname until prompted to use their first name.

GRAMMAR

Greek has a formal and an informal form of "you": **ya sas/ya sou**. The informal is used only between friends or when addressing children. Use the formal **ya sas** unless prompted to do otherwise.

Hello, we haven't met.	Χαίρετε, δεν γνωριζόμαστε. _kherete тнеn ghnoreezomaste_
My name is …	Λέγομαι … _leghome_
May I introduce …?	Να σας συστήσω … _na sas seesteeso_
John, this is …	Γιάννη, από εδώ ο/η … _yeeanee apo eтнo o/ee_
Pleased to meet you.	Χαίρω πολύ. _khero polee_
What's your name?	Πώς λέγεστε; _pos leyeste_
How are you?	Πώς είσαι (Πώς είστε); _pos eese (pos eeste)_
Fine, thanks. And you?	Καλά, ευχαριστώ. Εσύ; (Εσείς;) _kala, efkhareesto. esee (esees)_

– _ya sou, tee kanees?_
– _kala, efkhareesto. esee?_
– _kala, efkhareesto._

118

Where are you from?
Από πού είσαι (είστε);

Where do you come from?	Από πού είσαι (είστε); *apo poo eese (eeste)*
I'm from …	Είμαι από … *eeme apo*
Australia	την Αυστραλία *teen afstraleea*
Britain	την Βρεταννία *teen vretaneea*
Canada	τον Καναδά *ton kanaTHa*
England	την Αγγλία *teen angleea*
Ireland	την Ιρλανδία *teen eerlanTHeea*
Scotland	τη Σκωτία *tee skoteea*
the U.S.	τις Ηνωμένες Πολιτείες *tees eenomenes poleetee-es*
Wales	την Ουαλλία *teen ooaleea*
Where do you live?	Πού μένεις (μένετε); *poo menees (menete)*
What part of … are you from?	Από ποιό μέρος …. είσαι (είστε); *apo peeo meros …. eese (eeste)*
Greece	της Ελλάδας *tees elaTHas*
Cyprus	της Κύπρου *tees keeproo*
We come here every year.	Ερχόμαστε εδώ κάθε χρόνο. *erkhomaste eTHo kathe khrono*
It's my / our first visit.	Είναι η πρώτη μου/μας επίσκεψη. *eene ee protee moo/mas epeeskepsee*
Have you ever been to Britain / the U.S.?	Έχεις (έχετε) πάει ποτέ στη Βρεταννία/ στις Ηνωμένες Πολιτείες; *ekhees (ekhete) paee pote stee vretaneea/ stees eenomenes poleetee-es*
Do you like it here?	Σου (σας) αρέσει εδώ; *soo (sas) aresee eTHo*
I love (the) … here.	Μου αρέσει … εδώ. *moo aresee … eTHo*
I don't care for (the) … here.	Δεν με ενδιαφέρει … εδώ. *THen me enTHeeaferee … eTHo*
architecture	η αρχιτεκτονική *ee arkheetektoneekee*
countryside	η εξοχή *ee eksokhee*
cuisine	η κουζίνα *ee koozeena*

Who are you with?
Με ποιόν/ποιάν είσαι (είστε);

Who are you with?	Με ποιόν/ποιάν είσαι (είστε); *me peeon/pian eese (eeste)*
I'm on my own.	Είμαι μόνος/-η μου. *eeme monos/-ee moo*
I'm with a friend.	Είμαι με ένα φίλο/μια φίλη μου. *eeme me ena feelo/mia feelee moo*
I'm with my …	Είμαι με … μου. *eeme me … moo*
wife	τη γυναίκα *tee yeeneka*
husband	τον άνδρα *ton anthra*
family	την οικογένειά *teen eekoyeneea*
children	τα παιδιά *ta pethya*
parents	τους γονείς *toos ghonees*
boyfriend/girlfriend	το φίλο/τη φίλη *to feelo/tee feelee*
father/mother	τον πατέρα/τη μητέρα *ton patera/tee meetera*
son/daughter	το γιό/την κόρη *to yo/teen koree*
brother/sister	τον αδελφό/την αδελφή *ton athelfo/ teen athelfee*
uncle/aunt	το θείο/τη θεία *to theeo/tee theea*
Are you married?	Είσαι (είστε) παντρεμένος/-η; *eese (eeste) pandremenos/-ee*
I'm …	Είμαι … *eeme*
married/single	παντρεμένος(-η)/ελεύθερος(-η) *pandremenos(-ee)/eleftheros(-ee)*
divorced/separated	διαζευγμένος(-η) *deeazevghmenos(-ee)*
We live together.	Συζούμε. *seezoome*
Do you have any children?	Έχετε παιδιά; *ekhete pethya*
2 boys and a girl.	Δύο αγόρια και ένα κορίτσι. *theeo aghoreea ke ena koreetsee*
How old are they?	Πόσων χρονών είναι; *poson khronon eene*
They're 10 and 12.	Είναι δέκα και δώδεκα. *eene theka ke thotheka*

What do you do? Τι δουλειά κάνετε;

What do you do?	Τι δουλειά κάνεις (κάνετε); _tee_ THoo_lee_a ka_nees_ (ka_nete_)
What are you studying?	Τι σπουδάζεις (σπουδάζετε); _tee_ spoo_THa_zees (spoo_THa_zete)
I'm studying ...	Σπουδάζω ... spoo_THa_zo
I'm in ...	Είμαι ... _eeme_
business	στο εμπόριο sto _embo_reeo
engineering	στη μηχανική stee meekha_nee_kee
retail	στις λιανικές πωλήσεις stees leeanee_kes_ po_lee_sees
sales	στις πωλήσεις stees po_lee_sees
Who do you work for ...?	Για ποιόν δουλεύετε; ya pee_on_ THoo_leve_te
I work for ...	Δουλεύω για ... THoo_levo_ ya
I'm a/an ...	Είμαι ... _eeme_
accountant	λογιστής/λογίστρια lo_yees_tees/lo_yees_treea
housewife	(ν)οικοκυρά (n)eekoke_era_
student	φοιτητής/φοιτήτρια feetee_tees_/fee_tee_treea
I'm ...	Είμαι ... _eeme_
retired	συνταξιούχος seendaksee_oo_khos
self-employed	ελεύθερος επαγγελματίας e_lef_theros epangelma_tee_as
between jobs	μεταξύ εργασιών meta_ksee_ erghasee_on_
What are your hobbies/interests?	Ποιά είναι τα χόμπυ/ενδιαφέροντά σου (σας); pia _eene_ ta _khom_bee/ entheea_fe_ronda soo (sas)
I like ...	Μου αρέσει ... moo a_resee_
music	η μουσική ee moo_see_kee
reading	το διάβασμα to THee_a_vasma
sports	ο αθλητισμός o athleetee_zmos_
Would you like to play ...	Θέλεις (θέλετε) να παίξουμε ... _the_lees (_the_lete) na _pek_soome
cards/chess	χαρτιά/σκάκι khar_teea_/_ska_kee
backgammon	τάβλι _tav_lee

What weather! Τι καιρός!

What a lovely day!	Τι όμορφη ημέρα!	*tee omorfee eemera*
What awful weather!	Τι απαίσιος καιρός!	*tee apeseeos keros*
It's so cold/hot today!	Κάνει τόσο κρύο/τόση ζέστη σήμερα!	*kanee toso kreeo/tosee zestee seemera*
Is it usually this hot?	Κάνει συνήθως τόση ζέστη;	*kanee seeneethos tosee zestee*
Do you think it's going to ... tomorrow?	Νομίζεις (νομίζετε) ότι θα .... αύριο;	*nomeezees (nomeezete) otee tha ... avreeo*
be a nice day	είναι ωραία ημέρα	*eene orea eemera*
rain	βρέξει	*vreksee*
snow	χιονίσει	*kheeoneesee*
What is the weather forecast?	Τι λέει η πρόβλεψη του καιρού;	*tee lee-e ee provlepsee too keroo*
It's ...	Έχει ...	*ekhee*
sunny	ήλιο	*eeleeo*
cloudy	συννεφιά	*seenefeea*
foggy	ομίχλη	*omeekhlee*
wintry [frosty]	παγετό	*payeto*
icy	πάγο	*pagho*
rainy	βροχερό καιρό	*vrokhero kero*
snowy	χιόνι	*kheeonee*
stormy	καταιγίδες	*kateyeeтнes*
windy	αέρα	*aera*
Has the weather been like this for long?	Ο καιρός είναι έτσι εδώ και πολύ καιρό;	*o keros eene etsee етно ke polee kero*
There will be a heat-wave tomorrow.	Αύριο θα έχουμε καύσωνα.	*avreeo tha ekhoome kafsona*

ΠΡΟΒΛΕΨΗ ΚΑΙΡΟΥ	weather forecast

122

Enjoying your trip?
Περνάς (περνάτε) καλά στο ταξίδι σου (σας);

Κάνεις (κάνετε) διακοπές;	Are you on vacation?
Πώς ήρθες (ήρθατε) εδώ;	How did you get here?
Πώς ήταν το ταξίδι σου (σας);	How was your trip?
Πού μένεις (μένετε);	Where are you staying?
Πόσο καιρό είσαι (είστε) εδώ;	How long have you been here?
Πόσο καιρό θα μείνεις (μείνετε);	How long are you staying?
Τι έχεις (έχετε) κάνει μέχρι τώρα;	What have you done so far?
Πού θα πας (πάτε) μετά;	Where are you going next?
Περνάς (περνάτε) καλά τις διακοπές σου (σας);	Are you enjoying your vacation?

I'm here on …	Είμαι εδώ … *eeme* e**THO**
business	για δουλειά *ya* **THoo**lee**a**
vacation [holiday]	για διακοπές *ya* **TH**eea**ko**pes
We came by …	Ήρθαμε με … *eerthame me*
train/bus/plane	το τραίνο/το λεωφορείο/το αεροπλάνο *to* **tre**no/*to* leo**fo**reeo/*to* aero**pla**no
car/ferry	το αυτοκίνητο/το φέρρυ-μπωτ *to* afto**kee**neeto/*to* **fe**ree-bot
I have a rental [hire] car.	Έχω νοικιάσει αυτοκίνητο. *ekho* neekee**a**see afto**kee**neeto
We're staying in …	Μένουμε σε … *menoome se*
an apartment	διαμέρισμα **TH**eea**me**reezma
a hotel/campsite	σε ξενοδοχείο/σε κάμπιγκ *se* kseno**THo**kheeo/*se* **ka**mbeeng
with friends	με φίλους *me* **fee**loos
Can you suggest …?	Μπορείς (μπορείτε) να προτείνεις (προτείνετε) …; *borees (boreete) na* pro**tee**nees (pro**tee**nete)
things to do	κάτι να κάνουμε **ka**tee *na* **ka**noome
places to eat	μέρη για φαγητό **me**ree *ya* faye**to**
We're having a great/horrible time.	Περνάμε ωραία/απαίσια. per**na**me o**re**a/a**pe**seea

123

Invitations Προσκλήσεις

Would you like to have dinner with us on …?	Θέλεις (θέλετε) να έρθεις (έρθετε) για βραδινό στις …; _thelees (thelete) na erthees (erthete) ya vraTHeeno stees_
May I invite you to lunch?	Θα ήθελα να σε (σας) καλέσω για μεσημεριανό. _tha eethela na se (sas) kaleso ya meseemereeano_
Can you come for a drink this evening?	Μπορείς να έρθεις (μπορείτε να έρθετε) για ένα ποτό απόψε το βράδυ; _borees na erthees (boreete na erthete) ya ena poto apopse to vraTHee_
We are having a party. Can you come?	Κάνουμε ένα πάρτυ. Μπορείς να έρθεις; _kanoome ena "party". borees na erthees_
May we join you?	Να έρθουμε μαζί σας; _na erthoome mazee sas_
Would you like to join us?	Θέλεις να έρθεις (θέλετε να έρθετε) μαζί μας; _thelees na erthees (thelete na erthete) mazee mas_

Going out Έξοδος

What are your plans for …?	Ποιά είναι τα σχέδιά σου (σας) για …; _pia eene ta skheTHeea soo (sas) ya_
today / tonight	σήμερα/απόψε _seemera/apopse_
tomorrow	αύριο _avreeo_
Are you free this evening?	Είστε ελεύθερη απόψε; _eeste eleftheree apopse_
Would you like to …?	Θα ήθελες (θα θέλατε) να …; _tha eetheles (tha thelate) na_
go dancing	πάμε για χορό _pame ya khoro_
go for a drink / meal	πάμε για ένα ποτό/για φαγητό _pame ya ena poto/ya fayeeto_
go for a walk	πάμε ένα περίπατο _pame ena pereepato_
go shopping	πάμε για ψώνια _pame ya psoneea_
Where would you like to go?	Πού θα ήθελες (θα θέλατε) να πάμε; _poo tha eetheles (tha thelate) na pame_
I'd like to go to …	Θα ήθελα να πάω … _tha eethela na pao_
I'd like to see …	Θα ήθελα να δω … _tha eethela na THo_
Do you like …?	Σου αρέσει …; _soo aresee_

124

Accepting/Declining
Δέχομαι/Απορρίπτω την πρόταση

Thank you. I'd love to.	Θαύμα. Θα το ήθελα πολύ. *thavma. tha to eethela polee*
Thank you, but I'm busy.	Σας ευχαριστώ, αλλά είμαι πολύ απασχολημένος/-η. *sas efkhareesto ala eeme polee apaskholeemenos/-ee*
May I bring a friend?	Μπορώ να φέρω ένα φίλο/μια φίλη; *boro na fero ena feelo/mia feelee*
Where shall we meet?	Πού θα συναντηθούμε; *poo tha seenandeethoome*
I'll meet you …	Θα σε συναντήσω … *tha se seenandeeso*
in the bar	στο μπαρ *sto bar*
in front of your hotel	μπροστά στο ξενοδοχείο *brosta sto ksenoтноkheeo*
I'll call for you at 8.	Θα περάσω να σε πάρω στις οχτώ. *tha peraso na se paro stees okhto*
Could we make it a bit later/earlier?	Μπορούμε να πούμε λίγο αργότερα/νωρίτερα; *boroome na poome leegho arghotera/noreetera*
How about another day?	Τί θα έλεγες για άλλη μέρα; *tee tha eleyes ya alee mera*
That will be fine.	Εντάξει. *endaksee*

Dining out/in Τρώγοντας έξω/στο σπίτι

If you are invited to a Greek's home for a meal, always take a gift – flowers, something for the home, chocolates, etc. – as you can be sure a lot of effort will be put into feeding you well!

Let me buy you a drink.	Να σε κεράσω ένα ποτό. *na se keraso ena poto*
Do you like …?	Σου αρέσει …; *soo aresee*
What are you going to have?	Τί θα πάρεις; *tee tha parees*
Thank you for the meal.	Σε (σας) ευχαριστώ για το γεύμα. *se (sas) efkhareesto ya to yevma*
That was a lovely meal.	Ήταν ένα θαυμάσιο γεύμα. *eetan ena thavmaseeo yevma*

TIME ➤ 220

Encounters Συναντήσεις

Are you waiting for someone?	Περιμένετε κάποιον;	*pereemenete kapeeon*
Do you mind if I ...?	Σας πειράζει να ...;	*sas peerazee na*
sit here/smoke	καθήσω εδώ/καπνίσω	*katheeso etho/kapneeso*
Can I buy you a drink?	Μπορώ να σε (σου) κεράσω ένα ποτό;	*boro na se (sas) keraso ena poto*
I'd love to have some company.	Θα μου άρεσε πολύ η παρέα.	*tha moo arese polee ee parea*
Why are you laughing?	Γιατί γελάς (γελάτε);	*yatee yelas (yelate)*
Is my Greek that bad?	Τόσο άσχημα είναι τα Ελληνικά μου;	*toso askheema eene ta eleeneeka moo*
Shall we go somewhere quieter?	Πάμε κάπου πιο ήσυχα;	*pame kapoo peeo eeseekha*
Leave me alone, please!	Σας παρακαλώ, αφήστε με ήσυχη!	*sas parakalo afeeste me eeseekhee*
You look great!	Είσαι πολύ όμορφος/όμορφη!	*eese polee omorfos/omorfee*
May I kiss you?	Μπορώ να σε φιλήσω;	*boro na se feeleeso*
I'm not ready for that.	Δεν είμαι ακόμη έτοιμος/-η για αυτό.	*Then eeme akomee eteemos/-ee ya afto*
I'm afraid we've got to leave now.	Λυπάμαι, πρέπει να φύγουμε τώρα.	*leepame prepee na feeghoome tora*
Thanks for the evening.	Σε ευχαριστώ για τη βραδυά.	*se efkhareesto ya tee vratHya*
Can I see you again tomorrow?	Μπορώ να σε ξαναδώ αύριο;	*boro na se ksanatHo avreeo*
See you soon.	Θα σε δω σύντομα.	*tha se tHo seendoma*
Can I have your address?	Μπορώ να έχω τη διεύθυνσή σου (σας);	*boro na ekho tee tHee-eftheensee soo (sas)*
This is our address in the U.S./Britain.	Αυτή είναι η διεύθυνσή μας στις Ηνωμένες Πολιτείες/στη Βρεταννία.	*aftee eene ee tHee-eftheensee mas stees eenomenes poleetee-es/stee vretaneea*

Telephoning Στο τηλέφωνο

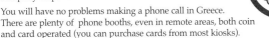

OTE (**orghaneezmos teelepeekeenoneeon elaтнos**) is the company responsible for Greek telecommunications.

You will have no problems making a phone call in Greece. There are plenty of phone booths, even in remote areas, both coin and card operated (you can purchase cards from most kiosks).

In addition kiosks often have metered phones. You don't need any change; simply make the phone call and pay after you've finished.

May I have your telephone number?	Μπορώ να έχω τον αριθμό τηλεφώνου σου (σας); boro na ekho ton areethmo teelefonoo soo (sas)
Here's my number.	Ορίστε ο αριθμός τηλεφώνου μου. oreeste o areethmos teelefonoo moo
Please call me.	Παρακαλώ, πάρε (πάρτε) με τηλέφωνο. parakalo pare (parte) me teelefono
I'll give you a call.	Θα σε (σας) πάρω τηλέφωνο. tha se (sas) paro teelefono
Where's the nearest telephone booth?	Πού είναι ο κοντινότερος τηλεφωνικός θάλαμος; poo eene o kondenoteros teelefoneekos thalamos
May I use your phone?	Μπορώ να χρησιμοποιήσω το τηλέφωνό σας; boro na khreeseemopee-eeso to teelefono sas
It's an emergency.	Είναι επείγον. eene epeeghon
Do you have a telephone directory for …?	Έχετε τηλεφωνικό κατάλογο για …; ekhete teelefoneeko katalogho ya
How much is it to phone the U.S./Britain?	Πόσο κάνει το τηλεφώνημα για τις Ηνωμένες Πολιτείες/Βρεταννία; poso kanee to telefoneema ya tees eenomenes poleetee-es/vretaneea
What's the number/ area [dialling] code for …?	Ποιός είναι ο αριθμός/κωδικός για …; peeos eene o areethmos/koтнeekos ya
I'd like a phone card, please.	Θα ήθελα μια τηλεκάρτα, παρακαλώ; tha eethela mia teelekarta parakalo
I'd like to call collect [reverse the charges].	Θα ήθελα να καλέσω με χρέωση στον παραλήπτη. tha eethela na kaleso me khreosee ston paraleeptee

Speaking Μιλώντας

Hello. This is …   Εμπρός. Είμαι ο/η …
embros. eeme o/ee

I'd like to speak to …   Θα ήθελα να μιλήσω με τον/την …
tha eethela na meeleeso me ton/teen

Extension …   Εσωτερική γραμμή …
esotereekee ghramee

Speak louder/more slowly, please.   Μιλάτε πιο δυνατά/πιο αργά, παρακαλώ.
meelate peeo тHeenata/peeo argha parakalo

Could you repeat that, please?   Μπορείτε να το επαναλάβετε;
boreete na to epanalavete

I'm afraid he's/she's not in.   Λυπάμαι, αλλά δεν είναι εδώ.
leepame ala тHen eene eтHo

You've got the wrong number.   Έχετε λάθος νούμερο.
ekhete lathos noomero

Just a moment.   Μισό λεπτό. _meeso lepto_

Hold on, please.   Περιμένετε, παρακαλώ.
pereemenete parakalo

When will he/she be back?   Πότε θα επιστρέψει;
pote tha epeestrepsee

Will you tell him/her that I called?   Μπορείτε να του/της πείτε ότι πήρα τηλέφωνο; _boreete na too/tees peete otee peera teelefono_

My name is …   Λέγομαι … _leghome_

Would you ask him/her to call me?   Μπορείτε να του/της ζητήσετε να με πάρει τηλέφωνο; _boreete na too/tees zeeteesete na me paree teelefono_

May I leave a message, please?   Μπορώ να αφήσω ένα μήνυμα, παρακαλώ; _boro na afeeso ena meeneema parakalo_

I must go now.   Πρέπει να πηγαίνω τώρα.
prepee na peeyeno tora

Nice to speak to you.   Χάρηκα πού μιλήσαμε.
khareeka poo meeleesame

I'll be in touch.   Θα έρθω σε επαφή. _tha ertho se epafee_

Bye.   Αντίο. _andeeo_

Stores & Services

Shopping can be a great pleasure in Greece. Apart from the standard department stores, you can wander through flea markets and seek out the small handicraft stores that line the narrow alleys of most islands and old towns. Haggling is expected in souvenir stores (don't be put off by the price tag), handicraft stores, and outdoor markets, but in other stores the prices are fixed.

ESSENTIAL

I'd like …	Θα ήθελα …	*tha eethela*
Do you have …?	Έχετε …;	*ekhete*
How much is that?	Πόσο κάνει αυτό;	*poso kanee afto*
Thank you.	Ευχαριστώ.	*efkhareesto*

ΑΝΟΙΧΤΟ	open
ΚΛΕΙΣΤΟ	closed

Stores and services
Καταστήματα και υπηρεσίες
Where is ...? Πού είναι ...;

Where's the nearest ...?	Πού είναι το κοντινότερο ...; *poo eene to kondeenoteroo*
Where's there a good ...?	Πού υπάρχει ένα καλό ...; *poo eeparkhee ena kalo*
Where's the shopping mall [centre]?	Πού είναι η εμπορική περιοχή; *poo eene ee emboreekee pereeokhee*
Is it far from here?	Είναι μακριά από δω; *eene makreea apo eTHo*
How do I get there?	Πώς πάνε εκεί; *pos pane ekee*

Stores Καταστήματα

antique store	το κατάστημα με αντίκες *to katasteema me anteekes*
bakery	το αρτοποιείο *to artopee-eeo*
bank	η τράπεζα *ee trapeza*
barber	το κουρείο *to kooreeo*
bookstore	το βιβλιοπωλείο *to veevleeopoleeo*
butcher	το κρεοπωλείο *to kreopoleeo*
camera store	το φωτογραφείο *to fotoghrafeeo*
clothing store [clothes shop]	το κατάστημα ρούχων *to katasteema rookhon*
delicatessen	τυριά-αλλαντικά *teerya alandeeka*
department store	το πολυκατάστημα *to poleekatasteema*
drugstore	το φαρμακείο *to farmakeeo*
fish store [fishmonger]	το ιχθυοπωλείο *to eekhtheeopoleeo*
florist	το ανθοπωλείο *to anthopoleeo*
gift store	το κατάστημα με είδη δώρων *to katasteema me eeTHee THoron*
greengrocer	το οπωροπωλείο *to oporopoleeo*
grocery store	παντοπωλείο *pandopoleeo*
health food store	το κατάστημα με υγιεινές τροφές *to katasteema me eeyee-eenes trofes*

jeweler	το κοσμηματοπωλείο
	to kozmeematopoleeo
kiosk	το περίπτερο
	to pereeptero
liquor store [off-licence]	το κατάστημα ποτών
	to katasteema poton
market	η αγορά *ee aghora*
pastry store	το ζαχαροπλαστείο
	to zakharoplasteeo
pharmacy [chemist]	το φαρμακείο *to farmakeeo*
record/music store	το δισκάδικο *to THeeskaTHeeko*
second-hand store	το κατάστημα μεταχειρισμένων ειδών
	to katasteema metakheereezmenon eeTHon
shoe store	το κατάστημα υποδημάτων
	to katasteema eepoTHeematon
shopping mall [centre]	η εμπορική περιοχή
	ee emboreekee pereeokhee
souvenir store	το κατάστημα σουβενίρ
	to katasteema "souvenir"
sporting goods store	το κατάστημα αθλητικών
	to katasteema athleeteekon
supermarket	το σουπερμάρκετ *to "supermarket"*
tobacconist	το καπνοπωλείο *to karnopoleeo*
toy store	το κατάστημα παιχνιδιών
	to katasteema pekhneeTHyon

Services Υπηρεσίες

clinic	η κλινική *ee kleeneekee*
dentist	ο οδοντίατρος *o oTHondeeatros*
doctor	ο γιατρός *o yatros*
dry cleaner	το καθαριστήριο *to kathareesteereeo*
hairdresser (ladies/men)	το κομμωτήριο *to komoteereeo*
hospital	το νοσοκομείο *to nosokomeeo*
library	η βιβλιοθήκη *ee veevleeotheekee*
optician	ο οπτικός *o opteekos*
police station	το αστυνομικό τμήμα
	to asteenomeeko tmeema
post office	το ταχυδρομείο *to takheeTHromeeo*
travel agency	το ταξιδιωτικό γραφείο
	to takseeTHeeooteeko ghrafeeo

Opening hours Ώρες λειτουργίας

Most stores are open daily from 8:30 a.m. to 3:00 p.m. in the winter and 8:00 a.m. to 2:30 p.m. in the summer. On Tuesdays, Thursdays and Fridays they reopen at 5:00 p.m. and stay open until 8:30 p.m. (5:30 p.m. until 9:00 p.m. in the summer). Most stores are open on Saturdays from 8:30 a.m. until 3:00 p.m. Supermarkets and department stores are open from 9:00 a.m. to 9:00 p.m. Monday through Saturday and some are open for a half day on Sunday.

When does the … open/shut?	Πότε ανοίγει/κλείνει ο/η/το …; *pote aneeyee/kleenee o/ee/to*
Are you open in the evening?	Είστε ανοιχτά το απόγευμα; *eeste aneekhta to apoyevma*
Do you close for lunch?	Κλείνετε το μεσημέρι; *kleenete to meseemeree*
Where is the …?	Πού είναι …; *poo eene*
cashier [cash desk]	το ταμείο *to tameeo*
elevator [lift]	το ασανσέρ *to asanser*
escalator	οι κυλιόμενες σκάλες *ee keeleeomenes skales*
store guide	ο οδηγός καταστήματος *o отнeeghos katasteematos*
It's in the basement.	Είναι στο υπόγειο. *eene sto eepoyeeo*
It's on the … floor.	Είναι στο … *eene sto*
first [ground (Brit.)]	ισόγειο *eesoyeeo*
second [first (Brit.)]	πρώτο όροφο *proto orofo*
Where's the … department?	Πού είναι το τμήμα …; *poo eene to tmeema*

ΑΝΟΙΧΤΟ ΟΛΗΜΕΡΙΣ	open all day
ΚΛΕΙΣΤΟ ΤΟ ΜΕΣΗΜΕΡΙ	closed for lunch
ΩΡΕΣ ΕΜΠΟΡΙΟΥ	business hours
ΕΙΣΟΔΟΣ	entrance
ΣΚΑΛΑ	stairs
ΕΞΟΔΟΣ	exit
ΕΞΟΔΟΣ ΚΙΝΔΥΝΟΥ	(emergency) exit
ΕΞΟΔΟΣ ΣΕ ΠΕΡΙΠΤΩΣΗ ΠΥΡΚΑΙΑΣ	fire exit

Service Εξυπηρέτηση

Can you help me?	Μπορείτε να με βοηθήσετε; *boreete na me voeetheesete*
I'm looking for ...	Ψάχνω για ... *psakhno ya*
I'm just browsing.	Απλώς κοιτάω. *aplos keetao*
It's my turn.	Είναι η σειρά μου. *eene ee seera moo*
Do you have any ...?	Έχετε καθόλου ...; *ekhete katholoo*
I'd like to buy ...	Θα ήθελα να αγοράσω ... *tha eethela na aghoraso*
Could you show me ...?	Μπορείτε να μου δείξετε ...; *boreete na moo THeeksete*
How much is this/that?	Πόσο κάνει αυτό/εκείνο; *poso kanee afto/ekeeno*
That's all, thanks.	Τίποτε άλλο. Ευχαριστώ. *teepote alo. efkhareesto*

Καλημέρα/καλησπέρα σας.	Good morning/afternoon.
Σας εξυπηρετεί κανείς;	Are you being served?
Τί θα θέλατε;	What would you like?
Μισό λεπτό να το ελέγξω.	One moment, I'll just check that for you.
Τίποτε άλλο;	Is that everything?/Anything else?

– *boro na sas voeetheeso?*
– *okhee, efkhareesto. aplos keetao.*
– *endaksee ...*
– *parakalo.*
– *ne. boro na sas voeetheeso?*
– *poso kanee afto?*
– *Mmm... meeso lepto na to elenkso ... kanee 6 evro.*

ΕΞΥΠΗΡΕΤΗΣΗ ΠΕΛΑΤΩΝ	customer service
ΑΥΤΟΕΞΥΠΗΡΕΤΗΣΗ	self-service
ΕΙΔΙΚΗ ΠΡΟΣΦΟΡΑ	clearance
ΕΚΠΤΩΣΕΙΣ	sale

Preference Προτίμηση

I want something …	Θέλω κάτι …	_thelo_ _katee_
It must be …	Πρέπει να είναι …	_prepee na_ _eene_
big / small	μεγάλο/μικρό	_meghalo/meekro_
cheap / expensive	φτηνό/ακριβό	_fteeno/akreevo_
dark / light	σκούρο/ανοιχτό	_skooro/aneekhto_
light / heavy	ελαφρύ/βαρύ	_elafree/varee_
oval / round / square	οβάλ/στρογγυλό/τετράγωνο	_oval/strongeelo/tetraghono_
genuine / imitation	αυθεντικό/απομίμηση	_afthendeeko/apomeemeesee_
I don't want anything too expensive.	Δεν θέλω κάτι πολύ ακριβό.	_THen thelo katee polee akreevo_
In the region of … euros.	Γύρω στις … ευρώ.	_yeero stees … evro_

Τί … θα θέλατε;	What … would you like?
χρώμα/σχήμα	color / shape
ποιότητα/ποσότητα	quality / quantity
Τί είδος θα θέλατε;	What sort would you like?
Περίπου σε τι τιμή σκεφτόσαστε;	What price range are you thinking of?

Do you have anything …?	Έχετε κάτι …;	_ekhete katee_
larger	μεγαλύτερο	_meghaleetero_
better quality	καλύτερης ποιότητας	_kaleeterees peeoteetas_
cheaper	φτηνότερο	_fteenotero_
smaller	μικρότερο	_meekrotero_
Can you show me …?	Μπορείτε να μου δείξετε …;	_boreete na moo THeeksete_
that / this one	εκείνο/αυτό	_ekeeno/afto_
these / those ones	αυτά/εκείνα	_afta/ekeena_
the one in the window / display case	αυτό στη βιτρίνα	_afto stee veetreena_
some others	μερικά άλλα	_mereeka ala_

Conditions of purchase Όροι αγοράς

Is there a guarantee?
Υπάρχει εγγύηση;
eeparkhee engee-eesee

Are there any instructions with it?
Υπάρχουν οδηγίες;
eeparkhoon oτHeeyee-es

Out of stock Εξαντλημένα

Λυπάμαι, δεν έχουμε άλλα.	I'm sorry, we don't have any.
Έχουν τελειώσει.	We're out of stock.
Μπορώ να σας δείξω κάτι άλλο/ένα άλλο είδος;	Can I show you something else/ a different sort?
Να σας το παραγγείλουμε;	Shall we order it for you?

Can you order it for me?
Μπορείτε να μου το παραγγείλετε;
boreete na moo to parangeelete?

How long will it take?
Πόσο καιρό θα πάρει;
poso kero tha paree?

Where else might I get ...?
Πού αλλού μπορώ να βρω ...;
poo aloo boro na vro?

Decision Απόφαση

That's not quite what I want.
Δεν είναι ακριβώς αυτό που θέλω.
τHen eene akreevos afto poo thelo

No, I don't like it.
Όχι, δεν μου αρέσει.
okhee, τHen moo aresee

That's too expensive.
Είναι πολύ ακριβό.
eene polee akreevo

I'd like to think about it.
Θα ήθελα να το σκεφτώ.
tha eethela na to skefto

I'll take it.
Θα το πάρω. *tha to paro*

– *boreete na moo τHeeksete ekeeno to ... ekee, parakalo?*
– *veveos. na sas to katevasso.*
– *efkhareesto. ... mmm, τHen eene akreevos afto poo thelo.*
– *ekhoome ala steel ke τHeeaforeteeka khromata.*
– *okhee. sas efkhareesto.*

Paying Πληρωμή

Most credit cards are accepted in large stores and hotels, and you can also use them in ATMs [cash machines] at major banks. Smaller businesses usually accept only cash.

Where do I pay?	Πού πληρώνω; *poo pleerono*
How much is that?	Πόσο κάνει; *poso kanee*
Could you write it down, please?	Μπορείτε να το γράψετε, παρακαλώ; *boreete na to ghrapsete parakalo*
Do you accept …?	Δέχεστε …; *THekheste*
traveler's checks [cheques]	ταξιδιωτικές επιταγές *takseeTHeeooteekes epeetayes*
I'll pay …	Θα πληρώσω … *tha pleeroso*
by cash	τοις μετρητοίς *tees metreetees*
by credit card	με πιστωτική κάρτα *me peestoteekee karta*
I don't have any smaller change.	Δεν έχω τίποτε μικρότερο. *THen ekho teepote meekrotero*
Sorry, I don't have enough money.	Συγγνώμη, δεν έχω αρκετά χρήματα. *seeghnomee, THen ekho arketa khreemata*

Πώς θα πληρώσετε;	How will you pay?
Η συναλλαγή δεν εγκρίθηκε/δεν έγινε δεκτή.	This transaction has not been approved/accepted.
Αυτή η κάρτα δεν ισχύει.	This card is not valid.
Μπορώ να έχω κάποια ταυτότητα;	May I have some identification?
Έχετε ψιλά/τίποτε μικρότερο;	Do you have any smaller change?

Could I have a receipt, please?	Μπορώ να έχω απόδειξη παρακαλώ; *boro na ekho apoTHeeksee parakalo*
I think you've given me the wrong change.	Νομίζω ότι μου δώσατε λάθος ρέστα. *nomeezo otee moo THosate lathos resta*

ΤΑΜΕΙΟ	cash desk
Η ΚΛΟΠΗ ΤΙΜΩΡΕΙΤΑΙ ΜΕ ΠΡΟΣΤΙΜΟ	shoplifters will be fined

Complaints Παράπονα

This doesn't work.	Αυτό είναι ελαττωματικό. *afto eene elatomateeko*
Where can I make a complaint?	Πού μπορώ να παραπονεθώ; *poo boro na paraponetho*
Can I exchange this, please?	Μπορείτε να μου το αλλάξετε; *boreete na moo to alaksete*
I'd like a refund.	Θα ήθελα την επιστροφή των χρημάτων μου. *tha eethela teen epeestrofee ton khreematon moo*
Here's the receipt.	Ορίστε η απόδειξη. *oreeste ee apoτHeeksee*
I don't have the receipt.	Δεν έχω την απόδειξη. *τHen ekho teen apoτHeksee*
I'd like to see the manager.	Θα ήθελα να δω το διευθυντή. *tha eethela na τHo to τHee-eftheendee*

Repairs/Cleaning Επισκευές/Καθαριστήριο

This is broken. Can you repair it?	Αυτό είναι σπασμένο. Μπορείτε να μου το διορθώσετε; *afto eene spazmeno. boreete na moo to τHeorthosete*
Do you have ... for this?	Έχετε ... γι' αυτό; *ekhete ... yafto*
a battery	μπαταρία *batareea*
replacement parts	ανταλλακτικά *andalakteeka*
There's a problem with the ...	Υπάρχει πρόβλημα με τον/την/το ... *eeparkhee provleema me ton/teen/to*
I'd like this ...	Θα ήθελα να μου ... αυτό. *tha eethela na moo ... afto*
cleaned	καθαρίσετε *kathareesete*
pressed	σιδερώσετε *seeτHerosete*
When will it/they be ready?	Πότε θα είναι έτοιμο; *pote tha eene eteemo*
This isn't mine.	Αυτό δεν είναι δικό μου. *afto τHen eene τHeeko moo*
There's ... missing.	Λείπει ένας/μια/ένα ... *leepee enas/mia/ena*

Bank/Currency exchange
Τράπεζα/Ανταλλαγή συναλλάγματος

Changing money in Greece is not a problem. All major foreign currencies, travelers checks [cheques] and Eurocheques are widely accepted at all banks and currency exchanges. In addition, automatic cash dispensers (look for theATM sign) can be found ouside most main banks and accept VISA, MasterCard, EC, American Express, Eurocard, etc.

Banks open at 7:30 a.m. or 8:00 a.m. and close at 2:30 p.m. (1:30 p.m. on Fridays). Centrally located banks are also open on Saturdays. Currency exchanges stay open until late at night.

Where's the nearest …?	Πού είναι η κοντινότερη …; *poo eene ee kondee**no**teree*
bank	η τράπεζα *ee trapeza*
currency exchange [bureau de change]	ανταλλαγή συναλλάγματος *anda**la**ghee seenalaghmatos*

ΩΘΗΣΑΤΕ/ΕΛΞΑΤΕ/ΠΙΕΣΑΤΕ	push/pull/press
ΑΝΟΙΧΤΟ/ΚΛΕΙΣΤΟ	open/closed
ΤΑΜΕΙΟ	cashiers

Changing money Αλλαγή χρημάτων

Can I exchange foreign currency here?	Μπορώ να αλλάξω ξένο συνάλλαγμα εδώ; *boro na alakso kseno seenalaghma eTHo*
I'd like to change some dollars/pounds into euros.	Θα ήθελα να αλλάξω μερικά δολλάρια/λίρες σε ευρώ. *tha eethela na alakso mereeka THolareea/leeres se evro*
I want to cash some traveler's checks [cheques].	Θα ήθελα να εξαργυρώσω μερικές ταξιδιωτικές επιταγές. *tha eethela na eksaryeeroso mereekes takseeTHyoteekes epeetayes*
What's the exchange rate?	Ποιά είναι η τιμή συναλλάγματος; *pia eene ee teemee seenalaghmatos*
How much commission do you charge?	Πόση προμήθεια χρεώνετε; *posee promeetheea khreonete*
I've lost my traveler's checks [cheques]. These are the numbers.	Έχασα τις ταξιδιωτικές επιταγές μου. Ορίστε οι αριθμοί. *ekhasa tees takseeTHyoteekes epeetayes moo. oreeste ee areethmee*

138

Security Ασφάλεια

Μπορώ να δω …;	Could I see …?
το διαβατήριο σας	your passport
την ταυτότητά σας	some identification
την τραπεζική κάρτα σας	your bank card
Ποιά είναι η διεύθυνσή σας;	What's your address?
Πού μένετε;	Where are you staying?
Συμπληρώστε αυτό το έντυπο, παρακαλώ.	Fill in this form, please.
Παρακαλώ υπογράψτε εδώ.	Please sign here.

ATMs [Cash machines]
Αυτόματες Ταμειολογιστικές Μηχανές (Α.Τ.Μ.)

Can I withdraw money
on my credit card here?

Μπορώ να κάνω ανάληψη με την πιστωτική κάρτα μου εδώ; *boro na kano analeepsee me teen peestoteekee karta moo eΤΗΟ*

Where are the ATMs
[cash machines]?

Πού είναι οι αυτόματες μηχανες; *poo eene ee aftomates meekhanes*

Can I use my … card in
the cash machine?

Μπορώ να χρησιμοποιήσω την κάρτα … σε αυτόματη μηχανή; *boro na khreeseemopee-eeso teen karta … se aftomatee meekhanee*

The cash machine has
eaten my card.

Η αυτόματη μηχανή πήρε την κάρτα μου. *ee aftomatee meekhanee peere teen karta moo*

ΞΕΝΟ ΣΥΝΑΛΛΑΓΜΑ	foreign currency
ΠΡΟΜΗΘΕΙΑ	bank charges

In 2002 the oldest currency in Europe, the Greek drachma, was replaced with the common European currency, the euro (ευρώ, pronounced *evro*), divided into 100 cents (λεπτό, *lepto*).

> *Coins*: 1, 2, 5, 10, 20, 50 c.; €1, 2
>
> *Notes*: €5, 10, 20, 50, 100, 200, 500

Pharmacy Φαρμακείο

All pharmacists in Greece must hold a pharmacology degree and are generally extremely helpful at treating minor ailments. Many medications that are prescription only in other countries can be bought over the counter. Additionally, insulin is free at all pharmacies.

Pharmacies work on a rota system and there will always be one open 24 hours a day. Read the list on display in all pharmacy windows to find the nearest.

Where's the nearest (all-night) pharmacy?	Πού είναι το κοντινότερο (εφημερεύον) φαρμακείο; *poo eene to kondeenotero (efeemerevon) farmakeeo*
What time does the pharmacy open/close?	Τί ώρα ανοίγει/κλείνει το φαρμακείο; *tee ora aneeyee/kleenee to farmakeeo*
Can you make up this prescription for me?	Μπορείτε να μου φτιάξετε αυτή τη συνταγή; *boreete na moo fteaksete aftee tee seendayee*
Shall I wait?	Να περιμένω; *na pereemeno*
I'll come back for it.	Θα επιστρέψω. *tha epeestrepso*

Dosage instructions Δοσολογία

How much should I take?	Πόσο πρέπει να πάρω; *poso prepee na paro*
How often should I take it?	Πόσο συχνά πρέπει να το παίρνω; *poso seekhna prepee na to perno*
Is it suitable for children?	Είναι κατάλληλο για παιδιά; *eene kataleelo ya peтнya*

Πάρτε … χάπια/… κουταλιές …	Take … tablets/… teaspoons …
πριν/μετά το γεύμα	before/after meals
με νερό	with water
ολόκληρα	whole
το πρωί/το βράδυ	in the morning/at night
για … ημέρες	for … days

ΔΗΛΗΤΗΡΙΟ	poison
ΜΟΝΟ ΓΙΑ ΕΞΩΤΕΡΙΚΗ ΧΡΗΣΗ	for external use only
ΔΕΝ ΠΑΙΡΝΕΤΑΙ ΑΠΟ ΤΟ ΣΤΟΜΑ	not to be taken internally

DOCTOR ➤ 161

Asking advice Ζητώντας συμβουλή

What would you recommend for …?	Τι συνιστάτε για … *tee* seenee*state* ya
a cold	το κρυολόγημα *to* kreeo*loyeema*
a cough	το βήχα *to* *veekha*
diarrhea	τη διάρροια *tee* THee*areea*
hay fever	την αλλεργία σε γύρη *teen* aler*yeea* se *yeeree*
insect bites	το τσίμπημα από έντομο *to* *tseembeema* a*po* *endomo*
motion [travel] sickness	ναυτία naf*teea*
a sore throat	πονόλαιμο po*no*lemo
sunburn	τα εγκαύματα ήλιου *ta* e*gav*mata *eel*eeoo
an upset stomach	το στομαχόπονο *to* stoma*kho*pono
Can I get it without a prescription?	Μπορώ να το πάρω χωρίς συνταγή γιατρού; bo*ro* na to *pa*ro kho*rees* seend*ayee* ya*troo*

Over-the-counter treatment
Εξυπηρέτηση στο φαρμακείο

Can I have a(n)/some …?	Μπορώ να έχω …; bo*ro* na *ekho*
antiseptic cream	μια αντισηπτική κρέμα *mia* andeeseep*teekee* *krema*
aspirin	μια ασπιρίνη *mia* aspee*reenee*
adhesive bandage [plaster]	αυτοκόλλητους επιδέσμους afto*ko*leetoos eree*THez*moos
condoms	προφυλακτικά profeelak*teeka*
cotton [wool]	βαμβάκι vam*va*kee
cough syrup	σιρόπι για το βήχα see*ro*pee ya to *veekha*
gauze [bandage]	γάζα *ghaza*
insect repellent/spray	εντομοαπωθητικό/εντομοκτόνο endomoapotheeteeko/endomoktono
pain killers	παυσίπονα paf*seepona*
vitamin tablets	βιταμίνες veeta*meenes*

Toiletries Καλλυντικά

I'd like a/an/ some … Θα ήθελα … *tha eethela*

after shave	ένα άφτερ σέιβ *ena "after-shave"*
after-sun lotion	το γαλάκτωμα για μετά την ηλιοθεραπεία *to ghalaktoma ya meta teen eeleeotherapeea*
deodorant	ένα αποσμητικό *ena apozmeeteeko*
razor blades	ξυραφάκια *kseerafakeea*
sanitary napkins [towels]	σερβιέττες *servee-etes*
soap	ένα σαπούνι *ena sapoonee*
suntan lotion	κρέμα/λάδι ήλιου *krema/laтнee eeleeoo*
tampons	ταμπόν *tambon*
tissues	χαρτομάντηλα *khartomandeela*
toilet paper	χαρτί υγείας *khartee eeyeeas*
toothbrush	μια οδοντόβουρτσα *mia oтнondovoortsa*
toothpaste	μια οδοντόκρεμα *mia oтнondokrema*

Haircare Φροντίδα για τα μαλλιά

comb	η χτένα *ee khtena*
conditioner	το γαλάκτωμα για τα μαλλιά *to ghalaktoma ya ta maleea*
hair brush	η βούρτσα *ee voortsa*
hair mousse	ο αφρός χτενίσματος, η μους *o afros khteneezmatos, ee moos*
hair spray	η λακ *ee lak*
shampoo	το σαμπουάν *to sampooan*

For the baby Για το μωρό

baby food	το φαγητό για μωρά *to fayeeto ya mora*
baby wipes	υγρά μαντηλάκια *eeghra mandeelakeea*
diapers [nappies]	οι πάνες μωρού *ee panes moroo*
sterilizing solution	το αποστειρωτικό διάλυμα *to aposteeroteeko тнeealeema*

Clothing Ρουχισμός

General Γενικά

I'd like ...   Θα ήθελα ... _tha eethela_

Do you have any ...?   Έχετε καθόλου ...;
                              ekhete katholoo

ΓΥΝΑΙΚΕΙΑ	ladieswear
ΑΝΔΡΙΚΑ	menswear
ΠΑΙΔΙΚΑ ΡΟΥΧΑ	childrenswear

Color Χρώμα

I'm looking for something in ...   Ψάχνω κάτι σε ...
                                    psakhno katee se

beige   μπεζ _bez_

black   μαύρο _mavro_

blue   μπλε _ble_

brown   καφέ _kafe_

green   πράσινο _praseeno_

gray   γκρίζο _greezo_

orange   πορτοκαλί _portokalee_

pink   ροζ _roz_

purple   μωβ _mov_

red   κόκκινο _kokeeno_

white   άσπρο _aspro_

yellow   κίτρινο _keetreeno_

light ...   ανοιχτό ... _aneekhto_

dark ...   σκούρο ... _skooro_

I want a darker/lighter shade.   Θέλω μια σκουρότερη/ανοιχτότερη
                                    απόχρωση. _thelo mia skooroteree/_
                                    aneekhtoteree apokhrosee

Do you have the same in ...?   Έχετε το ίδιο σε ...;
                                    ekhete to eeтнуo se

Clothes and accessories
Ρούχα και αξεσουάρ

belt	η ζώνη *ee zonee*
bikini	το μπικίνι *to beekeenee*
blouse	η μπλούζα *ee blooza*
bra	το σουτιέν *to sootee-en*
briefs	το κυλοτάκι/σλιπ *to keelotakee/sleep*
coat	το παλτό *to palto*
dress	το φόρεμα *to forema*
handbag	η τσάντα *ee tsanda*
hat	το καπέλλο *to kapelo*
jacket	το σακάκι *to sakakee*
jeans	το μπλου-τζην *to blootzeen*
leggings	ω κολλάν *to kolan*
pants (U.S.)	το παντελόνι *to pandelonee*
pantyhose [tights]	το καλτσόν *to kaltson*
scarf	το κασκώλ *to kaskol*
shirt	το πουκάμισο *to pookameeso*
shorts	το σόρτς *to sorts*
skirt	η φούστα *ee foosta*
socks	οι κάλτσες *ee kaltses*
suit (men's)	το κουστούμι *to koostoomee*
suit (women's)	το ταγιέρ *to tayer*
sunglasses	τα γυαλιά ήλιου *ta yaleea eeleeoo*
sweater	το πουλόβερ *to poolover*
sweatshirt	η αθλητική μπλούζα *ee athleeteekee blooza*
swimming trunks	το μαγιώ *to mayo*
swimsuit	το ολόσωμο μαγιώ *to olosomo mayo*
T-shirt	το μπλουζάκι *to bloozakee*
tie	η γραβάτα *ee ghravata*
trousers	το παντελόνι *to pandelonee*
with long/short sleeves	με μακριά/κοντά μανίκια *me makreea/konda maneekeea*
with a V-/round neck	με βε/με στρογγυλή λαιμόκοψη *me ve/me strongeelee lemokopsee*

Shoes Παπούτσια

boots	οι μπότες *ee botes*
flip-flops	οι σαγιονάρες *ee sayonares*
running [training] shoes	τα αθλητικά παπούτσια *ta athleeteeka papootseea*
sandals	τα πέδιλα *ta petнeela*
shoes	τα παπούτσια *ta papootseea*
slippers	οι παντόφλες *ee pandofles*

Walking / Hiking gear Εξοπλισμός για πεζοπορία

knapsack	το σακκίδιο *to sakeeтнeeo*
hiking boots	οι μπότες πεζοπορίας *ee botes pezoporeeas*
waterproof jacket	το αδιάβροχο *to атнeeavrokho*
windbreaker [cagoule]	το αδιάβροχο μπουφάν *to атнeeavrokho boofan*

Fabric Ύφασμα

I want something in …	Θέλω κάτι σε … *thelo katee se*
cotton	βαμβακερό *vamvakero*
denim	ντένιμ *"denim"*
lace	δαντέλλα *тнandela*
leather	δερμάτινο *тнermateeno*
linen	λινό *leeno*
wool	μάλλινο *maleeno*
Is this …?	Αυτό είναι …; *afto eene*
pure cotton	αγνό βαμβάκι *aghno vamvakee*
synthetic	συνθετικό *seentheteeko*
Is it hand / machine washable?	Πλένεται στο χέρι/στο πλυντήριο; *plenete sto kheree/sto pleendeereeo*

ΠΛΕΝΕΤΑΙ ΜΟΝΟ ΣΤΟ ΚΑΘΑΡΙΣΤΗΡΙΟ	dry clean only
ΠΛΕΝΕΤΑΙ ΣΤΟ ΧΕΡΙ	handwash only
ΜΗΝ ΤΟ ΣΙΔΕΡΩΣΕΤΕ	do not iron

Does it fit? Μου κάνει;

Can I try this on?	Μπορώ να το δοκιμάσω; *boro na to THokeemaso*
It fits well. I'll take it.	Μου κάνει. Θα το πάρω. *moo kanee. tha to paro*
It doesn't fit.	Δεν μου κάνει. *THen moo kanee*
It's too...	Είναι πολύ ... *eene polee*
short/long	κοντό/μακρύ *kondo/makree*
tight/loose	στενό/φαρδύ *steno/farTHee*
Do you have this in size ...?	Το έχετε στο μέγεθος ...; *to ekhete sto meyethos*
What size is this?	Τι μέγεθος είναι αυτό; *tee meyethos eene afto*
Could you measure me, please?	Μπορείτε να με μετρήσετε, παρακαλώ; *boreete na me metreesete parakalo*
I don't know Greek sizes.	Δεν ξέρω τα ελληνικά μεγέθη. *THen ksero ta eleeneeka meyethee*

Size Μέγεθος

Continental sizes are used in Greece. Use the tables below to convert, but remember that they are only a rough guide as sizes vary considerably.

	Dresses/Suits						Women's shoes			
American	8	10	12	14	16	18	6	7	8	9
British	10	12	14	16	18	20	$4^{1/2}$	$5^{1/2}$	$6^{1/2}$	$7^{1/2}$
Continental	36	38	40	42	44	46	37	38	40	41

	Shirts				Men's shoes								
American } **British**	15	16	17	18	5	6	7	8	$8^{1/2}$	9	$9^{1/2}$	10	11
Continental	38	41	43	45	38	39	41	42	43	43	44	44	45

εξαιρετικά μεγάλος	extra large (XL)
μεγάλος	large (L)
μέτριος	medium (M)
μικρός	small (S)

1 centimeter (cm.) = 0.39 in.	1 inch = 2.54 cm.
1 meter (m.) = 39.37 in.	1 foot = 30.5 cm.
10 meters = 32.81 ft.	1 yard = 0.91 m.

Health and beauty
Υγεία και ομορφιά

I'd like a …	Θα ήθελα … *tha eethela*
facial	έναν καθαρισμό προσώπου *enan kathareezmo prosopoo*
manicure	ένα μανικιούρ *ena maneekeeoor*
massage	ένα μασάζ *ena masaz*
waxing	μια χαλάουα *mia khalaooa*

Hairdresser / Hairstylist Στο κομμωτήριο

I'd like to make an appointment for …	Θα ήθελα να κλείσω ένα ραντεβού για … *tha eethela na kleeso ena randevoo ya*
Can you make it a bit earlier / later?	Μπορείτε λίγο νωρίτερα/αργότερα; *boreete leegho noreetera/arghotera*
I'd like a …	Θα ήθελα … *tha eethela*
cut and blow-dry	κούρεμα και πιστολάκι *koorema ke peestolakee*
shampoo and set	σαμπουάν και χτένισμα *sampooan ke khteneezma*
trim	διόρθωμα *THeeorthoma*
I'd like my hair …	Θα ήθελα … *tha eethela*
colored / tinted	να μου βάψετε τα μαλλιά *na moo vapsete ta maleea*
highlighted	ανταύγειες *andavyee-es*
permed	μια περμανάντ *mia permanand*
Don't cut it too short.	Μη τα κόψετε πολύ κοντά. *mee ta kopsete polee konda*
A little more off the …	Κόψτε λίγο ακόμα από … *kopste leegho akoma apo*
back / front	πίσω/μπρος *peeso/bros*
neck / sides	το λαιμό/τα πλάγια *to lemo/ta playa*
top	πάνω *pano*
That's fine, thanks.	Εντάξει, ευχαριστώ. *endaksee, efkhareesto*

Household articles
Είδη οικιακής χρήσεως

I'd like a(n)/some … Θα ήθελα ένα/λίγο …
tha eethela ena/leegho

alumin(i)um foil	αλουμινόχαρτο *aloomeenokharto*
bottle opener/corkscrew	ένα τιρμπουσόν *ena teermbooson*
can opener	ένα ανοιχτήρι *ena aneekhteeree*
candles	κεριά *kerya*
clothes pins [pegs]	μανταλάκια *mandalakeea*
light bulb	μια λάμπα *mia lamba*
matches	σπίρτα *speerta*
paper napkins	χαρτοπετσέτες *khartopetsetes*
plastic wrap [cling film]	διαφανή μεμβράνη *THeeafanee memvranee*
plug	μια πρίζα *mia preeza*
scissors	ένα ψαλίδι *ena psaleeTHee*
screwdriver	ένα κατσαβίδι *ena katsaveeTHee*

Cleaning items Είδη καθαρισμού

bleach	χλωρίνη *khloreenee*
dish cloth	πανί για τα πιάτα *panee ya ta piata*
dishwashing detergent [washing-up liquid]	υγρό πιάτων *eeghro piaton*
garbage [refuse] bags	σακκούλες σκουπιδιών *sakooles skoopeeTHeeon*
kitchen cloth	απορροφητική πετσέτα κουζίνας *aporofeeteekee petseta koozeenas*
detergent [washing powder]	απορρυπαντικό *aporeepandeeko*

Crockery/Cutlery Πιατικά/Μαχαιροπήρουνα

cups	τα φλυτζάνια *ta fleetzaneea*
forks	τα πηρούνια *ta peerooneea*
glasses	τα ποτήρια *ta poteerya*
knives	τα μαχαίρια *ta makherya*
plates	τα πιάτα *ta piata*
spoons	τα κουτάλια *ta kootaleea*
teaspoons	τα κουταλάκια *ta kootalakeea*

Jeweler Στο κοσμηματοπωλείο

Could I see …?	Μπορώ να δώ …; *boro na THO*
this/that	αυτό/εκείνο *afto/ekeeno*
It's in the window/ display cabinet.	Είναι στη βιτρίνα. *eene stee veetreena*
I'd like a(n)/some …	Θα ήθελα … *tha eethela*
alarm clock	ένα ξυπνητήρι *ena kseepneeteeree*
battery	μια μπαταρία *mia batareea*
bracelet	ένα βραχιόλι *ena vrakheeolee*
brooch	μια καρφίτσα *mia karfeetsa*
chain	μια αλυσίδα *mia aleeseeTHa*
clock	ένα ρολόι *ena roloee*
earrings	σκουλαρίκια *skoolareekeea*
necklace	ένα κολλιέ *ena kolee-e*
ring	ένα δαχτυλίδι *ena THakhteeleeTHee*
watch	ένα ρολόι *ena roloee*

Materials Υλικά

Is this real silver/gold?	Αυτό είναι αληθινό ασήμι/χρυσό; *afto eene aleetheeno aseemee/khreeso*
Is there any certification for it?	Υπάρχει σφραγίδα επάνω; *eeparkhee sfrayeeTHa epano*
Do you have anything in …?	Έχετε τίποτα σε … ; *ekhete teepota se*
copper	χαλκό *khalko*
crystal	κρύσταλλο *kreestalo*
cut glass	σκαλιστό γυαλί *skaleesto yalee*
diamond	διαμάντι *THyamandee*
gold	χρυσό *khreeso*
gold-plate	επίχρυσο *epeekhreeso*
pearl	μαργαριτάρι *marghareetaree*
pewter	κασσίτερο *kaseetero*
platinum	πλατίνα *plateena*
silver	ασήμι *aseemee*
silver-plate	επάργυρο *eparyeero*

Newsstand [Newsagent]/Bookstore
Περίπτερο/Βιβλιοπωλείο

Yellow-colored kiosks (**pereeptera**) can be found on most street corners and at key locations in towns and cities and are a ubiquitous part of everyday life. Greek and foreign newspapers and magazines are sold there as well as tobacco, candy, beer, bus tickets, and more. The more sophisticated kiosks also sell books, maps, guides, and souvenirs.

Do you sell English-language books/newspapers?	Πουλάτε αγγλικά βιβλία/αγγλικές εφημερίδες; *poolate angleeka veevleea/angleekes efeemereeτΗes*
I'd like a(n)/some …	Θα ήθελα … *tha eethela*
book	ένα βιβλίο *ena vevleeo*
candy [sweets]	καραμέλες *karameles*
chewing gum	μια τσίχλα *mia tseekhla*
chocolate bar	μια σοκολάτα *mia sokolata*
(pack of) cigarettes	ένα πακέτο τσιγάρα *ena paketo tseeghara*
cigars	πούρα *poora*
dictionary	ένα λεξικό *ena lekseeko*
Greek-English	Ελληνο-Αγγλικό *eleeno-angleeko*
guidebook of …	έναν τουριστικό οδηγό του/της … *enan tooreesteeko oτΗeegho too/tees*
lighter	έναν αναπτήρα *enan anapteera*
magazine	ένα περιοδικό *ena pereeoτΗeeko*
map of …	ένα χάρτη της … *ena khartee tees*
matches	σπίρτα *speerta*
newspaper	μια εφημερίδα *mia efeemereeτΗa*
American/English	αμερικάνικη/αγγλική *amereekaneekee/angleekee*
paper	χαρτί *khartee*
pen	ένα στυλό *ena steelo*
postcard	μια κάρτα *mia karta*
stamps	γραμματόσημα *ghramatoseema*
tobacco	καπνό *kapno*
writing pad	ένα μπλοκ *ena blok*

Photography Φωτογραφικά

I'm looking for a … camera. Ψάχνω για μια …
φωτογραφική μηχανή.
psakhno ya mia
fotohrafeekee meekahnee

automatic	αυτόματη *aftomatee*
compact	συμπαγής *seembayees*
disposable	μιας χρήσεως *mias khreeseos*
SLR	μονοοπτική ρεφλέξ *monoopteekee refleks*
battery	μπαταρία *batareea*
camera case	θήκη της μηχανής *theekee tees meekahnees*
(electronic) flash	(ηλεκτρονικό) φλας *(eelektroneeko) flas*
filter	φίλτρο *feeltro*
lens	φακός *fakos*
lens cap	κάλυμμα του φακού *kaleema too fakoo*

Film / Processing Φιλμ/Εμφάνιση

I'd like a … film for this camera. Θα ήθελα ένα … φιλμ για αυτή τη
φωτογραφική μηχανή. *tha eethela*
ena … "film" ya aftee tee
fotoghrafeekee meekahnee

black and white ασπρόμαυρο *aspromavro*

color έγχρωμο *enkhromo*

I'd like this film
developed, please. Θα ήθελα να μου εμφανίσετε αυτό το
φιλμ, παρακαλώ. *tha eethela na moo*
emfaneesete afto to "film" parakalo

Would you enlarge this, please? Μπορείτε να μου μεγεθύνετε αυτό,
παρακαλώ; *boreete na moo*
meyentheenete afto parakalo

How much do … exposures cost? Πόσο κοστίζουν οι … στάσεις;
poso kosteezoon ee … stasees

When will the photos be ready? Πότε θα είναι έτοιμες οι φωτογραφίες;
pote tha eene eteemes ee fotoghrafee-es

I'd like to collect my photos.
Here's the receipt. Θα ήθελα να πάρω τις φωτογραφίες
μου. Ορίστε η απόδειξη.
tha eethela na paro tees fotoghrafee-es
moo. oreeste ee apoTHeeksee

Police Αστυνομία

If you have witnessed or been the victim of a crime, report it to the tourist police or directly to the police. The tourist police always have an English-speaking interpreter on duty. If arrested for any reason you should ask for an interpreter. Note: possession of drugs is punishable by five years imprisonment and a large fine. Traffic offences are dealt with by a separate body known as the **trokhea**.

The emergency police number is 100.

Where's the nearest police station?	Πού είναι το κοντινότερο αστυνομικό τμήμα; poo eene to kondeenotero asteenomeeko tmeema
Does anyone here speak English?	Μιλάει κανείς εδώ Αγγλικά; meelaee kanees ετηο angleeka
I want to report an …	Θέλω να αναφέρω …. thelo na anafero
accident/attack	ένα ατύχημα/μια επίθεση ena ateekheema/mia epeethesee
My child is missing.	Λείπει το παιδί μου. leepee to peτΗee moo
Here's a photo of him/her.	Να μια φωτογραφία του/της. na mia fotoghrafeea too/tees
I need an English-speaking lawyer.	Χρειάζομαι έναν αγγλόφωνο δικηγόρο. khreeazome enan anglofono τΗeekeeghoro
I need to make a phone call.	Χρειάζεται να κάνω ένα τηλεφώνημα. khreeazete na kano ena teelefoneema
I need to contact the American/British consulate.	Χρειάζεται να έρθω σε επαφή με το … αμερικάνικο/βρεταννικό Προξενείο. khreeazete na ertho se epafee me to amereekaneeko/vretaneeko prokseneeo

Μπορείτε να τον/την περιγράψετε;	Can you describe him/her?
άνδρας/γυναίκα	male/female
ξανθός(-η)/μελαχρινός(-η)	blond/brunette
με κόκκινα/με γκρίζα μαλλιά	red-headed/gray-haired
με μακριά/κοντά μαλλιά/φαλακρός	long hair/short hair/balding
με ύψος περίπου …	approximate height …
ηλικίας (περίπου) …	aged (approximately) …
φορούσε …	he/she was wearing …

CLOTHES ➤ 144; COLORS ➤ 143

Lost property/Theft Απώλεια/Κλοπή

I want to report a theft/ break-in.	Θέλω να καταγγείλω μια κλοπή/μια διάρρηξη. *thelo na katangeelo mia klopee/mia THeeareeksee*
My car's been broken into.	Μού διέρρηξαν το αυτοκίνητο. *moo THee-ereeksan to aftokeeneeto*
I've lost my ...	Έχασα ... *ekhasa*
My ... has been stolen.	Μου έκλεψαν ... μου. *moo eklepsan ... moo*
camera	τη φωτογραφική μηχανή *tee fotoghrafeekee meekhanee*
(rental) car	το (νοικιασμένο) αυτοκίνητο *to (neekeeazmeno) aftokeeneeto*
credit cards	τις πιστωτικές κάρτες *tees peestoteekes kartes*
handbag	την τσάντα *teen tsanda*
money	τα χρήματα *ta khreemata*
passport	το διαβατήριο *to THeeavateereeo*
purse/wallet	το πορτοφόλι *to portofolee*
watch	το ρολόι *to roloee*
What shall I do?	Τί να κάνω; *tee na kano*
I need a police report for my insurance claim.	Χρειάζομαι ένα πιστοποιητικό της αστυνομίας για την ασφάλειά μου. *khreeazome ena peestopee-eeteeko tees asteenomeeas ya teen asfaleea moo*

Τί λείπει;	What's missing?
Πότε συνέβηκε;	When did it happen?
Πού μένετε;	Where are you staying?
Από πού το πήραν;	Where was it taken from?
Πού ήσασταν εκείνη την ώρα;	Where were you at the time?
Θα σας βρούμε ένα/ μια διερμηνέα.	We're getting an interpreter for you.
Θα κοιτάξουμε το ζήτημα.	We'll look into the matter.
Παρακαλώ, συμπληρώστε αυτό το έντυπο.	Please fill in this form.

Post office Ταχυδρομείο

Mailboxes are yellow and bear the initials ELTA. The post office is open from 8 a.m. to 8 p.m., except Wednesdays and Saturdays when it shuts at around 1 p.m. Main post offices are open Sunday mornings.

Stamps can also be bought at some kiosks and stores that sell postcards.

General queries Γενικές ερωτήσεις

Where is the nearest/ main post office?	Πού είναι το κοντινότερο/κεντρικό ταχυδρομείο; *poo eene to kondeenotero/ kendreeko takheeTHromeeo*
What time does the post office open/close?	Τί ώρα ανοίγει/κλείνει το ταχυδρομείο; *tee ora aneeyee/kleenee to takheeTHromeeo*
Does it close for lunch?	Κλείνει το μεσημέρι; *kleenee to meseemeree*
Where's the mailbox [postbox]?	Πού είναι το ταχυδρομικό κουτί; *poo eene to takheeTHromeeko kootee*

Buying stamps Αγοράζοντας γραμματόσημα

A stamp for this postcard / letter, please.	Ένα γραμματόσημο γι' αυτή τη κάρτα/ γράμμα, παρακαλώ. *ena ghramatoseemo yaftee teen karta/ghrama, parakalo*
A ...-cent stamp, please.	Ένα γραμματόσημο των ... λεπτών, παρακαλώ. *ena ghramatoseemo ton ... lepton parakalo*
What's the postage for a postcard/letter to ...?	Πόσο κάνει αυτή η κάρτα/αυτό το γράμμα για ...; *poso kanee aftee ee karta/afto to ghrama ya*
Is there a stamp machine here?	Υπάρχει μηχανή για γραμματόσημα εδώ; *eeparkhee meekhanee ya ghramatoseema eTHo*

– *kherete. tha eethela na steelo*
aftes tees kartes stees eenomenes poleetee-es.

– *poses?*

– *enea, parakalo.*

– *kanoon 50 x 9 (peneenda) lepta (epee enea):*
4.5 (teserameesee) evro, parakalo.

154

Sending parcels Στέλνοντας πακέτα

I want to send this package by ...	Θέλω να στείλω αυτό το πακέτο ... _thelo na steelo afto to paketo_
airmail	αεροπορικώς _aeroporeekos_
special delivery	επείγον _epeeghon_
registered mail	συστημένο _seesteemeno_
It contains ...	Περιέχει ... _peree-ekhee_

Παρακαλώ συμπληρώστε αυτήν την τελωνειακή δήλωση.	Please fill in the customs declaration.
Ποιά είναι η αξία;	What is the value?
Τί είναι μέσα;	What's inside?

Other services Άλλες υπηρεσίες

I'd like a phonecard, please.	Θα ήθελα μια τηλεκάρτα, παρακαλώ. _tha eethela mia teelekarta parakalo_
20 / 50 / 100 units	Είκοσι/πενήντα/εκατό μονάδες _eekosee/peneenda/ekato monaTHes_
Do you have a photocopier / fax machine here?	Έχετε φωτοτυπικό/φαξ εδώ; _ekhete fototeepeeko/"fax" eTHo_
I'd like to send a message by fax / e-mail.	Θα ήθελα να στείλω ένα φαξ/"e-mail". _tha eethela na steelo ena "fax"/ "e-mail"_
Can I access the Internet here?	Μπορώ να έχω πρόσβαση στο Ιντερνέτ από εδώ; _boro na ekho prosvasee sto "internet" apo eTHo_
What are the charges per hour?	Πόσο χρεώνεται η ώρα; _poso khreonete ee ora_
How do I log on?	Πώς συνδέομαι; _pos seenTHeome_

ΓΡΑΜΜΑΤΟΣΗΜΑ	stamps
ΤΗΛΕΓΡΑΦΗΜΑΤΑ	telegrams
ΟΛΕΣ ΟΙ ΥΠΗΡΕΣΙΕΣ	all transactions
ΠΟΣΤ ΡΕΣΤΑΝΤ	general delivery [poste restante]
ΕΠΟΜΕΝΗ ΣΥΛΛΟΓΗ	next collection ...
ΠΑΚΕΤΑ	parcels

Gifts Δώρα

Typical local souvenirs
Παραδοσιακά σουβενίρ

You can buy some imaginative and unusual souvenirs for a reasonable price. Shop around at souvenir stalls, and don't be afraid to haggle. Many of the handicrafts, especially jewelry and pottery, are handmade, so quality, design, and price will vary from store to store. Greek jewelry is intricate and beautifully made, some of the designs being copies of Byzantine jewelry bearing the dolphin, lion, ram, snake, and owl – the five animal symbols of ancient Greece.

You will also find a range of leather goods: belts, sandals, wallets, and bags. Hand-woven rugs and carpets of all sizes, embroidered tablecloths, decorative lace, icons and as a more unusual souvenir, a wooden backgammon board, all make good presents.

Some food products also make excellent gifts. Here are a few exportable products:

olives	ελιές *elee-es*
olive oil	λάδι *laᴛнee*
thyme honey	Θυμαρίσιο μέλι *theemareeseeo melee*
Turkish delight	λουκούμι *lookoomee*
ground Greek coffee	ελληνικός καφές *eleeneekos kafes*
dried Corinthian currants	κορινθιακή σταφίδα *koreentheeakee stafeeᴛна*
pistachio nuts	φυστίκια *feesteekeea*
halva	χαλβάς *khalvas*

Note that there is a ban on the export of all wild bulbs and orchids and endangered wildlife, including bird's eggs, tortoise shell, feathers, and stuffed animals.

Gifts Δώρα

bottle of wine	ένα μπουκάλι κρασί *ena bookalee krasee*
box of pastries	ένα κουτί γλυκά *ena kootee ghleeka*
calendar	ένα ημερολόγιο *ena eemeroloyeeo*
key ring	ένα μπρελόκ *ena brelok*
postcard	μια κάρτα *mia karta*
T-shirt	ένα μπλουζάκι *ena bloozakee*

Music Μουσική

I'd like a ...	Θα ήθελα ... *tha eethela*
cassette	μια κασέτα *mia kaseta*
compact disc	ένα κόμπακτ ντισκ *ena "CD"*
record	ένα δίσκο *ena THeesko*
videocassette	μια βιντεοκασέτα *mia veendeokaseta*
Which singers are popular? And which bands?	Ποιοί τραγουδιστές είναι δημοφιλείς; Και ποιά συγκροτήματα; *pee-ee traghooTHeestes eene THeemofeelees? ke pia seengroteemata*

Toys and games Παιχνίδια

I'd like a toy/game ...	Θα ήθελα ένα παιχνίδι ... *tha eethela ena pekhneeTHee*
for a boy	για ένα αγόρι *ya ena aghoree*
for a 5-year-old girl	για ένα πεντάχρονο κορίτσι *ya ena pendakhrono koreetsee*
pail and shovel [bucket and spade]	ο κουβάς και το φτυαράκι *o koovas ke to fteearakee*
chess/backgammon set	ένα σκάκι/τάβλι *ena skakee/tavlee*
doll	μια κούκλα *mia kookla*
electronic game	ένα ηλεκτρονικό παιχνίδι *ena eelektroneeko pekhneeTHee*
teddy bear	ένα αρκουδάκι *ena arkooTHakee*

Antiques Αντίκες

There are restrictions on exporting certain antiques and antiquities, so it is best to check in advance with the customs authorities before purchasing.

How old is this?	Πόσο παλιό είναι αυτό; *poso paleo eene afto*
Can you send it to me?	Μπορείτε να μου το στείλετε; *boreete na moo to steelete*
Will I have problems with customs?	Θα έχω προβλήματα με το τελωνείο; *tha ekho provleemata me to teloneeo*
Is there a certificate of authenticity?	Υπάρχει πιστοποιητικό αυθεντικότητας; *eeparkhee peestopee-eeteeko afthendeekoteetas*

Supermarket/Minimart
Σουπερμάρκετ/Παντοπωλείο

Large-scale self-service hypermarkets and supermarkets can be
found on the outskirts of most towns and smaller ones nearer city
centers. There are several large chains, including: **alfaveeta**,
vaseelopoolos, **veropoolos**, **mareenopoolos**, and **hellas spar**. They are all
good value. Note: there will usually be someone to serve you in smaller
local stores, so it's better not to pick things up yourself.

At the supermarket Στο σουπερμάρκετ

Excuse me. Where can I find …?	Συγγνώμη. Πού μπορώ να βρω …; *seeghnomee. poo boro na vro*
Do I pay for this here or at the checkout?	Να πληρώσω για αυτό εδώ ή στο ταμείο; *na pleeroso ya afto etho ee sto tameeo*
Where are the shopping carts [trolleys]/baskets?	Πού είναι τα καροτσάκια/καλάθια; *poo eene ta karotsakeea/kalatheea*
Is there a … here?	Υπάρχει τμήμα με … εδώ; *eeparkhee tmeema me … etho*
delicatessen	τυριά-αλλαντικά *teerya alandeeka*
pasta section	ζυμαρικά *zeemareeka*

ΨΩΜΙ ΚΑΙ ΓΛΥΚΑ	bread and cakes
ΕΙΔΗ ΚΑΘΑΡΙΣΜΟΥ	cleaning products
ΓΑΛΑΚΤΟΚΟΜΙΚΑ	dairy products
ΦΡΕΣΚΑ ΨΑΡΙΑ	fresh fish
ΦΡΕΣΚΟ ΚΡΕΑΣ	fresh meat
ΦΡΕΣΚΑ ΠΡΟΙΟΝΤΑ	fresh produce
ΚΑΤΕΨΥΓΜΕΝΑ	frozen foods
ΕΙΔΗ ΟΙΚΙΑΚΗΣ ΧΡΗΣΕΩΣ	household goods
ΠΟΥΛΕΡΙΚΑ	poultry
ΕΙΔΙΚΗ ΠΡΟΣΦΟΡΑ	special promotion
ΚΟΝΣΕΡΒΕΣ ΦΡΟΥΤΩΝ/ ΛΑΧΑΝΙΚΩΝ	canned fruit/vegetables
ΠΟΤΑ	wines and spirits

Weights and measures
- 1 kilogram or kilo (**kg.**) = 1000 grams (**g.**); **100 g.** = 3.5 oz.; **1 kg.** = 2.2 lb;
  1 oz. = 28.35 g.; 1 lb. = 453.60 g.
- 1 liter (l.) = 0.88 imp. quart or 1.06 U.S. quart; 1 imp. quart = 1.14 l.;
  1 U.S. quart = 0.951 l.; 1 imp. gallon = 4.55 l.; 1 U.S. gallon = 3.8 l.

Food hygiene Διατροφή

ΚΑΤΑΝΑΛΩΣΗ ... ΗΜΕΡΕΣ ΜΕΤΑ ΤΟ ΑΝΟΙΓΜΑ	eat within ... days of opening
ΔΙΑΤΗΡΕΙΤΑΙ ΣΤΟ ΨΥΓΕΙΟ	keep refrigerated
ΚΑΤΑΛΛΗΛΟ ΓΙΑ ΦΟΥΡΝΟΥΣ ΜΙΚΡΟΚΥΜΑΤΩΝ	microwaveable
ΞΑΝΑΘΕΡΜΑΝΕΤΕ ΠΡΙΝ ΤΗΝ ΚΑΤΑΝΑΛΩΣΗ	reheat before eating
ΑΝΑΛΩΣΗ ΜΕΧΡΙ ...	sell by ...
ΚΑΤΑΛΛΗΛΟ ΓΙΑ ΧΟΡΤΟΦΑΓΟΥΣ	suitable for vegetarians

At the minimart Στο παντοπωλείο

I'd like some of that/those.	Θα ήθελα μερικά από αυτά/εκείνα. *tha eethela mereeka apo afta/ekeena*
That's all, thanks.	Τίποτε άλλο. Ευχαριστώ. *teepote alo. efkhareesto*
I'd like a(n)/some ...	Θα ήθελα ... *tha eethela*
kilo of apples	ένα κιλό μήλα *ena keelo meela*
half-kilo of tomatoes	μισό κιλό ντομάτες *meeso keelo domates*
100 grams of cheese	εκατό γραμμάρια τυρί *ekato ghramareea teeree*
liter of milk	ένα λίτρο γάλα *ena leetro ghala*
six eggs	έξι αυγά *eksee avgha*
... slices of ham	... μερικές φέτες ζαμπόν *... mereekes fetes zambon*
bottle of wine	ένα μπουκάλι κρασί *ena bookalee krasee*
carton of milk	ένα κουτί γάλα *ena kootee ghala*
jar of jam	ένα βάζο μαρμελάδα *ena vazo marmelaтна*
bag of potato chips [crisps]	ένα πακέτο τσιπς *ena paketo "chips"*

– tha <u>ee</u>thela mee<u>so</u> <u>kee</u>lo a<u>po</u> af<u>to</u> to
tee<u>ree</u>, paraka<u>lo</u>.
– af<u>to</u>?
– ne, teen <u>fe</u>ta, paraka<u>lo</u>.
– ve<u>ve</u>os. tee<u>po</u>te <u>a</u>lo?
– ke <u>te</u>sera ko<u>ma</u>teea spana<u>ko</u>peeta,
paraka<u>lo</u>.
– o<u>ree</u>ste.

Provisions/Picnic Τρόφιμα/Πικνίκ

apples	τα μήλα ta <u>mee</u>la
bananas	οι μπανάνες ee ba<u>na</u>nes
beer	η μπύρα ee <u>bee</u>ra
bottle of wine	το μπουκάλι κρασί to boo<u>ka</u>lee kra<u>see</u>
butter	το βούτυρο to <u>voo</u>teero
cheese	το τυρί to tee<u>ree</u>
chocolate	η σοκολάτα ee soko<u>la</u>ta
cookies [biscuits]	τα μπισκότα ta bees<u>ko</u>ta
grapes	τα σταφύλια ta sta<u>fee</u>leea
ice cream	το παγωτό to pagho<u>to</u>
instant coffee	ο νεσκαφές o neska<u>fes</u>
milk	το γάλα to <u>gha</u>la
oranges	τα πορτοκάλια ta porto<u>ka</u>leea
potato chips [crisps]	τα τσιπς ta "chips"
salt	το αλάτι to a<u>la</u>tee
soft drink/soda	το αναψυκτικό to anapseek<u>tee</u>ko
sugar	η ζάχαρη ee <u>za</u>kharee
tea bags	τα φακελλάκια τσαγιού ta fake<u>la</u>keea tsa<u>yoo</u>
yogurt	το γιαούρτι to ya<u>oo</u>rtee

Some of the most common types of bread are:

χωριάτικο khor<u>ya</u>teeko: Brown bread

ολικής αλέσεως olee<u>kees</u> a<u>le</u>seos: Wholegrain bread

άσπρο/πολυτελείας <u>a</u>spro/poleete<u>lee</u>as: Both are types of white bread.
poleete<u>lee</u>as is made from more refined flour than **aspro** and is more
expensive

σιμιγδαλένιο seemeeghtha<u>le</u>neeo Semolina bread

Health

Doctors in Greece are well trained but sometimes poor facilities affect the quality of healthcare. However, for simple ailments you should be in good hands. The E111 form will cover all EU citizens on the Greek national health service for any emergency treatment (including dental treatment). Non-EU citizens should take out a health insurance policy before traveling.

No immunization is necessary before coming to Greece, but it is best to make sure you are up-to-date on your tetanus shots.

Doctor (General) Γιατρός (Γενικά)

Where can I find a doctor/dentist?	Πού μπορώ να βρώ ένα γιατρό/οδοντίατρο; _poo boro na vro ena yatro/oтноndeeatro_
Where's there a doctor who speaks English?	Πού υπάρχει γιατρός που να μιλά Αγγλικά; _poo eeparkhee yatros poo na meela angleeka_
What are the office [surgery] hours?	Ποιές είναι οι ώρες ιατρίου; _pee-es eene ee ores eeatreeoo_
Could the doctor come to see me here?	Μπορεί να έρθει να με δει εδώ ο γιατρός; _boree na erthee na me тнee тно o yatros_
Can I make an appointment for … ?	Μπορώ να κλείσω ένα ραντεβού για … ; _boro na kleeso ena randevoo ya_
tomorrow	αύριο _avreeo_
as soon as possible	όσο το δυνατόν πιο σύντομα _oso to тнeenaton peeo seendoma_
It's urgent.	Είναι επείγον. _eene epeeghon_
I've got an appointment with Doctor …	Έχω ραντεβού με τον κύριο/κυρία … _ekho randevoo me ton keereeo/keereea_

TIME ➤ *220; DATE* ➤ *218*

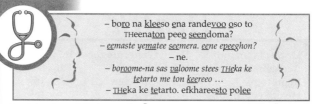

– bo<u>ro</u> na <u>klee</u>so <u>e</u>na rande<u>voo oso</u> to
THee<u>na</u>ton pee<u>o</u> <u>seen</u>doma?
– <u>ee</u>maste <u>ye</u>matee <u>see</u>mera. <u>ee</u>ne epe<u>egh</u>on?
– ne.
– bo<u>roo</u>me-na sas <u>va</u>loome stees THeka ke
<u>te</u>tarto me ton <u>kee</u>reeo …
– THeka ke <u>te</u>tarto. efkhar<u>ee</u>sto pol<u>ee</u>

Accident and injury Ατύχημα και τραυματισμός

My … is hurt/injured.	… μου χτύπησε/τραυματίστηκε. *moo khteepeese/travmateesteeke*
husband/wife	Ο άνδρας/η γυναίκα *o anTHras/ee yeeneka*
son/daughter	ο γιος/η κόρη *o yos/ee koree*
friend	Ο φίλος/η φίλη *o feelos/ee feelee*
baby	Το μωρό *to moro*
He/She is …	Είναι … *eene*
unconscious	αναίσθητος/-η *anestheetos/-ee*
(seriously) injured	σοβαρά τραυματισμένος/-η *sovara travmateezmenos/-ee*
He/she is bleeding (heavily)	Αιμορραγεί σοβαρά. *emorayee sovara*
I have a(n) …	Έχω … *ekho*
blister	μια φουσκάλα *mia fooskala*
boil	ένα σπυρί *ena speeree*
bruise	μια μελανιά *mia melaneea*
burn	ένα έγκαυμα *ena egavma*
cut	ένα κόψιμο *ena kopseemo*
graze	μια γρατζουνιά *mia ghratzooneea*
insect bite	ένα τσίμπημα από έντομο *ena tseembeema apo endomo*
lump	ένα σβώλο *ena zvolo*
rash	ένα εξάνθημα *ena eksantheema*
sting	ένα τσίμπημα *ena tseembeema*
swelling	ένα πρήξιμο *ena preekseemo*
wound	μια πληγή *mia pleeyee*
My … hurts.	Με πονάει … *me ponaee*

Symptoms Συμπτώματα

I've been feeling ill for … days.	Αισθάνομαι άρρωστος εδώ και … ημέρες _esthanome_ _arostos_ e<small>THO</small> ke … _eemeres_
I feel …	Αισθάνομαι … _esthanome_
feverish	σαν να έχω πυρετό _san na ekho peereto_
sick	άρρωστος _arostos_
I feel …	Έχω … _ekho_
dizzy	ζαλάδες _zalaThes_
faint	λιποθυμίες _leepotheemee-es_
I've been vomiting.	Έκανα εμετό. _ekana emeto_
I've got diarrhea.	Έχω διάρροια. _ekho THeeareea_
It hurts here.	Με πονάει εδώ. _me ponaee eTHO_
I have (a/an) …	Έχω … _ekho_
backache	πόνο στη πλάτη _pono steen platee_
cold	κρυολόγημα _kreeoloyeema_
earache	πόνο στο αυτί _pono sto aftee_
headache	πονοκέφαλο _ponokefalo_
sore throat	πονόλαιμο _ponolemo_
stomachache	στομαχόπονο _stomakhopono_
sunstroke	ηλίαση _eeleeasee_

Health conditions Κατάσταση υγείας

I am …	Έχω … _ekho_
asthmatic	άσθμα _asthma_
handicapped	αναπηρία _anapeereea_
I am …	Είμαι … _eeme_
deaf	κουφός/-ή _koofos/-ee_
diabetic	διαβητικός/-ή _THeeaveeteekos/-ee_
epileptic	επιληπτικός/-ιά _epeeleepteekos/-eea_
(… months) pregnant	(… μηνών) έγκυος _(meenon) engeeos_
I have a heart condition / high blood pressure.	Έχω πρόβλημα καρδιάς/υψηλή πίεση _ekho provleema karTHyas/ eepseelee pee-esee_

Doctor's inquiries Ερωτήσεις γιατρού

Πόσο καιρό αισθάνεστε έτσι;	How long have you been feeling like this?
Είναι η πρώτη φορά που το παθαίνετε;	Is this the first time you've had this?
Παίρνετε άλλα φάρμακα;	Are you taking any other medication?
Είστε αλλεργικός σε τίποτα;	Are you allergic to anything?
Έχετε κάνει εμβόλιο τετάνου;	Have you been vaccinated against tetanus?
Έχει κοπεί η όρεξή σας;	Have you lost your appetite?

Examination Εξέταση

Θα πάρω τη θερμοκρασία/ την πίεσή σας.	I'll take your temperature/ blood pressure.
Σηκώστε το μανίκι σας παρακαλώ.	Roll up your sleeve, please.
Παρακαλώ γδυθείτε ως τη μέση.	Please undress to the waist.
Παρακαλώ ξαπλώστε.	Please lie down.
Ανοίξτε το στόμα σας.	Open your mouth.
Πάρτε μια βαθιά αναπνοή.	Breathe deeply.
Παρακαλώ βήξτε.	Cough, please.
Πού πονάει;	Where does it hurt?
Πονάει εδώ;	Does it hurt here?

Diagnosis Διάγνωση

Θέλω να βγάλετε μια ακτινογραφία.	I want you to have an X-ray.
Θέλω ένα δείγμα αίματος/ κοπράνων/ούρων.	I want a specimen of your blood/stools/urine.
Θέλω να δείτε έναν ειδικό.	I want you to see a specialist.
Θέλω να πάτε στο νοσοκομείο.	I want you to go to a hospital.
Είναι ...	It's ...
σπασμένο/στραμπουληγμένο	broken/sprained
εξαρθρωμένο/σχισμένο	dislocated/torn

Έχετε	You have (a/an) …
σκωληκοειδίτιδα	appendicitis
κυστίτιδα	cystitis
γρίππη	flu
τροφική δηλητηρίαση	food poisoning
κάταγμα	fracture
γαστρίτιδα	gastritis
κοίλη	hernia
φλεγμονή του/της …	inflammation of …
ιλαρά	measles
πνευμονία	pneumonia
ισχυαλγία	sciatica
αμυγδαλίτιδα	tonsilitis
όγκο	tumor
αφροδισιακό νόσημα	venereal disease
Είναι μολυσμένο.	It's infected.
Είναι μεταδοτικό.	It's contagious.

Treatment Θεραπεία

Θα σας δώσω …	I'll give you …
ένα αντισηπτικό	an antiseptic
ένα παυσίπονο	a painkiller
Θα σας γράψω συνταγή για …	I'm going to prescribe …
μια δόση αντιβιοτικά	a course of antibiotics
υπόθετα	(some) suppositories
Είσαστε αλλεργικός/-ή σε κανένα φάρμακο;	Are you allergic to any medication?
Παίρνετε … κάθε … ώρες/ πριν τα γεύματα.	Take … every … hours/ before meals.
Θέλω να επιστρέψετε σε … ημέρες.	I'd like you to come back in … days.
Συμβουλευτείτε ένα γιατρό όταν επιστρέψετε στην πατρίδα σας.	Consult a doctor when you get home.

Parts of the body
Μέρη του σώματος

arm	χέρι _kheree_
back	πλάτη _platee_
bone	οστό _osto_
breast/chest	στήθος _steethos_
ear	αυτί _aftee_
eye	μάτι _matee_
face	πρόσωπο _prosopo_
finger	δάχτυλο _THakhteelo_
foot	πόδι _poTHee_
hand	χέρι _kheree_
head	κεφάλι _kefalee_
heart	καρδιά _karTHya_
jaw	σαγόνι _saghonee_
kidney	νεφρό _nefro_
knee	γόνατο _ghonato_
leg	πόδι _poTHee_
liver	ήπαρ (medical), συκώτι _eepar, seekotee_
mouth	στόμα _stoma_
muscle	μυς _mees_
neck	αυχένας _afkhenas_
nose	μύτη _meetee_
rib	πλευρό _plevro_
shoulder	ώμος _omos_
skin	δέρμα _THerma_
spine	σπονδυλική στήλη _sponTHeeleekee steelee_
stomach	στομάχι _stomakhee_
throat	λαιμός _lemos_
thumb	αντίχειρας _andeekheeras_
toe	δάχτυλο ποδιού _THakhteelo poTHyoo_
tongue	γλώσσα _ghlosa_
vein	φλέβα _fleva_

Gynecologist Στο γυναικολόγο

I have ...   Έχω ... _ekho_

abdominal pains   πόνους στη κοιλιά
                                   ponoos steen keeleea

period pains   πόνους περιόδου
                                   ponoos pereeoτΗοο

a vaginal infection   κολπική μόλυνση _kolpeekee moleensee_

I haven't had my period   Δεν έχω περίοδο εδώ και ... μήνες.
for ... months.   _τΗen ekho pereeoτΗο eτΗο ke ... meenes_

I'm on the Pill.   Παίρνω το αντισυλληπτικό χάπι.
                                   perno to andeeseeleepteeko khapee

Hospital Νοσοκομείο

Please notify my family.   Παρακαλώ ειδοποιήστε την οικογένειά
                                   μου. _parakalo eeτΗopee-eeste teen
                                   eekoyeneea moo_

What are the visiting hours?   Ποιές είναι οι ώρες επισκεπτηρίου;
                                   pee-es eene ee ores epeeskepteereeoo

I'm in pain.   Πονάω. _ponao_

I can't eat / sleep.   Δεν μπορώ να φάω/κοιμηθώ.
                                   τΗen boro na fao/keemeetho

When will the doctor come?   Πότε θα έρθει ο γιατρός;
                                   pote tha erthee o yatros

Which ward is ... in?   Σε ποιά πτέρυγα είναι ο/η ... ;
                                   se pia ptereegha eene o/ee

Optician Στον οφθαλμίατρο

I'm near- [short-] sighted /   Είμαι μύωπας/πρεσβύωπας.
far- [long-] sighted.   _eeme meeopas/prezveeopas_

I've lost ...   Έχασα ... _ekhasa_

one of my contact lenses   έναν από τους φακούς επαφής μου.
                                   enan apo toos fakoos epafees moo

my glasses   τα γυαλιά μου _ta yaleea moo_

a lens   ένα φακό _ena fako_

Could you give me   Μπορείτε να μου το αντικαταστήσετε;
a replacement?   _boreete na moo to andeekatasteesete_

Dentist Οδοντίατρος

I have a toothache.	Έχω πονόδοντο. _ekho poноTHonto_
This tooth hurts.	Αυτό το δόντι με πονάει. _afto to THondee me ponaee_
I've lost/broken a tooth/crown/cap.	Έχασα/έσπασα ένα δόντι/μια κορώνα/ένα σφράγισμα. _ekhasa/espasa ena THondee/mia korona/ena sfrayeezma_
I've lost a filling.	Έχασα ένα σφράγισμα. _ekhasa ena sfrayeezma_
Can you repair this denture?	Μπορείτε να φτιάξετε αυτή την τεχνητή οδοντοστοιχία; _boreete na fteeaksete aftee teen tekhneetee оTHondosteekheea_
I don't want it extracted.	Δεν θέλω να μου το βγάλετε. _THen thelo na moo to vghalete_

Θα σας κάνω μια ένεση/ ένα τοπικό αναισθητικό.	I'm going to give you an injection/ a local anesthetic.
Χρειάζεστε ένα σφράγισμα/ μια κορώνα.	You need a filling/cap/crown.
Πρέπει να το βγάλω.	I'll have to take it out.
Μπορώ να το διορθώσω μόνο προσωρινά.	I can only fix it temporarily.
Ελάτε σε ... ημέρες.	Come back in ... days.
Μη φάτε τίποτα για ... ώρες.	Don't eat anything for ... hours.

Payment and insurance Πληρωμή και ασφάλεια

How much do I owe you?	Τι σας οφείλω; _tee sas ofeelo_
I have insurance.	Έχω ασφάλεια. _ekho asfaleea_
Can I have a receipt for my health insurance?	Μπορώ να έχω μια απόδειξη για την ασφάλεια υγείας μου; _boro na ekho mia apoTHeeksee ya teen asfaleea eeyeeas moo_
Do you have... ?	Έχετε ... ; _ekhete_
Form E111/health insurance	το έντυπο E111/ασφάλεια υγείας _to endeepo epseelon ekaton endeka/ asfaleea eeyeeas_

Dictionary
English – Greek

Most terms in this dictionary are either followed by an example or cross-referenced to pages where the word appears in a phrase. The notes below provide some basic grammar guidelines.

Nouns

The gender of a noun is indicated by the article preceding it: **o** for masculine (m), **ee** for feminine (f), and **to** for neuter (n).

masculine	ο καφὲς	**o kafes**	the coffee
feminine	η μπὺρα	**ee beera**	the beer
neuter	το τρὲνο	**to treno**	the train

There is no easy way to form the plural but if you clearly state a number along with the noun (➤ 216), then you will be easily understood.

Greek nouns have cases – that is a noun's ending is dependent on the position of the word in the sentence, for example whether it is the subject or the object. For this reason you will see the same noun with slightly different endings in different phrases. Don't worry too much about this. Use the form given in the dictionary if in doubt.

Adjectives

Adjectives agree with the noun they are describing in gender, case, and number. In this dictionary the (nominative) masculine form is given. The most common ending for a feminine adjective is **-ee** and for the neuter **-o**.

Verbs

Verbs are shown in the first person singular (I eat, I go, etc.). Below are three of the main categories of regular verbs in the present tense. Using the endings indicated after **-**, you can use a large number of verbs competently. Greeks generally use the polite "you" form of verbs (**esees**). The informal form (**esee**) is used amongst friends and with children, but don't worry too much – you will not be considered rude, just friendly!

Verb ends in:	-ω **-o** *(I have)*	-ὼ **-o** *(I am thirsty)*	-όμαι **-ome** *(I think)*
egho *(I)*	**ekh-o**	**THeeps-o**	**skeft-ome**
esee *(you, informal)*	**ekh-ees**	**THeeps-as**	**skeft-ese**
aftos/aftee/afto *(he/she/it)*	**ekh-ee**	**THeeps-a** (**-aee**)	**skeft-ete**
emees *(we)*	**ekh-oume**	**THeeps-oume**	**skeft-omaste**
esees *(you, formal & pl.)*	**ekh-ete**	**THeeps-ate**	**skeft-este**
aftee/aftes/afta *(they m/f/n)*	**ekh-oon**	**THeeps-oon**	**skeft-onde**

A a few λίγα leegha 15

a little λίγο leegho 15

a lot πολύ polee 15

a.m. π.μ. pro meseemvreeas

about (approximately) περίπου, γύρω pereepoo 15

abscess απόστημα n aposteema

abseiling αναρρίχηση f anareekheesee

access πρόσβαση f prozvasee 100

accessories αξεσουάρ n aksesooar 144

accident ατύχημα n ateekheema 92, 152; **accidentally** κατά λάθος kata lathos 28

accompaniments συνοδεία φαγητού f seenoTHeea fagheetoo 38

accompany, to συνοδεύω seenoTHevo 65

accountant λογιστής m loyeestees

ace (cards) άσσος m asos

acne ακμή f akmee

adaptor προσαρμοστής m prosarmostees 26

address διεύθυνση f THe-eeftheensee 84, 93, 94, 126

adhesive bandages αυτοκόλλητοι επίδεσμοι mpl, λευκοπλάστ aftokoleetee epeeTHezmee, lefkoplast 141

adjoining room διπλανό δωμάτιο n THeeplano THomateeo 22

admission: what's the admission charge? πόσο κάνει η είσοδος; poso kanee ee eesoTHos 114

adult ενήλικας eneeleekas 81, 100

aerial (car/tv) κεραία f keraya

after (place) μετά meta 95; (time) μετά meta 13

after-sun lotion γαλάκτωμα για μετά την ηλιοθεραπεία n ghalaktoma ya meta teen eeleeotherapeea 142

afternoon, in the το απόγευμα to apoyevma 221

age ηλικία f eeleekeea 152

ago πριν από, εδώ και preen apo, eTHo ke 13

agree: I agree συμφωνώ seemfono

air conditioning κλιματισμός m kleemateezmos 22, 24

air pump αντλία αέρος f andleea aeros 87

air-freshener αποσμητικό χώρου n apozmeeteeko khoroo

airline αεροπορία f aeroporeea

airmail αεροπορικώς aeroporeekos 155

airport αεροδρόμιο n aeroTHromeeo 96

airsteward/hostess αεροσυνοδός aeroseenoTHos

aisle seat διάδρομος m THeeaTHromos 69

Albania Αλβανία f alvaneea

alcoholic (drink) οινοπνευματώδες (ποτό) eenopnevmatoTHes (poto)

all όλοι olee

allergic, to be είμαι αλλεργικός/-ή eeme alergheekos/-ee 164, 165

allergy αλλεργία f alergeea

allowed: is it allowed? επιτρέπεται; epeetrepete

alone μόνος monos 120

alphabet αλφάβητο n alfaveeto

already ήδη eeTHee 28

also επίσης epeesees 19

aluminium foil αλουμινόχαρτο n aloomeenokharto 148

always πάντα panda 13

am: I am είμαι eeme

amazing καταπληκτικό katapleekteeko 101

ambassador πρεσβευτής m prezveftees

amber κεχριμπάρι n kekhreembaree

ambulance ασθενοφόρο n asthenoforo 92

American (adj) αμερικάνικος amereekaneekos 150, 152; (n) Αμερικαν-ός, -ίδα amereekan-os, -eeTHa

amount ποσό n poso 42

amusement arcade αίθουσα ψυχαγωγίας f ethoosa pseekhaghoyeeas 113

and και ke 19

angling ψάρεμα n psarema

animal ζώο n zo-o 106

another άλλο allo 21; **~ time** άλλη φορά alee fora 125

antibiotics αντιβιοτικά n andeeveeoteeka 165

anticeptic αντισηπτικό n andeeseepteeko 165

antique αντίκα f anteeka 157; **~ store** κατάστημα με αντίκες n katasteema me anteekes 130

antiquities αρχαιολογικός χώρος m arkheoloyeekos khoros

antiseptic cream αντισηπτική κρέμα f andeeseepteekee krema 141

anyone else κανείς άλλος kanees alos 93

anything cheaper κάτι φτηνότερο katee fteenotero 21

apartment διαμέρισμα n THeeamereezma 28

apologize: I apologize ζητώ συγγνώμη zeeto seeghnomee

appendicitis σκωληκοειδίτιδα f skoleekoeeTHeeteeTHa 165

appendix σκωληκοειδίτιδα f skoleekoeeTHeeteeTHa

appetizer ορεκτικό n oreekteeko 43

apple μήλο n meelo 160

appointment ραντεβού n randevoo 161; **to make an ~** κλείνω ένα ραντεβού kleeno ena randevoo 147

approximately περίπου pereepoo 152

April Απρίλιος m apreeleeos 218

archery τοξοβολία f toksovoleea

architect αρχιτέκτονας arkheetektonas 104; **architecture** αρχιτεκτονική f arkheetektoneekee 119

are you ... είστε ...; eeste

area code κωδικός m koTHeekos 127

arm χέρι n kheree 166

around (time) περίπου pereepoo

arrange: can you arrange it? μπορείτε να το κανονίσετε; boreete na to kanoneesete

arrest, to be under είσαστε υπό σύλληψη eesaste eepo seeleepsee

arrive, to φτάνω ftano 68, 71, 76

art τέχνη f tekhnee; **~ gallery** γκαλερί τέχνης f galeree tekhnees 99

artificial sweetener ζακχαρίνη f zak-khareenee 38

artist καλλιτέχνης kaleetekhnees 104

as soon as possible όσο το δυνατόν πιο σύντομα oso to THeenaton peeo seendoma

ashore, to go πάω στην ξηρά pao steen kseera

ashtray σταχτοδοχείο n stakhtoTHokheeo 39

ask: I asked for ... ζήτησα ... zeeteesa 41

asleep, to be κοιμάμαι keemame

aspirin (soluble) ασπιρίνη (διαλυόμενη) f aspeereenee (THealeeomenee) 141

asthmatic, to be έχω άσθμα ekho asthma 163

astringent στυπτικό n steepteeko

at (time) στις stees 13; **at least** τουλάχιστον toolakheeston 23

athletics αθλήματα στίβου npl athleemata steevoo 114

attack (criminal) επίθεση f epeethesee 152; (medical) κρούσμα kroozma

attendant βοηθός voeethos

attractive ελκυστικός elkeesteekos

August Αύγουστος m avghoostos 218

aunt θεία f theea 120

Australia Αυστραλία f afstraleea 119

Australian (n) Αυστραλός afstralos

authenticity αυθεντικότητα f afthendeekoteeta 157

A-Z

automatic (car) αυτόματο (αυτοκίνητο) aftomato (aftokeeneeto) 86

automatic camera αυτόματη φωτογραφική μηχανή f aftomatee fotoghrafeekee meekhanee 151

autumn φθινόπωρο n ftheenoporo 219

B **baby** μωρό n moro 39, 113, 162; **~ seat** καρέκλα μωρού f karekla moroo; **~ food** φαγητό για μωρά n fayeeto ya mora 142

back πλάτη f platee 166; **~ache** πόνος στη πλάτη ponos steen platee 163

backgammon τάβλι n tavlee 121

bad κακό kako 14

baggage πράγματα npl, αποσκευές fpl pragmata, aposkeves 32, 67, 69, 71; **~ reclaim** παραλαβή αποσκευών f paralavee aposkevon 71; **~ check** φύλαξη αποσκευών f feelaksee aposkevon 73

baked στο φούρνο sto foorno

bakery αρτοποιείο n / φούρνος m artopee-eeo/ foornos 130

balcony μπαλκόνι n balkonee 29

ballet μπαλλέτο n baleto 108, 111

banana μπανάνα f banana 160

band (musical group) συγκρότημα n seengroteema 111, 157

bandage γάζα f ghaza 141

bank τράπεζα f trapeza 130, 138; **~ account** λογαριασμός τραπέζης m logharyazmos trapezees; **~ loan** τραπεζικό δάνειο n trapezeeko THaneeo

bar μπαρ n "bar" 26, 112

barber κουρείο n kooreeo 130

basement υπόγειο n eepoyeeo 132

basket καλάθι n kalathee 158

basketball μπάσκετ μπολ m, καλαθοσφαίρηση f basket bol, kalathosfereesee 114

bath: to take a ~ κάνω μπάνιο kano baneeo

bathroom μπάνιο n baneeo 26, 29

battery μπαταρία f batareea 137, 151

battle site πεδίο μάχης n peTHeeo makhees

be able, to μπορώ boro 18

be, to (see also am, are) είμαι eeme

beach παραλία f paraleea 116

beans όσπρια npl ospreea 47

beard γένια npl yeneea

beautiful όμορφος omorfos 101

because επειδή epeeTHee 15; **because of** λόγω logho 15

bed κρεββάτι krevatee 21; **~ and breakfast** διαμονή με πρωινό THeeamonee me proeeno 24

bedding σεντόνια npl sendoneea 29

bedroom υπνοδωμάτιο n eepnoTHomateeo 29

bee μέλισσα f meleesa

beer μπύρα f beera 40, 160

before (time) πριν (από) preen (apo) 13, 221

beginner αρχάριος arkhareeos 117

beginning αρχή f arkhee

beige μπεζ bez 143

belong: this belongs to me αυτό μου ανήκει afto moo aneekee

belt ζώνη f zonee 144

berth κουκέτα f kooketa 74, 77

better καλύτερο kaleetero 14

bib ποδιά μωρού f poTHya moroo

bicycle ποδήλατο n poTHeelato 83; **bicycle parts** 82

bidet μπιντέ n beeTHe

big μεγάλος meghalos 14, 134, 117; **bigger** μεγαλύτερο meghaleetero 24

bikini μπικίνι n "bikini" 144

bill λογαριασμός m logharyazmos 32

binoculars κυάλια n keealeea

bird πουλί n poolee 106

biscuits μπισκότα npl beeskota 160

bite (insect) τσίμπημα n tseembeema

bitten: I've been bitten by a dog με δάγκωσε ένας σκύλος me THangose enas skeelos

bitter πικρός peekros 41

black μαύρος mavros 143; (coffee) σκέτος m sketos 40; ~ **and white film** (camera) ασπρόμαυρο φιλμ aspromavro "film" 151

bladder ουροδόχος κύστη f ooroTHokhos keestee

blanket κουβέρτα f kooverta 27

bleach χλωρίνη f khloreenee 148

bleeding, to be αιμορραγώ emoragho 92, 162

blinds περσίδες fpl perseeTHes 25

blister φουσκάλα f fooskala 162

blocked, to be έχει βουλώσει ekhee voolosee 25

blood αίμα n ema 164; ~ **group** ομάδα αίματος f omaTHa ematos; ~ **pressure** πίεση f pee-esee 163

blouse μπλούζα f blooza 144

blue μπλε ble 143

boarding card κάρτα επιβιβάσεως f karta epeeveevaseos 70

boat πλοίο n pleeo 81; ~ **trip** ταξίδι με πλοίο n takseeTHee me pleeo 81

body: parts of the ~ μέρη του σώματος meree too somatos 166

boil σπυρί n speeree 162

boiled βραστό vrasto

boiler θερμοσίφωνας m thermoseefonas 29

bone οστό n osto 166

book βιβλίο n veevleeo 11, 150

book, to (reserve) κλείνω kleeno; **booked up, to be** όλα κλεισμένα ola kleezmena 115; **booking** (restaurant) κράτηση f krateesee

booklet of tickets δεσμίδα εισιτηρίων f THezmeeTHa eeseeteereeon 79

bookstore βιβλιοπωλείο n veevleeopoleeo 130, 150

boots μπότες fpl botes 115, 145

border (country) σύνορα npl seenora

boring βαρετό vareto 101

born: I was born ... Γεννήθηκα ... yeneetheeka

borrow: may I borrow the ...? Μπορώ να δανειστώ το/τη ...; boro na THaneesto to/tee

botanical garden βοτανικός κήπος m votaneekos keepos 99

bottle μπουκάλι n bookalee 37, 159; ~ **of wine** μπουκάλι κρασί n bookalee krasee 156, 160; ~-**opener** τιρμπουσόν n teerbooson 148

bow (ship) πλώρη f ploree

bowel έντερο n endero

box office γραφείο κρατήσεων n ghrafeeo krateeseon

boxing μποξ n boks

boy αγόρι n aghoree 120, 157

boyfriend φίλος m feelos 120

bra σουτιέν n sootee-en 144

bread ψωμί n psomee 38

break, to σπάζω spazo 28

break-in διάρρηξη f THeeareeksee 153

breakdown (car) βλάβη f vlavee 88

breakfast πρωινό n proeeno 26, 27

breast στήθος n steethos 166

breathe, to αναπνέω anapneo 92

breathtaking φαντασμαγορικό fandazmaghoreeko 101

bridge γέφυρα f ghefeera 96, 107

bridge (cards) μπριτζ n "bridge"

briefcase τσάντα γραφείου f, χαρτοφύλακας m tsanda ghrafeeoo,

briefs κυλοτάκι, σλιπ n keelotakee, sleep 144

bring, to φέρνω ferno

Britain Βρεταννία f vretaneea 119

British (adj) βρεταννικός vretaneekos 152; (n) Βρεταννός vretanos

brochure φυλλάδιο n feelaTHeeo

broken σπασμένος spazmenos 137, 164

bronchitis βρογχίτιδα f vronkheeteeτHα

broom σκούπα f skoopa

brother αδελφός m ατHelfos 120

brown καφέ kafe 143

browse, to κοιτάω keetao 133

bruise μελανιά f melaneea 162

brush βούρτσα f voortsa

buffet car τραπεζαρία τραίνου f trapezareea trenoo

build, to κτίζω kteezo 104

building κτίριο n kteereeo

Bulgaria Βουλγαρία f voolghareea

bureau de change γραφείο συναλλάγματος n ghrafeeo seenalaghmatos 138

burger χάμπουργκερ n khamboorger 40

burglary (see also **theft**) κλοπή f klopee

burn έγκαυμα n engavma 162

burst pipe σπασμένος σωλήνας m spazmenos soleenas

bus λεωφορείο n leoforeeo 70, 78, 79, 98; **~ route** διαδρομή λεωφορείων f τΗeeaτΗromee leoforeeon 96; **~ station** σταθμός λεωφορείων m statHmos leoforeeon 78; **~ stop** στάση λεωφορείου f stasee leoforeeoo 65, 96

business: on ~ για δουλειά ya τHooleea 66; **~ class** μπίζνες "business" 68; **~ trip** ταξίδι για δουλειά takseeτΗee ya τHooleea 123

busy (occupied) απασχολημένος apaskholeemenos 125

but αλλά ala 19

butane gas υγραέριο n eeghraereeo 30, 31

butcher shop κρεοπωλείο n kreopoleeo 130

butter βούτυρο n vooteero 38, 43, 160

button κουμπί n koombee

buy, to αγοράζω aghorazo 67, 80

by (time) μέχρι mekhree 13; **by car** με το αυτοκίνητο me to aftokeeneeto 17, 94; **by cash** τοις μετρητοίς tees metreetees 136; **by credit card** με πιστωτική κάρτα me peestoteekee karta 17

bye! αντίο! andeeo

cabaret καμπαρέ n "cabaret" 112

cabin καμπίνα f kambeena 81

café καφετέρια f kafetereea 35, 40

cagoule αδιάβροχο μπουφάν n ατHeeavrokho boofan 145

cake κέηκ n "cake" 40

calendar ημερολόγιο n eemeroloyeeo 156

call, to καλώ kalo 92; (telephone) παίρνω τηλέφωνο perno teelefono 127, 128; **call the police!** καλέστε την αστυνομία! kaleste teen asteenomeea 92; **~ collect** με χρέωση του παραλήπτη me khreosee too paraleeptee 127

camcorder φορητή βιντεοκάμερα f foreetee videokamera

camera φωτογραφική μηχανή f fotoghrafeekee meekhanee 151; **~ case** θήκη μηχανής f theekee meekhanees 151; **~ store** φωτογραφικά npl, κατάστημα με φωτογραφικά είδη n fotoghrafeeka, katasteema me fotoghrafeeka eeτHee 151

campbed κρεββάτι εκστρατείας n krevatee ekstrateeas 31

camping κατασκήνωση f, κάμπινγκ n kataskeenosee, "camping" 30, 31; **~ equipment** εξοπλισμός κάμπινγκ eksopleezmos "camping" 31

campsite χώρος κάμπινγκ/για κατασκήνωση m khoros "camping"/ya kataskeenosee 30

can: can I? μπορώ; bo<u>ro</u> 18; **can I have?** μπορώ να έχω; bo<u>ro</u> na <u>e</u>kho 18; **can you help me?** μπορείτε να με βοηθήσετε; bo<u>ree</u>te na me voee<u>thee</u>sete 18; **can you recommend?** μπορείτε να συστήσετε; bo<u>ree</u>te na sees<u>tee</u>sete 112

can opener ανοιχτήρι n anee<u>khtee</u>ree 148

Canada Καναδάς m kana<u>THas</u> 119

Canadian (n) Καναδός kana<u>THOS</u>

canal κανάλι n ka<u>na</u>lee

cancel, to ακυρώνω akee<u>ro</u>no 68

cancer (disease) καρκίνος m kar<u>kee</u>nos

candle κερί n ke<u>ree</u> 148

candy καραμέλα f kara<u>me</u>la 150

canoe κανώ ka<u>no</u>

capital city πρωτεύουσα f prote<u>voo</u>sa

captain (boat) καπετάνιος kape<u>ta</u>neeos

car αυτοκίνητο n afto<u>kee</u>neeto 81, 86, 87, 88, 89, 90, 153; **by ~** με το αυτοκίνητο me to afto<u>kee</u>neeto 95; **~ alarm** συναγερμός αυτοκινήτου m seenayer<u>mos</u> aftokee<u>nee</u>too; **~ ferry** φέρυ-μποτ n "ferry" bot; **~ rental** ενοικίαση αυτοκινήτων f eneek<u>ee</u>ase aftokee<u>nee</u>ton 70, 86; **~ park** χώρος στάθμευσης m <u>kho</u>ros <u>stath</u>mefsees 87; **~wash** πλύσιμο αυτοκινήτου n <u>plee</u>seemo afto<u>kee</u>neetoo

carafe καράφα f ka<u>ra</u>fa 37

caravan (trailer) τροχόσπιτο n tro<u>kho</u>speeto 30, 81

cards χαρτιά npl khart<u>ee</u>a 121

careful: be careful! Πρόσεχε! <u>pro</u>sekhe

carpet (fitted) μοκέτα f mo<u>ke</u>ta; (rug) χαλί n kha<u>lee</u>

carry-cot καροτσάκι (μωρού) n karo<u>tsa</u>kee (mo<u>roo</u>)

carton κουτί n koo<u>tee</u> 159

cartoon γελοιογραφία f yeleeogh<u>ra</u>feea

cash, to εξαργυρώνω eksarghee<u>ro</u>no 138; **cash desk** ταμείο n ta<u>mee</u>o 132, 136

casino καζίνο n "casino" 112

cassette κασέτα f ka<u>se</u>ta 157

castle κάστρο(n) <u>kast</u>ro 99

casualty dept. τμήμα πρώτων βοηθειών n <u>tmee</u>ma <u>pro</u>ton voee<u>thee</u>on

cat γάτα f <u>gha</u>ta

catch, to (bus) παίρνω <u>per</u>no

cathedral καθεδρικός ναός(m) kathe<u>THree</u>kos na<u>os</u> 99

cave σπήλαιο(f) <u>spee</u>leeo 107

cent λεπτό n lep<u>to</u> 139

change, to αλλάζω a<u>la</u>zo 75

cheap φτηνό ftee<u>no</u> 14

cheese τυρί n tee<u>ree</u> 49

check (bill) λογαριασμός m loghar<u>ya</u>zmos 32

check [cheque] (bank) επιταγή f epeeta<u>ghee</u> 138

chips [crisps] τσιπς n, πατατάκια "chips", pata<u>ta</u>keea 160

Christmas Χριστούγεννα khree<u>stoo</u>ghena 219

clean καθαρό katha<u>ro</u> 14

clothing store κατάστημα ρούχων n ka<u>tas</u>teema <u>roo</u>khon 130

cold (temperature) κρύος <u>kree</u>os 14, 41, 122

cold (flu) κρυολόγημα n kreeo<u>lo</u>yeema 141, 163

collapse: he's collapsed κατέρρευσε ka<u>te</u>refse

collect, to παίρνω <u>per</u>no 151

color χρώμα n <u>khro</u>ma 134, 143; **~ film** έγχρωμο φιλμ <u>enkhro</u>mo film 151

comb χτένα f <u>khte</u>na 142

come, to έρχομαι <u>er</u>khome 36; **~ back** (return) επιστρέφω epee<u>stre</u>fo 165

commission προμήθεια f pro<u>mee</u>theea 138

communion Μετάληψη f me<u>ta</u>leepsee

compact disk CD, κόμπακτ ντισκ n "CD", "compact disk" 157

A-Z

company *(business)* εταιρία f etereea; *(companionship)* παρέα f parea 126

complain: where can I make a complaint? πού μπορώ να παραπονεθώ; poo boro na paraponetho 137

complaints *(restaurant)* παράπονα npl parapona 41

concert συναυλία f seenavleea 108, 111; **~ hall** αίθουσα συναυλιών f ethoosa seenavleeon 111

concession μειωμένο εισιτήριο n meeomeno eeseeteereeo 100

concussion, to have έχω διάσειση ekho THeeaseesee

conditioner γαλάκτωμα για τα μαλλιά n ghalaktoma ya ta malea 142

condom προφυλακτικό n profeelakteeko 141

conductor διευθυντής ορχήστρας THeeeftheendees orkheestras 111

conference συνέδριο n seeneTHreeo

confirm, to *(reservation)* επιβεβαιώνω epeevenevono 22, 68

congratulations! συγχαρητήρια! seenkhareeteereea

conscious, to be έχω τις αισθήσεις μου ekho tees estheesees moo

constipation δυσκοιλιότητα f THeeskeeleeoteeta

Consul Πρόξενος m proksenos ; **Consulate** Προξενείο n prokseneeo 152

consult, to συμβουλεύομαι seemvoolevome 165

contact, to επικοινωνώ epeekeenono 28

contact lens φακός επαφής m fakos epafees 167; **~ fluid** υγρό για φακούς επαφής n eeghro ya fakoos epafees

contagious μεταδοτικός metaTHoteekos 165

contain, to περιέχω peree-ekho 39, 69, 155

contemporary dance μοντέρνος χορός m mondernos khoros 111

contraceptive αντισυλληπτικό n andeeseeleepteeko

cook book βιβλίο μαγειρικής n veevleeo mayeereekees

cook *(chef)* μάγειρας mayeeras

cook, to μαγειρεύω mayeerevo

cooker κουζίνα f koozeena 28, 29

cookies μπισκότα n beeskota 160

copper χαλκός m khalkos 149

corkscrew τιρμπουσόν n teerbooson 148

corn plaster αυτοκόλλητος επίδεσμος για κάλους m aftokoleetos epeeTHezmos ya kaloos

corner γωνία f ghoneea 95

correct *(see also right)* σωστό sosto

cosmetics καλλυντικά n kaleendeeka

cot παιδικό κρεββάτι n peTHeeko krevatee 22

cotton [wool] βαμβάκι n vamvakee 141

cough βήχας m veekhas 141; **~ syrup** σιρόπι για το βήχα n seeropee ya to veekha 141

cough, to βήχω veekho 164

could I have ...? μπορώ να έχω ...; boro na ekho 18

counter ταμείο n tameeo

country *(nation)* χώρα f khora

countryside εξοχή f eksokhee 119

couple *(pair)* ζευγάρι n zevgharee

courier *(guide)* κούριερ "courier"

course *(meal)* πιάτο n piato

court house δικαστήριο n THeekasteereeo

cousin ξάδελφος m ksaTHelfos

cramp κράμπα f kramba

crèche βρεφονηπιακός σταθμός m vrefoneepeeakos stathmos

credit card πιστωτική κάρτα f peestoteekee karta 42, 109, 136

crib παιδικό κρεββάτι n peTHeeko krevatee 22

crisps τσιπς n, πατατάκια
"chips", pata*takee*a 160

crockery πιατικά npl
piatee*ka* 29, 148

crossroad σταυροδρόμι n
stavro*thro*mee 95

crowded έχει πολύ κόσμο *e*khee po*lee
*ko*zmo 31

crown *(dental)* κορώνα f ko*ro*na 168

cruise κρουαζιέρα f krooa*zye*ra

crutches δεκανίκια n тнеka*neekee*a

crystal κρύσταλλο n *kree*stalo 149

cuisine κουζίνα f koo*zee*na 119

cup φλυτζάνι n flee*tzane*e 39

cupboard ντουλάπα f doo*la*pa

curlers μπικουτί n beekoo*tee*

currency νόμισμα n *no*meezma 67;
~ exchange συνάλλαγμα(n)
seen*a*laghma 70; **~ exchange office**
γραφείο συναλλάγματος n ghra*fee*o
seen*a*laghmatos 138

curtains κουρτίνες f koor*tee*nes

cushion μαξιλάρι n makseel*a*ree

customs τελωνείο n telon*ee*o 67, 157;
~ declaration τελωνειακή δήλωση f
telonee*ake*e тнее*lo*see 155

cut *(wound)* κόψιμο n
*ko*pseemo 162

cut and blow-dry κούρεμα και
πιστολάκι n *koo*rema ke
peestol*a*kee 147

cut glass σκαλιστό γυαλί n
skal*eesto* ya*lee* 149

cutlery μαχαιροπήρουνα npl
makhero*pee*roona 29, 148

cycle helmet κράνος (ποδηλατιστού) n
*kra*nos (ротнeelatee*stoo*)

cycling ποδηλασία f роtнeel*asee*a 114

cyclist ποδηλατιστής роtнeelatee*stees*

Cypriot *(n)* Κύπριος *kee*preeos

Cyprus Κύπρος f *kee*pros 119

cystitis κυστίτιδα f kee*stee*teeтнa 165

---

damage ζημιά f zeemee*a*

damaged χαλασμένος
khala*zme*nos 28

dance *(performance)* παράσταση χορού f
pa*ra*stasee kho*roo* 111

dancing, to go πάω για χορό
*pa*o ya kho*ro* 124

dangerous επικίνδυνος
epee*keen*тнeenos

dark *(color)* σκούρος *skoo*ros 14, 134;
(room) σκοτεινό skotee*no* 24

daughter κόρη f *ko*ree 120, 162

dawn ξημερώματα npl
kseemer*o*mata 221

day ημέρα/μέρα f ee*me*ra / *me*ra 97;
~ trip ημερήσια εκδρομή eemeree*see*a
ekтн*rome*e

deaf, to be είμαι κουφός *ee*me
koo*fos* 163

December Δεκέμβριος m
тнe*kem*vreeos 218

decide: we haven't decided yet
δεν έχουμε αποφασίσει ακόμη
тнen *e*khoome apofa*see*see a*ko*mee

deck *(ship)* κατάστρωμα n
kat*a*stroma; **~ chair** σεζ-λονγκ f
sez-long 116

declare, to δηλώνω
тнее*lo*no 67

deduct, to *(money)* αφαιρώ afe*ro*

defrost, to ξεπαγώνω ksepagh*o*no

degrees *(temperature)* βαθμοί mpl
vath*mee*

delay καθυστέρηση f
katheest*e*reesee 70

delicatessen τυρία-αλλαντικά
teerya-alandee*ka* 130, 158

delicious νόστιμο *no*steemo 14

deliver, to παραδίδω
parath*ee*тно

dental floss κλωστή f klo*stee*

---

dentist οδοντίατρος οποndeeatros 131, 168

dentures τεχνητή οδοντοστοιχία f tekhneetee οποndosteekheea 168

deodorant αποσμητικό n apozmeeteeko 142

department (in store) τμήμα n tmeema 132; **~ store** πολυκατάστημα n poleekatasteema 130

departure (train/airplane) αναχώρηση (τραίνου) f anakhoreesee (trenoo) 76; **~ lounge** αίθουσα αναχωρήσεων f ethoosa anakhoreesoon

depend: it depends on εξαρτάται eksartate

deposit προκαταβολή f prokatavolee 24, 115

describe, to περιγράφω pereeghrafo 152

designer σχεδιαστής skheTHeeastees

desserts επιδόρπια npl epeeTHorpeea 49

detergent απορρυπαντικό n aporeepandeeko

develop, to (photos) εμφανίζω emfaneezo 151

diabetes διαβήτης m THeeaveetees

diabetic διαβητικός/-ή THeeaveeteekos/ -ee 39, 163

diagnosis διάγνωση f THeeaghnosee 164

dialling code κωδικός m κοTHeekos 127

diamond διαμάντι n THyamandee 149

diamonds (cards) καρώ karo

diapers πάνες μωρού f panes moroo 142

diarrhoea διάρροια f THeeareea 141; **to have ~** έχω διάρροια ekho THeeareea 163

dice ζάρια npl zarya

dictionary λεξικό n lekseeko 150

diesel ντηζελ "diesel" 87

diet: I'm on a κάνω δίαιτα kano THee-eta

difficult δύσκολο THeeskolo 14

dining car εστιατόριο στο τραίνο n esteeatoreeo sto treno 75, 77

dining room τραπεζαρία f trapezareea 26, 29

dinner βραδινό n vraTHeeno 124; **~ jacket** βραδινό κοστούμι n vraTHeeno kostoomee

direct κατευθείαν kateftheean 75; **~-dial telephone** απευθείας κλήση apeftheeas kleesee

direct, to κατευθύνω kateftheeno 18

direction of, in the στην/προς την κατεύθυνση steen/pros teen kateftheensee 95

directions κατεύθυνση f kateftheensee 95

director (film) σκηνοθέτης skeenothetees; (of company) διευθυντής THee-eftheendees

directory (telephone) τηλεφωνικός κατάλογος m teelefoneekos kataloghos

dirty βρώμικος vromeekos 14, 28

disabled (npl) άτομα με ειδικές ανάγκες npl atoma me eeTHeekes ananges 22, 100

discotheque ντισκοτέκ f "discotheque" 112

dish (meal) πιάτο n piato 37; **~ cloth** πανί για τα πιάτα n panee ya ta piata 148

dishwashing detergent υγρό πιάτων n eeghro piaton 148

dislocated, to be είναι εξαρθρωμένος eene eksarthromenos 164

display case/cabinet βιτρίνα f veetreena 134, 149

disposable camera μιας χρήσεως φωτογραφική μηχανή f mias khreeseos fotoghrafeekee meekhanee 151

distilled water απεσταγμένο νερό n apestaghmeno nero

district περιφέρεια f pereefereea

disturb: don't disturb μην ενοχλείτε meen eno<u>khlee</u>te

diving equipment εξοπλισμός για υποβρύχιο κολύμπι m eksoplee<u>zmos</u> ya eepo<u>vreekheeo</u> ko<u>leembee</u> 116

divorced, to be διαζευγμένος THeeazevgh<u>menos</u> 120

dizzy, to feel έχω ζαλάδες <u>e</u>kho za<u>la</u>THes 163

do: do you accept ...? δέχεστε ...; <u>THe</u>kheste 136; **do you have ...?** έχετε ...; <u>e</u>khete...? 37; **things to do** κάτι να κάνουμε <u>ka</u>tee na <u>ka</u>noome 123

dock προκυμαία f prokee<u>mea</u>

doctor γιατρός ya<u>tros</u> 131, 161, 167

dog σκύλος m <u>skee</u>los

doll κούκλα f <u>kook</u>la 157

dollar δολλάριο n THo<u>lareeo</u> 67, 138

door πόρτα f <u>por</u>ta 25

dosage δοσολογία f THosolo<u>yee</u>a 140

double διπλός THee<u>plos</u>; **~ bed** διπλό κρεββάτι THee<u>plo</u> kre<u>vatee</u> 21; **~ room** διπλό δωμάτιο THee<u>plo</u> THo<u>mateeo</u> 21

downtown area κέντρο της πόλης n <u>kendro</u> tees <u>polees</u> 99

dozen ντουζίνα f doo<u>zeena</u> 217

drain υπόνομος m ee<u>ponomos</u>

dress φόρεμα n <u>forema</u> 144

drink(s) (n) ποτό n po<u>to</u> 41, 70, 124, 125, 126; **alcoholic ~** οινοπνευματώδη npl eenopnevma<u>toTHee</u> 50, 51

drinking water πόσιμο νερό n <u>poseemo</u> ne<u>ro</u> 30

drip: the faucet [tap] drips η βρύση στάζει ee <u>vreesee</u> <u>stazee</u>

drive, to οδηγώ oTHee<u>gho</u> 93

drop off, to (children) αφήνω a<u>feeno</u> 113

drowning: someone is drowning κάποιος πνίγεται <u>kapeeos</u> <u>pnee</u>yete

drugstore φαρμακείο n farma<u>kee</u>o 130

drunk μεθυσμένος meTHee<u>zmenos</u>

dry cleaner καθαριστήριο n kathareestee<u>reeo</u> 131

dry cut κούρεμα n <u>koorema</u> 147

dry clean στεγνό καθάρισμα stegh<u>no</u> ka<u>thareesma</u> 147

dubbed, to be μεταγλωττισμένος metaghlotee<u>zmenos</u> 110

dummy (pacifier) πιπίλα f pee<u>peela</u>

dustbins τενεκέδες mpl tene<u>keTHes</u> 30

dusty σκονισμένος skonee<u>zmenos</u>

duty: to pay ~ πληρώνω φόρο pleer<u>ono</u> <u>foro</u> 67; **~-free goods** αφορολόγητα είδη npl aforo<u>loyeeta</u> <u>ee</u>THee ; **~-free shop** κατάστημα αφορολόγητων ειδών n ka<u>tasteema</u> aforo<u>loyeeton</u> ee<u>THon</u> ; **~-free shopping** αγορά αφορολόγητων ειδών f agho<u>ra</u> aforo<u>loyeeton</u> ee<u>THon</u> 67

duvet πάπλωμα n <u>paploma</u>

E **each: how much each?** πόσο το καθένα; <u>poso</u> to ka<u>thena</u>

ear αυτί n a<u>ftee</u> 166; **~ drops** σταγόνες για τα αυτιά sta<u>ghones</u> ya ta a<u>fteea</u>; **~ache** πόνος στο αυτί m <u>ponos</u> sto a<u>ftee</u> 163

early νωρίς no<u>rees</u> 14, 221; **earlier** νωρίτερα no<u>reetera</u> 125, 147

east ανατολικά anatolee<u>ka</u> 95

Easter Πάσχα n <u>paskha</u> 219

easy εύκολο <u>efkolo</u> 14

eat, to τρώω <u>tro</u>-o 41; **places to ~** μέρη για φαγητό <u>meree</u> ya fayee<u>to</u> 123; **we've already eaten** έχουμε ήδη φάει <u>ekhoome</u> <u>ee</u>THee <u>fa</u>ee

economical οικονομικός eekonomee<u>kos</u>

economy class τουριστική θέση tooreestee<u>kee</u> <u>thesee</u> 68

egg αυγό n av<u>gho</u> 44

eight οχτώ o<u>khto</u> 216

eighteen δεκαοχτώ THekao<u>khto</u> 216

eighty ογδόντα oghᴛʜonda 217

elastic *(adj)* ελαστικός elasteekos

electric: ~ **blanket** ηλεκτρική κουβέρτα f eelektreekee kooverta; ~ **fire** αερόθερμο n aerothermo; ~ **shaver** ξυριστική μηχανή f kseereesteekee meekhanee

electricity meter ρολόι ηλεκτρικού ρεύματος n roloee eelektreekoo revmatos 28

electronic game ηλεκτρονικό παιχνίδι n eelektroneeko pekhneeᴛʜee 157

elevator ασανσέρ n asanser 26, 132

eleven έντεκα endeka 216

embark, to *(boat)* επιβιβάζομαι epeeveevazome

embassy πρεσβεία f prezveea

emerald σμαράγδι n zmaraghᴛʜee

emergency επείγον epeeghon 127; ~ **exit** έξοδος κινδύνου f eksoᴛʜos keenᴛʜeenoo; **it's an emergency** είναι έκτακτη ανάγκη eene ektaktee anangee

empty άδειο aᴛʜyo 14

end, to τελειώνω teleeono 109

engine μηχανή f meekhanee 88

engineer μηχανικός meekhaneekos

England Αγγλία f angleea 119

English Αγγλικά angleeka 11, 67, 110, 150, 152, 161; ~-**speaking** Αγγλόφωνος anglofonos 98, 152

enjoy, to ευχαριστιέμαι efkhareesteeeme 110; **μου αρέσει** moo aresee 121; **περνάω καλά** pernao kala 123

enlarge, to *(photos)* μεγεθύνω meghenᴛʜeeno 151

enough αρκετά arketa 15, 42, 136

ensuite bathroom μπάνιο σουίτα n baneeo sooeeta

entertainment guide οδηγός θεαμάτων m oᴛʜeeghos theamaton

entrance fee είσοδος f eesoᴛʜos 100

entry visa βίζα f veeza

epileptic είμαι επληπτικός/-ια eeme epeeleepteekos/-eea 163

equally εξίσου ekseesoo 17

error λάθος n lathos

escalator κυλιόμενες σκάλες fpl keeleeomenes skales 132

essential απαραίτητα apareteeta 89

estate agent κτηματομεσίτης m kteematomeseetees

EU Ευρωπαϊκή Ένωση f evropaeekee enosee

euro ευρώ n evro 139

evening: in the ~ το βράδυ to vraᴛʜee 221; ~ **dress** βραδυνό ένδυμα n vraᴛʜeeno enᴛʜeema 112

every week κάθε εβδομάδα kathe evᴛʜomaᴛʜna 13

examination *(medical)* ιατρική εξέταση f eeatreekee eksetasee

example, for για παράδειγμα ya paraᴛʜeeghma

excess baggage υπέρβαρο n eepervaro 69

exchange, to *(money)* αλλάζω alazo 138; ~ **rate** τιμή συναλλάγματος teemee seenalaghmatos 138

excluding meals χωρίς γεύματα khorees ghevmata 24

excursion εκδρομή f ekᴛʜʀomee 97, 98

excuse me *(apology)* συγγνώμη seeghnomee 10; *(attention)* παρακαλώ parakalo 10, 94

exhausted, to be είμαι ξεθεωμένος eeme ksetheomenos 106

exhibition έκθεση f ekthesee

exit έξοδος f eksoᴛʜos 70; **at the ~** στην έξοδο steen eksoᴛʜo

expensive ακριβός akreevos 14, 134

expiration [expiry] date ημερομηνία λήξεως emeromeeneea leekseos 109

exposure *(photos)* στάση f stasee 151

express *(mail)* εξπρές, επείγον "express", epeeghon 155

extension *(number)* εσωτερική γραμμή esotereekee ghramee 128

extra *(additional)* άλλο ένα, ένα ακόμη allo ena, ena akomee 23

extracted *(tooth)* βγάζω (δόντι) vghazo (THondee) 168

eye μάτι n matee 166; **~liner** μολύβι ματιών n moleevee mateeon; **~shadow** σκιά ματιών f skeea mateeon

F **face** πρόσωπο n prosopo 166
facial καθαρισμός προσώπου m kathareezmos prosopoo 147

facilities ευπηρέτηση, διευκόλυνση ekseepeereteesee, THee-efkoleensee 22, 30

faint, to feel έχω λιποθυμίες ekho leepotheemee-es 163

fall: he's had a fall έπεσε epese

fall *(autumn)* φθινόπωρο n ftheenoporo 219

family οικογένεια f eekoyenea 66, 74, 120

famous φημισμένος feemeesmenos

fan ανεμιστήρας m anemeesteeras 25

far μακριά makreea 95; **how far is it?** πόσο απέχει; poso apekhee 73

fare: how much is the fare? πόσο κάνει το εισιτήριο; poso kanee to eeseeteereeo 79

farm φάρμα f farma 107

fast γρήγορα ghreeghora 93; **~ food** φαστ φουντ "fast food" 40; **~ food restaurant** φαστ φουντ n "fast food" 35; **you were driving too ~** οδηγούσατε πολύ γρήγορα oTHeeghoosatee polee ghreeghora

fat λίπος n leepos 39

father πατέρας m pateras 120

faucet βρύση f vreesee 25

fault: it's my/your ~ ήταν λάθος μου/σας eetan lathos moo/sas

faulty ελαττωματικό elatomateeko 137

favorite αγαπημένος aghapeemenos

fax φαξ n "fax" 155;
~ facilities υπηρεσία φαξ f eepeereseea "fax" 22

February Φεβρουάριος m fevrooareeos 218

feed, to ταΐζω taeezo 39; **feeding bottle** μπιμπερό n beembero

feel ill/sick δεν αισθάνομαι καλά THen esthanome kala 98, 163

female γυναίκα yeeneka 152

fence φράχτης m frakhtees

ferry φέρυ-μπωτ n "ferry" bot 81

festival φεστιβάλ n festeeval

feverish, to feel αισθάνομαι σαν να έχω πυρετό esthanome san na ekho peereto 163

few λίγο leegho 15

fiancé(e) αρραβωνιαστικός/-ιά aravoneeasteekos/-eea

field χωράφι f khorafee 107

fifteen δεκαπέντε THekapende 216

fifth πέμπτος pemptos 217

fifty πενήντα peneenda 217

filling *(dental)* σφράγισμα n sfragheezma 168

film *(camera)* φιλμ n "film" 151; *(movie)* ταινία f teneea 108, 110

filter φίλτρο n feeltro 151; **~ paper (for coffee)** φίλτρο (καφέ) n feeltro (kafe)

find out: could you find out ...? μπορείτε να βρείτε ...; boreete na vreete

fine *(penalty)* πρόστιμο prosteemo 93

fine *(well)* καλά kala 118

finger δάχτυλο n THakhteelo 166

fire: ~ alarm συναγερμός πυρκαγιάς m seenaghermos peerkayas; **~ brigade** πυροσβεστική f peerozvesteekee 92; **~ escape** έξοδος κινδύνου f eksoTHos keenTHeenoo; **~ extinguisher** πυροσβεστήρας m peerozvesteeras; **~place** τζάκι n tzakee; **~wood** καυσόξυλα npl kafsokseela; **there's a fire!** Φωτιά! foteea

first πρώτος protos 68, 75, 81, 217; **~ class** πρώτη θέση protee thesee 68, 74
first-aid kit κουτί πρώτων βοηθειών n kootee proton voeetheeon

fish ψάρι n psaree 45, 158; **~ store [fishmonger]** ιχθυοπωλείο n eekhtheeopoleeo 130

fishing: to go ~ πάω για ψάρεμα pao ya psarema; **~ rod** καλάμι ψαρέματος n kalamee psarematos

fit, to (clothes) μου κάνει moo kanee 146

five πέντε pende 216

flag σημαία f seemea

flash (electronic) (ηλεκτρονικό) φλας n (eelektroneeko) flas 151

flashlight φακός m fakos 31

flat (puncture): **I have a ~** παθαίνω λάστιχο patheno lasteekho 88

flat (apartment) διαμέρισμα n THeeamereezma

flea ψύλλος m pseelos

flight πτήση f pteesee 70; **~ number** αριθμός πτήσεως m areethmos pteeseos 68

flip-flops σαγιονάρες fpl sayonares 145

flood πλημμύρα f pleemeera

floor (storey) όροφος m orofos 132

floor mop σφουγγαρόπανο n sfoongaropano

floor show ζωντανό σόου n zondano "show" 112

florist ανθοπωλείο n anthopoleeo 130

flower λουλούδι n looloothee 106

flu γρίππη f ghreepee 165

flush: the toilet won't flush το καζανάκι δε δουλεύει to kazanakee THen THoolevee

fly (insect) μύγα f meegha

foggy, to be έχει ομίχλη ekhee omeekhlee 122

folk: ~ art λαϊκή τέχνη f laeekee tekhnee; **~ dance** δημοτικός/παραδοσιακός χορός m THeemoteekos/paraTHoseeakos khoros 111; **~ music** δημοτική/παραδοσιακή μουσική f THeemoteekee/paraTHoseeakee mooseekee 111

follow, to ακολουθώ akolootho 95

food φαγητό n fayeeto 39, 41; **~ poisoning** τροφική δηλητηρίαση f trofeekee THeeleeteereeasee 165

foot πόδι n roTHee 166

football (soccer) ποδόσφαιρο n poTHosfero 114

footpath μονοπάτι f monopatee 107

for: for a day για μια ημέρα ya mia mera 86; **for a week** για μια εβδομάδα ya mia evTHomaTHa 86

forecast πρόβλεψη provlepsee 122

foreign ξένος ksenos; **~ currency** ξένο συνάλλαγμα n kseno seenalaghma 138

forest δάσος f THasos 107

forget, to ξεχνώ ksekhno 41; **I forgot** ξέχασα ksekhasa 42

fork πηρούνι n peeroonee 39, 41, 148; (in the road) διασταύρωση f THeeastavrosee

form έντυπο n endeepo 153, 168

formal evening dress βραδυνό ένδυμα n vraTHeeno epTHeema 111

forms έντυπα n endeepa 23

fortnight δεκαπενθήμερο n THekapentheemero

fortunately ευτυχώς efteekhos 19

forty σαράντα saranda 217

forward: please forward my mail παρακαλώ διαβιβάστε την αλληλογραφία μου parakalo THeeaveevaste teen aleeloghrafeea moo

fountain συντριβάνι n seendreevanee 99

four τέσσερις, τέσσερα <u>tes</u>erees, <u>tes</u>era 216; **~-door car** τετράπορτο αυτοκίνητο n te<u>tra</u>porto afto<u>kee</u>neeto 86; **~-wheel drive** τετρακινητήριο tetrakeenee<u>tee</u>reeo 86

fourteen δεκατέσσερα THeka<u>tes</u>era 216

fourth τέταρτος <u>tet</u>artos 217

frame *(glasses)* σκελετός (γυαλιών) m skele<u>tos</u> (yale<u>on</u>)

free *(available)* ελεύθερος e<u>lef</u>theros 36, 77, 124

freezer κατάψυξη f ka<u>tap</u>seeksee 29

frequent: how frequent? πόσο συχνά; <u>po</u>so see<u>khna</u> 76; **frequently** συχνά see<u>khna</u> 13

fresh φρέσκος <u>fres</u>kos 14, 41

Friday Παρασκευή f paraske<u>vee</u> 218

fridge ψυγείο n psee<u>yee</u>o 29

fried τηγανητός teeghanee<u>tos</u>

friend φίλος/-η <u>fee</u>los/-ee 162; **friendly** φιλικός feelee<u>kos</u>

fries πατάτες τηγανητές fpl pa<u>ta</u>tes teeghanee<u>tes</u> 38, 40

frightened, to be είμαι φοβισμένος <u>ee</u>me foveez<u>me</u>nos

from από a<u>po</u> 12; **from ... to** *(time)* από ... (έ)ως a<u>po</u> ... (<u>e</u>)os 13

frosty, to be έχει παγετό <u>e</u>khee paye<u>to</u> 122

fruit φρούτο n <u>froo</u>to 48, 158; **~ juice** χυμός φρούτων m khee<u>mos</u> <u>froo</u>ton 40

frying pan τηγάνι n tee<u>gha</u>nee 29

fuel *(gasoline)* καύσιμα npl <u>kaf</u>seema 86

full γεμάτο ye<u>ma</u>to 14; **~ board** *(A.P.)* με πλήρη διατροφή me <u>plee</u>ree THeeatro<u>fee</u> 24; **~ insurance** ολική ασφάλεια f olee<u>kee</u> as<u>fa</u>leea 86

fun, to have περνάω καλά per<u>nao</u> ka<u>la</u>

furniture έπιπλα npl <u>ep</u>eepla

further: how much further to Athens? πόσο απέχει ακόμη η Αθήνα; <u>po</u>so a<u>pe</u>khee a<u>ko</u>mee ee a<u>thee</u>na

fuse ασφάλεια f as<u>fa</u>leea 28; **~ box** κουτί με τις ασφάλειες n koo<u>tee</u> me tees as<u>fa</u>lee-es 28; **~ wire** καλώδειο ασφάλειας n ka<u>lo</u>THeeo as<u>fa</u>leeas

G gallon γαλλόνι n ghal<u>o</u>nee
gambling χαρτοπαιξία f khartopek<u>see</u>a

game *(toy)* παιχνίδι n pekh<u>nee</u>THee 157

garage γκαράζ n ga<u>raz</u> 26; συνεργείο n seener<u>yee</u>o 88

garden κήπος m <u>kee</u>pos

gardener κηπουρός keepoo<u>ros</u>

gardening κηπουρική f keepooree<u>kee</u>

gas: ~ bottle μπουκάλα γκαζιού f boo<u>ka</u>la gaz<u>ee</u>oo; **I smell gas!** μυρίζω γκάζι! mee<u>ree</u>zo <u>ga</u>zee

gas station βενζινάδικο n venzee<u>na</u>Theeko 87

gasoline βενζίνη f ven<u>zee</u>nee 87

gastritis γαστρίτιδα f gha<u>stree</u>teeTHa 165

gate *(airport)* έξοδος f <u>ek</u>soTHos 70

gay club κλαμπ για ομοφυλόφιλους n "club" ya omofee<u>lo</u>feeloos 112

genuine αυθεντικός afthendee<u>kos</u> 134

get off, to *(transport)* κατεβαίνω kate<u>ve</u>no 79

get out, to *(of vehicle)* βγαίνω <u>vye</u>no 83

get to, to φτάνω <u>fta</u>no 77; **how do I get to ...?** πώς πάνε στο ...; pos <u>pa</u>ne sto ...? 73, 94

gift δώρο n <u>THo</u>ro 67, 156; **~ store** κατάστημα με είδη δώρων n ka<u>ta</u>steema me <u>ee</u>THee <u>THo</u>ron 130

girl κορίτσι n ko<u>ree</u>tsee 120, 157

girlfriend φίλη f <u>fee</u>lee 120

give, to δίνω <u>THee</u>no

glass ποτήρι n po<u>tee</u>ree 37, 39, 148

glasses *(optical)* γυαλιά n yale<u>a</u> 167

glove γάντι n <u>gha</u>ndee

A-Z

go πάμε; ~ **away!** φύγε! feeghe; ~ **back** *(turn around)* γυρίζω πίσω/επιστρέφω gheereezo peeso/epeestrefo 95; ~ **for a walk** πάω για ένα περίπατο pao ena pereepato 124; ~ **shopping** πάω για ψώνια pao ya psoneea 124; **let's go!** πάμε!

goggles γυαλιά npl yaleea

gold χρυσός m khreesos 149; **~-plate** επίχρυσο epeekhreeso 149

golf γκόλφ n "golf" 114; ~ **course** γήπεδο γκολφ yeepeтно "golf" 115

good καλός kalos 14, 35; ~ **morning** καλημέρα kalemera 10; ~ **afternoon** καλησπέρα kaleespera 10; ~ **evening** καλησπέρα kaleespera 10; ~ **night** καληνύχτα kaleeneekhta 10; ~ **value** καλή τιμή kalee teemee 101

good-bye αντίο, χαίρετε, γειά σας andeeo, kherete, ya sas 10

gram γραμμάριο n ghramareeo 159

grandparents παππούς και γιαγιά papoos ke yaya

grapes σταφύλια n stafeeleea 160

grass γρασίδι n, χόρτο n ghraseeтнa, khorto

gratuity φιλοδώρημα n feeloтноreema

graze γρατζουνιά f ghratzooneea 162

greasy *(hair, skin)* λιπαρό leeparo

Greece Ελλάδα f elaтнa 119

Greek *(adj)* Ελληνικά eleeneeka; *(n)* 110 Έλλην-ας/-ίδα eleen-as/-eeтнa; *(language)* Ελληνικά eleeneeka 11, 126

green πράσινος praseenos 143

greengrocer οπωροπωλείο n oporopoleeo 130

gray γκρι, γκρίζος gree, greezos 143

grilled στη σχάρα stee skhara

grocery store παντοπωλείο n pandopoleeo 130, 159

ground *(earth)* έδαφος n eтнafos 31; **~cloth [~sheet]** μουσαμάς για το έδαφος m moosamas ya to eтнafos 31

group γκρουπ n "group" 66

guarantee εγγύηση f engee-eesee 135; **is it guaranteed?** έχει εγγύηση; ekhee engee-eesee

guide *(tour)* ξεναγός ksenaghos 98; **~book** τουριστικός οδηγός m tooreesteekos oтнeeghos 150; **guided tour** ξενάγηση f ksenayeesee 100

guitar κιθάρα f keethara

gum *(mouth)* ούλο n oolo

guy rope σκοινί της τέντας n skeenee tees tendas 31

gynaecologist γυναικολόγος yeenekologhos 167

H **hair** μαλλιά npl maleea 147; ~ **brush** βούρτσα f voortsa 142; ~ **dryer** σεσουάρ n sesooar; ~ **mousse** αφρός χτενίσματος, μους για τα μαλλιά f afros khteneesmatos, "mousse" ya ta maleea 142; ~ **spray** λακ f lak 142; **~cut** κούρεμα n koorema 147; **~dresser** κομμωτήριο n komoteereeo 131, 147

half μισό meeso 217; ~ **board** *(M.A.P.)* με ημιδιατροφή me eemeeтнeeatrofee 24; ~ **fare** μισό εισιτήριο meeso eeseeteereeo; ~ **past** ... και μισή ... ke meesee 220

hammer το σφυρί n sfeeree 31

hand χέρι n kheree 166; ~ **cream** γαλάκτωμα χεριών n ghalaktoma kheryon; ~ **luggage** αποσκευές χειρός fpl aposkeves kheeros 69; ~ **towel** πετσέτα χεριών f petseta kheryon

handbag τσάντα f tsanda 144

handicrafts λαϊκή τέχνη f laeekee tekhnee

handkerchief χαρτομάντηλο n khartomandeelo

handle πόμολο n pomolo

hanger κρεμάστρα f kremastra 27

happen: what happened? τι συνέβη; tee seenevee 93

harbor λιμάνι n leemanee 99; **~ front** προκυμαία f prokeemea 96

hat καπέλλο n kapelo 144

have, to έχω ekho 18, 133

have to: do I have to ... ? χρειάζεται να ... ; khreeazete 75, 79

hayfever αλλεργία σε γύρη f aleryeea se yeeree 141

head κεφάλι n kefalee 166; **~ache** πονοκέφαλος m ponokefalos 163; **~ waiter** αρχισερβιτόρος arkheeserveetoros 41

head, to (travel) πηγαίνω προς peeyeno pros 83

health: ~ food store κατάστημα με υγιεινές τροφές katasteema me eeyeeeenes trofes 130; **~ insurance** ασφάλεια υγείας f asfaleea eeyeeas 168

hearing aid ακουστικό βαρυκοΐας n akoosteeko vareekoeeas

heart καρδιά f kartHya 166; **~ attack** καρδιακό έμφραγμα n kartHyako emfraghma; **~ condition** πρόβλημα καρδιάς n provleema kartHeeas 163

hearts (cards) κούπα koopa

heat (n) θέρμανση f thermansee 25; **~wave** καύσωνας kafsonas 122

heater (water) θερμοσίφωνας m thermoseefonas

heating θέρμανση f thermansee 25

heavy βαρύ varee 14

height ύψος n eepsos 152

helicopter ελικόπτερο n eleekoptero

hello χαίρετε kherete 10, 118

help, to βοηθώ voeetho 18; **can you ~ me?** μπορείτε να με βοηθήσετε; boreete na me voeetheesete 71, 92

her (her friend) της tees 16; (for/to her) αυτήν, της, την afteen, tees, teen 16;

herbs βότανα npl votana 48

here εδώ etHo 12, 17

hernia κοίλη f keelee 165

hers δικό της tHeeko tees 16; **it's hers** είναι δικό της eene tHeeko tees

hi! γειά σας ya sas 10

highlighted (hair) ανταύγειες fpl andavyee-es 147

highway Εθνική Οδός f/ αυτοκινητόδρομος m ethneekee otHos/aftokeeneetotHromos 94

hike, to (walk) κάνω πεζοπορία kano pezoporeea 106

hiking πεζοπορία f pezoporeea

hill λόφος m lofos 107

him (for/to him) αυτόν, του, τον afton, too, ton 16

hindu ινδουιστής intHooeestees

hire, to νοικιάζω neekeeazo; **I'd like to hire ...** θα ήθελα να νοικιάσω ... tha eethela na nekeeaso ...

his (his name) του too 16; **it's his** είναι δικό του eene tHeeko too

history ιστορία f eestoreea

hitchhiking ώτο-στοπ oto-stop 83

HIV-positive HIV-θετικός HIV-theteekos

hobby (pastime) χόμπυ n "hobby" 121

hold on, to περιμένετε pereemenete 128

hole (in clothes) τρύπα f treepa

holiday διακοπές fpl tHeeakopes 123; **on ~** για διακοπές ya tHeeakopes 66; **~ resort** τόπος διακοπών topos tHeeakopon

home: I'm going ~ επιστρέφω epeestrefo

homeopathic remedy ομοιοπαθητική θεραπεία omeopatheeteekee therapeea

homosexual (adj) ομοφυλόφιλος omofeelofeelos

honeymoon, to be on είμαι στο μήνα του μέλιτος eeme sto meena too meleetos

hopefully ελπίζω να ... elpeezo na 19

horse άλογο n alogho; **~racing** ιπποδρομίες fpl eeprotHromee-es 114

hospital νοσοκομείο n nosokomeeo 131, 164, 167

hot *(weather)* ζεστό ze<u>sto</u>
14, 122; **~ dog** χοτ-ντογκ n
"hot-dog" 110; **~ spring**
θερμή πηγή f therm<u>ee</u>
peegh<u>ee</u>; **~ water** ζεστό νερό
ze<u>sto</u> ne<u>ro</u> 25; **~ water bottle**
θερμοφόρα f thermof<u>o</u>ra

hotel ξενοδοχείο n
ksenoтн<u>o</u>kheeo 21

hour ώρα f <u>o</u>ra 76, 97

household articles είδη οικιακής
χρήσεως npl ee<u>тн</u>ee eekeea<u>kees</u>
<u>khreeseos</u> 148

housewife (ν)οικοκυρά f (n)eekoky<u>ra</u>

how? πώς; pos 17; **how are you?** τι
κάνεις (κάνετε *formal*); tee <u>ka</u>nees
(<u>ka</u>nete *formal*) 118; **how far?** πόσο
απέχει; <u>poso</u> ap<u>e</u>khee 94; **how long?**
(time) πόση ώρα; posee <u>o</u>ra 76, 78, 88,
94, 98; **how many?** πόσοι; posee 15,
80; **how much?** πόσο κάνει; <u>poso</u>
<u>kane</u>e 21, 84, 109; **how often?** πόσο
συχνά; <u>poso</u> seek<u>hna</u> 140; **how old?**
πόσων χρονών; <u>poson khronon</u> 120

hundred εκατό ek<u>ato</u> 217

hungry, to be πεινάω peen<u>ao</u>

hurt: to be ~ είμαι χτυπημένος <u>ee</u>me
khteepee<u>menos</u> 92; **it hurts** πονάει
pon<u>ae</u>e 162

husband άντρας m <u>a</u>ndras 120, 162

hypermarket υπεραγορά f eeperagh<u>o</u>ra

I I'd like ... θα ήθελα tha <u>ee</u>thela
18, 36, 37, 40

I'll have ... θα πάρω ... tha <u>pa</u>ro 37

ice πάγος m <u>pa</u>ghos 38; **~ dispenser**
μηχανή πάγου f meek<u>ha</u>nee <u>pa</u>ghoo;
~ lolly γρανίτα f ghran<u>ee</u>ta; **~ rink**
παγοδρόμιο n pagho<u>тн</u>romeeo

ice cream παγωτό n pagh<u>oto</u> 40, 160; **~
cone** παγωτό χωνάκι n pagh<u>oto</u>
khon<u>a</u>kee

icy, to be έχει πάγο <u>e</u>khee <u>pa</u>gho 122

identification ταυτότητα f taft<u>o</u>teeta 136

illegal: it's illegal είναι παράνομο <u>ee</u>ne
par<u>a</u>nomo

illness αρρώστεια f ar<u>o</u>steea

imitation απομίμηση f apomeemeesee 134

immediately αμέσως am<u>e</u>sos 13

impressive εντυπωσιακό
endeepose<u>a</u>ko 101

in *(place)* στο(-η) sto (-ee) 12;
(time) σε se 13

in-law: father/mother-in-law, πεθερ-ός/-ά
pether-<u>os</u>/-<u>a</u>

included: is ... included?
συμπεριλαμβάνεται το ...;
seembereelamv<u>a</u>nete to 86, 98

inconvenient: it's inconvenient δεν είναι
βολικό тнen <u>ee</u>ne vole<u>ek</u>o

indigestion δυσπεψία f deespeps<u>ee</u>a

indoor εσωτερικός esotere<u>ek</u>os; **~ pool**
κλειστή πισίνα klee<u>stee</u> pees<u>ee</u>na 116

inexpensive φτηνός ftee<u>nos</u> 35

infected μολυσμένος
molee<u>zmenos</u> 165

inflammation φλεγμονή f
flegh<u>monee</u> 165

informal *(dress)* πρόχειρο <u>pro</u>kheero 15

information πληροφορίες fpl
pleerofor<u>ee</u>-es 97; **~ office** γραφείο
πληροφοριών n ghraf<u>ee</u>o
pleerofore<u>on</u> 73, 96

injection ένεση f <u>e</u>nese 168

injured, to be είμαι τραυματισμένος
<u>ee</u>me travmatee<u>zmenos</u> 92, 162

innocent αθώος ath<u>o</u>-os

insect bite τσίμπημα από έντομο n
<u>tsee</u>mbeema ap<u>o</u> <u>e</u>ndomo 141, 162

insect repellent/spray εντομοαπωθητικό n,
εντομοκτόνο n endomoapotheeteek<u>o</u>,
endom<u>ok</u>tono 141

inside μέσα <u>me</u>sa 12; **~ lane** εσωτερική
λωρίδα f esotere<u>ek</u>ee lor<u>ee</u>тна

insist: I insist επιμένω epee<u>me</u>no

insomnia αϋπνία f aee<u>p</u>neea

instant coffee νεσκαφέ m neska*fe* 160

instead of αντί and*ee*

instructions οδηγίες fpl οτΗεε*yee*-es 135

instructor εκπαιδευτής, δάσκαλος ekpeΤΗef*tees*, ΤΗaskalos

insulin ινσουλίνη f eensoo*lee*nee

insurance certificate πιστοποιητικό της ασφάλειας n peestopee-eetee*ko* tees as*fa*leeas 93

insurance ασφάλεια f as*fa*leea 86, 89, 93, 168; **~ claim** ασφάλεια f as*fa*leea 153; **~ company** ασφαλιστική εταιρία f asfaleestee*kee* ete*ree*a 93

interest *(hobby)* ενδιαφέρον enΤΗeea*fe*ron 121

interest rate επιτόκιο n epee*to*keeo

interesting ενδιαφέρον enΤΗeea*fe*ron 101

international διεθνής ΤΗee-eth*nees*; **International Student Card** διεθνής φοιτητική κάρτα f ΤΗee-eth*nees* feetetee*kee* karta 29

interpreter διερμηνέας ΤΗee-ermee*ne*as 93, 153

intersection σταυροδρόμι n stavroΤΗromee 95

interval διάλειμμα n ΤΗee*a*leema

introduce: may I introduce ...? να συστήσω .... na see*stee*so 118

introductions συστάσεις see*sta*sees 118

invitation πρόσκληση f *pro*skleesee 124

invite, to καλώ ka*lo* 124

involved, to be είμαι αναμεμειγμένος *ee*me anamemee*ghme*nos 93

iodine ιώδειο n ee*o*THeeo

Ireland Ιρλανδία f eerlanΤΗeea 119

Irish Ιρλανδός eerlan*THos*

iron, to σιδερώνω seeΤΗe*ro*no

is there ...? υπάρχει ...; ee*par*khee 17

it is ... είναι ... *ee*ne 16, 17

Italian *(restaurant)* ιταλικό eetalee*ko* 35

itemized bill αναλυτικός λογαριασμός m analeetee*kos* logharya*zmos* 32

J **jack** *(cards)* βαλές va*les*

jam μαρμελάδα f marme*la*THa 43,159

jammed, to be έχει σφηνώσει *e*khee sfee*no*see 25

January Ιανουάριος m eeanoo*a*reeos 218

jar βάζο n *va*zo 159

jaw σαγόνι n sa*gho*nee 166

jeans μπλου-τζην n bloo-tzeen 144

jellyfish μέδουσα f *me*THoosa

jet-ski τζετ-σκι n "jet-ski" 116

jeweller κοσμηματοπωλείο n kozmeematopo*lee*o 131, 149

jewish *(adj)* εβραϊκός evrae*ekos*

job: what's your job? τί δουλειά κάνετε; tee ΤΗoolee*a* kanete

jogging: to go ~ πάω τζόγκινγκ *pa*o ya "jogging"; **~ pants** φόρμα για τζόγκινγκ *for*ma ya "jogging"

join: may we join you? να έρθουμε μαζί σας; na *er*thoome ma*zee* sas 124

joint passport κοινό διαβατήριο n kee*no* ΤΗeeava*tee*reeo 66

joke ανέκδοτο n a*nek*THoto

joker *(cards)* μπαλαντέρ m balan*der*

journalist δημοσιογράφος ΤΗeemoseeo*ghra*fos

journey ταξίδι n tak*see*THee 76, 78, 123

July Ιούλιος m ee*oo*leeos 218

jump leads καλώδια μπαταρίας npl ka*lo*THeea bata*ree*as

jumper πουλόβερ n poo*lo*ver 144

junction *(intersection)* κόμβος m, έξοδος f *kom*vos, *ek*soTHos

June Ιούνιος m ee*oo*neeos 218

K **keep: keep the change!** Κρατήστε τα ρέστα! kra*tee*ste ta *re*sta

kerosene stove καμινέτο n kamee*ne*to 31

key κλειδί n klee<u>тнее</u> 27, 28, 71, 88; **~ ring** μπρελόκ n brel<u>o</u>k 156

kharto<u>fee</u>lakas

kidney νεφρό n ne<u>fro</u> 166

kilo(gram) κιλό n kee<u>lo</u> 69, 159

kind: what kind of ...? τί είδους ...; tee <u>ee</u>тноos ...

king (cards) ρήγας m <u>ree</u>ghas; (chess) βασιλιάς m vaseel<u>ee</u>as

kiosk περίπτερο n pe<u>ree</u>ptero

kiss, to φιλώ fee<u>lo</u> 126

kitchen κουζίνα f koo<u>zee</u>na 29; **~ paper** χαρτί κουζίνας n khar<u>tee</u> koo<u>zee</u>nas

kitchenette κουζινούλα f koozee<u>noo</u>la

knapsack σάκκος m <u>sa</u>kos 31

knave (cards) βαλές va<u>les</u>

knee γόνατο n <u>gho</u>nato 166

knife μαχαίρι n ma<u>khee</u>ree 39, 41, 148

knight (chess) ιππότης m ee<u>po</u>tees

know: I don't know δεν ξέρω тнen <u>kse</u>ro 15

L

label ετικέτα f etee<u>ke</u>ta

ladder σκάλα f <u>ska</u>la

ladies (toilet) γυναικών yeene<u>kon</u>

lake λίμνη f <u>leem</u>nee 107

lamp λάμπα f <u>lam</u>ba 29

land, to προσγειώνομαι prozyee<u>o</u>nome 70

landlord σπιτονοικοκύρης speetoneeko<u>ky</u>rees

language course σειρά μαθημάτων ξένης γλώσσας f see<u>ra</u> mathee<u>ma</u>ton <u>kse</u>nees <u>ghlo</u>sas

large μεγάλος me<u>gha</u>los 40, 110

last (adj) τελευταίος telef<u>tee</u>os 68, 75, 80, 81

late αργά ar<u>gha</u> 14; αργότερα ar<u>gho</u>tera 221; **it will be late** θα αργήσει ar<u>ghee</u>see 70; **later** αργότερα ar<u>gho</u>tera 125, 147

laugh, to γελώ ye<u>lo</u> 126

laundry service υπηρεσία πλυντηρίου f eepeere<u>see</u>a pleende<u>ree</u>oo 22

lavatory μπάνιο n <u>ba</u>neeo

lawyer δικηγόρος m тнeekee<u>gho</u>ros 152

laxative καθαρτικό n kathartee<u>ko</u>

lead, to (road) πηγαίνω pee<u>ye</u>no 94

lead-free (gas [petrol]) αμόλυβδη a<u>mo</u>leevтнee 87

leaflet φυλλάδιο n fee<u>la</u>тнeeo 97

leak, to (roof/pipe) στάζω <u>sta</u>zo

learn, to (language/sport) μαθαίνω ma<u>the</u>no

leave me alone! αφήστε με ήσυχο/-η a<u>fee</u>ste me <u>ee</u>seekho/-ee 126

leave, to (deposit) αφήνω a<u>fee</u>no 71, 73, 86; (depart) φεύγω <u>fe</u>vgo 32, 68, 70, 98, 126

lecturer λέκτωρας <u>le</u>ktoras

left: on the ~ στα αριστερά sta arees<u>te</u>ra 76, 95; **~hand side** στην αριστερή μεριά steen arees<u>te</u>ree me<u>ree</u>a 95; **~-handed** αριστερόχειρας arees<u>te</u>rokheeras

left-luggage office φύλαξη αποσκευών f <u>fee</u>laksee aposke<u>von</u> 73

leg πόδι n <u>po</u>тнee 166

legal: it's legal είναι νόμιμο <u>ee</u>ne <u>no</u>meemo

leggings κολλάν n ko<u>lan</u> 144

lemon λεμόνι n le<u>mo</u>nee 38

lend: could you lend me ...? μπορείτε να μου δανείσετε ...; bo<u>ree</u>te na moo тнa<u>nee</u>sete ...

length μήκος n <u>mee</u>kos

lens φακός m fa<u>kos</u> 151, 167; **~ cap** κάλυμμα φακού n <u>ka</u>leema fa<u>koo</u> 151

lesbian club κλαμπ για λεσβίες n "club" ya lez<u>vee</u>es

less λιγότερο lee<u>gho</u>tero 15

letter γράμμα n <u>ghra</u>ma 154; **~box** γραμματοκιβώτιο n ghramatokee<u>vo</u>teeo

level (even) ομαλό oma<u>lo</u> 31

library βιβλιοθήκη f
veevleeotheekee 131
lie down, to ξαπλώνω ksaplono
lifebelt σωσίβιο n soseeveeo
lifeboat ναυαγοσωστική λέμβος f
navaghososteekee lemvos
lifeguard ναυαγοσώστης
navaghosostees 116
lifejacket σωσίβιο n soseeveeo
lift (elevator) ασανσέρ n asanser 26, 132;
~ **pass** άδεια (σκι) aтнeea "ski" 117
light (color) ανοιχτό aneekhto 14, 134;
(not heavy) ελαφρύ elafree 14, 134;
lighter(color) ανοιχτότερος
aneekhtoteros 143
light (electric) φως (ηλεκτρικό) n fos
(eelektreeko) 25; ~ **bulb** λάμπα f
lamba 148; **lights** (bicycle) φώτα
(ποδηλάτου) n fota (poтнeelatoo) 83
lighter (cigarette) αναπτήρας m
anapteeras 150
lighthouse φάρος m faros
lightning αστραπή f astrapee
like (similar to): ~ **this** σαν αυτό san afto
like: I'd like (to) ... θα ήθελα ... tha
eethela 124, 133
line (metro) γραμμή f ghramee 80;
(telephone): **an outside line, please** μια
εξωτερική γραμμή, παρακαλώ mia
eksotereekee ghramee, parakalo
lips χείλη n kheelee; **lipstick** κραγιόν n
krayon
liqueur λικέρ m leeker
liter λίτρο n leetro 87, 159
little μικρός meekros
live together, to συζώ seezo 120
liver ήπαρ (medical) n, συκώτι n
eepar, seekotee 166
living room σαλόνι n salonee 29
local τοπικός topeekos 35, 37;
~ **anaesthetic** τοπικό αναισθητικό n
topeeko anestheeteeko 168
lock (canal) φράγμα n, υδατοφράκτης m
fraghma, eeтнatofraktees

lock (key) κλειδαριά f
kleeтнarya 25; **it's**
locked είναι
κλειδωμένο eene
kleeтнomeno; **lock oneself**
out, to κλειδώνομαι έξω
kleeтнonome ekso 27
locker θυρίδα f theereeтнa
London Λονδίνο n lonтнeeno
long μακρύς makrees 146; ~-**distance**
bus υπεραστικό λεωφορείο n
eeperasteeko leoforeeo 78; ~-**distance**
call υπεραστικό τηλεφώνημα n
eeperasteeko teelefoneema; ~-**sighted**
πρεσβύωπας prezveeopas 167; **how**
long? πόσο καιρό; poso kero 164;
how much longer? πόση ώρα ακόμη;
posee ora akomee 41
look: I'm just looking απλώς κοιτάω
aplos keetao; ~ **for** ψάχνω psakhno
18; ~ **forward:** I'm looking forward to it
Το περιμένω με χαρά To pereemeno
me khara; **to have a ~** ρίχνω μια
ματιά reekhno mia mateea 89
loose (fitting) φαρδύς
farтнees 117, 146
lorry φορτηγό n forteegho
lose, to χάνω khano 28; I've lost ...
έχασα ... ekhasa 153; it's lost ...
χάθηκε khatheeke 71
loss απώλεια f apoleea 71
lost-and-found [lost property] office
γραφείο απωλεσθέντων αντικειμένων
n ghrafeeo apolesthendon
andeekeemenon 41
lotion λοσιόν f loseeon
lots πολύ polee
loud: it's too loud έχει πολύ θόρυβο
ekhee polee thoreevo; **louder** πιο
δυνατά peeo тнeenata 128
love: I love Greek food μου αρέσει το
ελληνικό φαγητό moo aresee to
eleeneeko fayeeto; I love you σε αγαπώ
se aghapo

low-fat χαμηλό σε λιπαρά khamee<u>lo</u> se leepa<u>ra</u>
lower *(berth)* κάτω (κουκέτα) <u>ka</u>to (koo<u>ke</u>ta) 74
lubricant λιπαντικό n leepandee<u>ko</u>
luck: good luck! καλή επιτυχία! ka<u>lee</u> epeeteek<u>hee</u>a 219
luggage αποσκευές fpl aposke<u>ves</u>; ~ **locker** θυρίδα f theer<u>ee</u>THa 71; ~ **carts (trolleys)** καροτσάκια αποσκευών n karot<u>sa</u>keea aposke<u>von</u> 71
lump σβώλος m <u>svo</u>los 162
lunch μεσημεριανό n meseemerya<u>no</u> 98
lung πνεύμονας m <u>pne</u>vmonas
luxury πολυτέλεια f polee<u>te</u>leea

M magazine περιοδικό n pereeo<u>THee</u>ko 150
magnificent μεγαλοπρεπές meghalop<u>re</u>pes 101
maid καμαριέρα f kama<u>rye</u>ra 27
maiden name πατρικό όνομα n patree<u>ko</u> <u>o</u>noma
mail αλληλογραφία f aleelogh<u>ra</u>feea 27; **by ~** με επιστολή me epeesto<u>lee</u> 22; **~box** ταχυδρομικό κουτί n takheeTHromee<u>ko</u> koo<u>tee</u> 154
main κύριος <u>kee</u>reeos 130; ~ **rail station** κεντρικός σιδηροδρομικός σταθμός n kendree<u>kos</u> seeTHeeroTHromee<u>kos</u> stath<u>mos</u> 73; ~ **street** κύριος δρόμος <u>kee</u>reeos <u>THro</u>mos 95
mains κεντρικός διακόπτης m kendree<u>kos</u> THeea<u>ko</u>ptees
make *(brand)* μάρκα f <u>ma</u>rka
make an appointment, to κλείνω ένα ραντεβού <u>klee</u>no <u>e</u>na rande<u>voo</u> 161
make-up μακιγιάζ n makee<u>yaz</u>
male άνδρας <u>an</u>THras 152
mallet κόπανος m <u>ko</u>panos 31
man *(male)* άνδρας <u>an</u>THras; *(mankind)* άνθρωπος <u>an</u>thropos

manager διευθυντής THee-ef<u>thee</u>n<u>dees</u> 25, 137
manicure μανικιούρ n maneekee<u>oor</u> 147
manual *(car)* χειροκίνητος kheero<u>kee</u>neetos
map χάρτης m <u>kha</u>rtees 94, 106, 150
March Μάρτιος m <u>ma</u>rteeos 218
market αγορά f agho<u>ra</u> 99, 131; ~ **day** ημέρα λαϊκής αγοράς ee<u>me</u>ra laee<u>kees</u> agho<u>ras</u>
married, to be είμαι παντρεμένος <u>ee</u>me pandre<u>me</u>nos 120
mask *(diving)* μάσκα f <u>ma</u>ska
mass λειτουργία f leetoor<u>yee</u>a 105
massage μασάζ n "massage" 147
match *(game)* αγώνας m /παιχνίδι n a<u>gho</u>nas / pekh<u>nee</u>THee 114
matches σπίρτα npl <u>spee</u>rta 31, 148, 150
material *(cloth)* ύφασμα n <u>ee</u>fasma
matinée απογευματινή παράσταση apoyevmatee<u>nee</u> pa<u>ra</u>stasee 109
matter: it doesn't matter δεν πειράζει THen pee<u>ra</u>zee; **what's the matter?** τι πρόβλημα υπάρχει; tee <u>pro</u>vleema ee<u>pa</u>rkhee
mattress *(air)* στρώμα (αέρα) n <u>stro</u>ma (a<u>e</u>ra) 31
May Μάιος m <u>ma</u>eeos 218
may I ...? μπορώ ...; bo<u>ro</u> ...? 18, 37
maybe ίσως <u>ee</u>sos
me *(for/to me)* εμένα, μου, με e<u>me</u>na, moo, me 16
meal γεύμα n <u>ye</u>vma 42, 125; φαγητό n faye<u>to</u> 38
mean, to σημαίνω see<u>me</u>no 11
measles ιλαρά f eela<u>ra</u> 165
measure, to μετρώ me<u>tro</u> 146
measurement μέτρηση f <u>me</u>treesee
meat κρέας n <u>kre</u>as 41, 46, 158
medication φάρμακα npl <u>fa</u>rmaka 164, 165
medium *(adj)* κανονικός kanonee<u>kos</u> 40

medium *(steak)* μέτρια ψημένο metreea pseemeno

meet, to συναντώ seenando 106, 125; **pleased to meet you** χαίρω πολύ khero polee 118

member *(of club)* μέλος n (του κλαμπ) melos (too "club") 112, 115

memorial μνημείο n mneemeeo 99

men *(toilets)* ανδρών anTHron

mend, to διορθώνω THeeorthono 137

mention: don't mention it παρακαλώ, τίποτα parakalo, teepota 10

message μήνυμα n meeneema 27, 128

metal μέταλλο n metalo

metro *(subway)* μετρό n (υπόγειος σιδηρόδρομος, ηλεκτρικός) m "metro" (eepoyeeos seeTHeeroTHromos, eelektreekos) 80; **~ station** σταθμός μετρό m stathmos "metro" 80

microwave *(oven)* (φούρνος) μικροκυμάτων (foornos) meekrokeematon

midday μεσημέρι n meseemeree

midnight μεσάνυχτα npl mesaneekhta 220

migraine ημικρανία f eemeekraneea

mileage τα χιλιόμετρα ta kheeleeometra 86

milk γάλα n ghala 43, 160; **with ~** με γάλα me ghala 40

milk of magnesia γάλα μαγνησίας n ghala maghneeseeas

million εκατομμύριο ekatomeereeo 217

mind: do you mind? σας πειράζει; sas peerazee 77, 126

mine δικό μου THeeko moo 16

mine: it's mine είναι δικό μου eene THeeko moo

mineral water εμφιαλωμένο νερό n emfeealomeno nero 40

mini-bar μίνι-μπαρ n "mini-bar" 32

minimart παντοπωλείο n pandopoleeo 158

minimum n ελάχιστο elakheesto

minister πάστορας pastoras

minor road δευτερεύων δρόμος m THefterevon THromos

minute λεπτό n lepto 76

mirror καθρέφτης m kathreftees

missing, to be λείπω leepo 137, 152

mistake λάθος n lathos 32, 41, 42

misunderstanding: there's been a ~ έγινε κάποια παρεξήγηση eyene kapia parekseeyeesee

modern art σύγχρονη τέχνη f seenkhronee tekhnee

modern μοντέρνο monderno 14

moisturizer *(cream)* υδατικό γαλάκτωμα n eeTHateeko ghalaktoma

monastery μοναστήρι, η μονή *(on road signs)* monasteeree / monee 99

Monday Δευτέρα f THeftera 218

money order ταχυδρομική επιταγή f takheeTHromeekee epeetayee

money χρήματα npl khreemata 42

money-belt ζώνη για χρήματα f zonee ya khreemata

month μήνας m meenas 218

monument μνημείο n mneemeeo 99

moped μοτοποδήλατο n motopoTHeelato 83

more παραπάνω parapano 15; **I'd like some more** θα ήθελα λίγο ακόμη tha eethela leegho akomee 39

morning, in the το πρωί to proee 221

morning-after pill χάπι της "επομένης" n khapee tees epomenees 167

Moslem *(adj)* μωαμεθανός moamethanos

mosquito κουνούπι n koonoopee; **~ bite** τσίμπημα κουνουπιού n tseembeema koonoopeeoo

mother μητέρα f meetera 120

motorbike μοτοσυκλέτα f motoseekleta 83

motorboat εξωλέμβιο f eksolemveeo 116

motorway Εθνική Οδός f/ αυτοκινητόδρομος m ethneekee oΤΗos/ aftokeeneetoΤΗromos 94

mountain βουνό, όρος (on maps) n voono, oros 107; ~ **pass** ορεινό πέρασμα f oreeno perazma 107

mountaineering ορειβασία f oreevaseea

mousetrap φάκα f faka

moustache μουστάκι n moostakee

mouth στόμα n stoma 166; ~ **ulcer** αύτρ(ι)α f aftr(ee)a

move, to (room) μετακομίζω metakomeezo 25; **don't move him!** μην τον μετακινήσετε! meen ton metakeeneesete 92

movie theatre κινηματογράφος m keeneematoghrafos

Mr. κύριος keereeos

Mrs. κυρία keereea

much πολύ polee 15

multiple journey (ticket) (εισιτήριο για) πολλαπλά ταξίδια (eeseeteereeo ya) polapla takseeΤΗeea 79

muscle μυς m mees 166

museum μουσείο n mooseeo 99

music μουσική f mooseekee 111; ~ **box** μουσικό κουτί n mooseeko kootee

musician μουσικός mooseekos

must: I must πρέπει prepee

mustard μουστάρδα f moostarΤΗa 38

my μου moo 16

N **nail: ~ polish** βερνίκι νυχιών n verneekee neekheeon; ~ **scissors** ψαλιδάκι νυχιών n psaleeΤΗakee neekheeon

name όνομα n onoma 22, 36, 93; **my name is** λέγομαι leghome 118; **what's your name?** πώς λέγεστε; pos leyeste 118

napkin πετσέτα f petseta 39

nappies πάνες μωρού f panes moroo 142

narrow στενό steno 14

national εθνικός ethneekos

nationality υπηκοότητα f eepeekooteeta

nature: ~ reserve εθνικός δρυμός m ethneekos ΤΗreemos 107; ~ **trail** μονοπάτι n monopatee 107

nausea ναυτία f nafteea

near κοντά konda 12; **nearby** εδώ κοντά eΤΗo konda 21; **nearest** κοντινότερος kondeenoteros 80, 88, 92, 130, 140

necessary απαραίτητα apareeteeta 89

neck (part of body) αυχένας m afkhenas 166; (clothing) λαιμόκοψη f lemokopsee 144

need: do we need to ...? χρειάζεται να ...; khreeazete na 112; **I need to ...** χρειάζομαι ... khreeazome 18

neighbor γείτονας yeetonas

nephew ανηψιός aneepseeos

nerve νεύρο n nevro

never ποτέ pote 13; ~ **mind** δεν πειράζει ΤΗen peerazee 10

New Zealand Νέα Ζηλανδία f nea zeelanΤΗeea

new καινούργιο kenooryo 14; **New year** Καινούριος Χρόνος m kenooryos khronos 219

newsdealer [newsagent] περίπτερο n pereeptero 150

newspaper εφημερίδα f efeemereeΤΗa 150

next επόμενος epomenos 68, 75, 78, 80, 81, 87; ~ **stop!** η επόμενη στάση! ee epomenee stasee 79

next to δίπλα ΤΗeepla 12, 95

niece ανηψιά aneepseea

night: at ~ τη νύχτα tee neekhta 221; ~**club** νυχτερινό κέντρο n neekhtereeno kendro 112

nightdress νυχτικό n neekhteeko

nine εννέα enea 216

nineteen δεκαεννέα ΤΗekaenea 216

ninety ενενήντα ene_neen_da 217

no όχι _okh_ee 10

noisy θορυβώδες thoree_vo_τHes 14, 24

non-smoking μη καπνίζοντες mee
kap_nee_zondes 36; **non-smoking (area)**
(περιοχή για) μη καπνίζοντες
(pereeo_khee_ ya) mee kap_nee_zondes 69

none, no one κανένας, καμμία, κανένα
ka_ne_nas/ka_mee_a/ka_ne_na 15, 16

noon μεσημέρι mesee_me_ree 220

normal allowance επιτρεπόμενα όρια npl
epeetre_po_mena _o_reea 67

north βόρεια _vo_reea 95

Northern Ireland Βόρεια Ιρλανδία
_vo_reea eerlan_THee_a

nose μύτη f _mee_tee 166; **~bleed**
αιμορραγία μύτης f emora_yee_a
_mee_tees

not yet όχι ακόμη _okh_ee a_ko_mee 13

nothing else τίποτε άλλο _tee_pote _a_lo 15

November Νοέμβριος m
no_em_vreeos 218

now τώρα _to_ra 13, 84

nudist beach παραλία γυμνιστών f
para_lee_a yeemnee_ston_

number (telephone) τηλέφωνο n
tee_le_fono 84

nurse νοσοκόμα f noso_ko_ma

O **o'clock: it's ... ~** είναι ... η ώρα
_ee_ne ... ee _o_ra 220

occupied κατειλημμένο kateelee_me_no 14

October Οκτώβριος m ok_to_vreeos 218

of course βεβαίως ve_ve_os 19

office γραφείο n gra_fee_o

often συχνά see_khna_ 13

okay εντάξει en_da_ksee 10, 19

old (not new) παλιό pa_leeo_ 14; (not
young) γέρος _ye_ros 14; **~ town** παλιά
πόλη f pa_leea_ _po_lee 96, 99; **~-
fashioned** ντεμοντέ demon_de_ 14

olive oil ελαιόλαδο n eleo_la_THo

omelet ομελέττα f ome_le_ta 40

on (date) στις stees 13;
(day) την teen 13;
~ board (transport)
μέσα στο τραίνο _me_sa
sto _tre_no 74; **~ foot** με τα
πόδια me ta _po_THya 17, 95;
~ the left στα αριστερά sta arees_te_ra
12; **~ the right** στά δεξιά sta THe_ksee_a
12; **~ the other side of** από την άλλη
μεριά _apo_ teen _a_lee mer_ya_ 95

once μία φορά mia fo_ra_ 217

one ένας, μια, ένα _enas_, _mia_, _ena_ 216;
~-way ticket απλό εισιτήριο n a_plo_
eesee_tee_reeo 68, 79

open (adj) ανοιχτό anee_khto_ 14; **~ to the
public** ανοιχτό στο κοινό anee_khto_ sto
kee_no_ 100; **~-air pool** ανοιχτή πισίνα
anee_khtee_ pee_see_na 116

open, to ανοίγω a_nee_gho 132, 140

opening hours ώρες λειτουργίας fpl
_o_res leetoor_yee_as 100

opera όπερα f _o_pera 108, 111; **~ house**
όπερα f _o_pera 99, 111

opposite απέναντι a_pe_nandee 12

optician οφθαλμίατρος
oftha_lmee_atros 131, 167

or ή ee 19

orange πορτοκάλι n
porto_ka_lee 143, 160

orchestra ορχήστρα f or_khee_stra 111

order, to παραγγέλνω para_gel_no 37, 89,
135; **I ordered** παρήγγειλα pa_ree_geela
41; **to ~ a taxi** καλώ ένα ταξί ka_lo_ ena
tak_see_ 32

organized οργανωμένος
orghano_me_nos 106

others άλλα _a_la 134

our μας mas 16

ours δικό μας THee_ko_ mas 16

out: he's out είναι έξω _ee_ne _ekso_

outdoor εξωτερικός eksotere_ee_kos

outside lane εξωτερική λωρίδα f
eksotere_ee_kee lo_ree_τHa

outside έξω _ekso_ 12, 36

oval οβάλ o_val_ 134

oven φούρνος m f_oornos_

over: ~ **there** εκεί e_kee_ 76; ~ **the road** απέναντι apen_andee_ 12

overdone (adj) πολύ ψημένο pol_ee_ psee_meno_ 41

overnight ένα βράδυ n ena vra_THee_ 23

owe: how much do I owe you? πόσο σας χρωστώ; poso sas khros_to_

own: on my ~ μόνος/-η μου m_onos_/-ee moo 65

owner κάτοχος k_atokhos_

P **p.m.** μ.μ. meta mesee_mvre_eas

pacifier μπίλα f peep_eela_

pack of cards τράπουλα f tr_apoola_

pack, to (baggage) φτιάχνω τις βαλίτσες ftee_akhno_ tees val_eetses_ 69

packet of cigarettes πακέτο τσιγάρα n pak_eto_ tsee_ghara_ 150

paddling pool ρηχή πισίνα f reekh_ee_ pees_eena_ 113

padlock λουκέτο n look_eto_

pain, to be in πονάω pon_ao_ 167

painkiller παυσίπονο n pafs_eepono_ 141, 165

paint, to ζωγραφίζω zoghraf_eezo_ 104; **painter** ζωγράφος zoghr_afos_ 104

pair of ένα ζευγάρι n ena zevgh_aree_ 217

pajamas πιτζάμες f peetz_ames_

palace ανάκτορα npl an_aktora_ 99

panorama πανόραμα f pan_orama_ 107

pants (trousers) παντελόνι n pandel_onee_ 144

panty hose καλτσόν n kalts_on_ 144

paper χαρτί n khart_ee_ 150; ~ **napkin** χαρτοπετσέτα f khartopets_eta_ 148

paraffin παραφινέλαιο n parafeen_eleo_ 31

paralysis παραλυσία f paralees_eea_

parcel πακέτο n, δέμα n pak_eto_, TH_ema_ 155

pardon? ορίστε; or_ee_ste 11

parents γονείς mpl ghon_ees_ 120

park πάρκο n p_arko_ 96, 99, 107; ~ **ranger** δασοφύλακας THasof_eelakas_

parking χώρος στάθμευσης m kh_oros_ stathmef_sees_ 87; ~ **meter** παρκόμετρο n park_ometro_ 87; ~ **lot** χώρος στάθμευσης m kh_oros_ stathmef_sees_ 87

parliament building Βουλή f vool_ee_ 99

partner (boyfriend/girlfriend) σύντροφος seend_rofos_

parts (components) ανταλλακτικά n andalakt_eeka_ 89

party (social) πάρτυ n "party" 124

pass, to περνώ per_no_ 77; ~ **through** περνώ per_no_ 66

passenger επιβάτης epee_vatees_

passport διαβατήριο n THeeavat_eereeo_ 66, 69

pastry store ζαχαροπλαστείο n zakharoplast_eeo_ 113

path μονοπάτι f monop_atee_ 107

pay, to πληρώνω pleer_ono_ 42, 136; ~ **a fine** πληρώνω πρόστιμο pleer_ono_ pr_osteemo_ 93

paying πληρωμή f pleer_omee_ 42, 136

peak κορυφή f koreef_ee_ 107

pearl μαργαριτάρι n margharee_taree_ 149

pebbly (beach) με χαλίκια me khal_eekeea_ 116

pedestrian: ~ **crossing** διάβαση πεζών f THee_avasee_ pez_on_ 96; ~ **zone** ο πεζόδρομος(m) o pez_oTHromos_ 96

pen στυλό n steel_o_ 150

penfriend φίλος μέσω αλληλογραφίας f_eelos_ meso aleelloghraf_eeas_

penknife σουγιάς m soo_yas_

pensioner συνταξιούχος seendakseeo_okhos_ 100

pepper (seasoning) μπέρι n peep_eree_ 38

per: ~ day την ημέρα teen ee<u>me</u>ra 30, 83, 86, 87, 115; ~ **hour** την ώρα teen <u>o</u>ra 87, 115; ~ **night** τη βραδιά tee vra<u>thya</u> 21; ~ **week** την εβδομάδα teen ev<u>th</u>o<u>ma</u>tha 83, 86

perhaps *(menstrual)* ίσως <u>ee</u>sos 19

period *(menstrual)* περίοδος f pe<u>ree</u>othos 167; ~ **pains** πόνοι περιόδου m <u>po</u>nee pe<u>ree</u>othoo 167

period *(of time)* περίοδος f pe<u>ree</u>othos 104

perm περμανάντ f perma<u>nand</u>

permed περμανάντ f perma<u>nand</u> 147

permit άδεια f <u>a</u>thea

petrol βενζίνη f ven<u>zee</u>nee 87, 88; ~ **station** βενζινάδικο n venzee<u>na</u>theeko 87

pewter κασσίτερος m ka<u>see</u>teros 149

phone *(see also **telephone**)*: ~ **call** τηλεφώνημα n teele<u>fo</u>neema 152; ~ **card** τηλεκάρτα f teele<u>ka</u>rta 127, 155

photo φωτογραφία f fotoghra<u>fee</u>a; **passport-size** ~ φωτογραφία διαβατηρίου fotoghra<u>fee</u>a THeeavatee<u>ree</u>oo 8

photo, to take a φωτογραφίζω fotoghra<u>fee</u>zo

photocopier φωτοτυπικό n fototee<u>pee</u>ko 155

phrase φράση f <u>fra</u>see 11

pick up, to παίρνω <u>per</u>no 28, 113

pickup truck ημιφορτηγό n eemeefortee<u>gho</u>

picnic area περιοχή για πικνίκ f pereeo<u>khee</u> ya "picnic" 107

piece τεμάχιο n te<u>ma</u>kheeo 69; **a piece of** ... ένα κομμάτι ... ena ko<u>ma</u>tee 40

Pill *(contraceptive)*: **to be on the** ~ παίρνω το αντισυλληπτικό χάπι <u>per</u>no to andeeseelee<u>ptee</u>ko <u>kha</u>pee 167

pillow μαξιλάρι n maksee<u>la</u>ree 27; ~ **case** μαξιλαροθήκη f makseelaro<u>thee</u>kee

pilot light φλόγιστρο n <u>flo</u>yeestro

pink ροζ roz 143

pipe *(smoking)* πίπα f <u>pee</u>pa; ~ **cleaners** καθαριστής πίπας m kathare<u>estees</u> <u>pee</u>pas; ~ **tobacco** καπνός πίπας m ka<u>pnos</u> <u>pee</u>pas

pity: it's a pity κρίμα <u>kree</u>ma

pizzeria πιτσαρία f peetsa<u>ree</u>a 35

place *(space)* θέση f <u>the</u>see 29

place a bet, to βάζω στοίχημα <u>va</u>zo <u>stee</u>kheema 114

plain *(not patterned)* απλό a<u>plo</u>

plane αεροπλάνο n aero<u>pla</u>no 68

plans σχέδια npl <u>skhe</u>THeea 124

plant φυτό n fee<u>to</u>

plastic bag πλαστική σακούλα f plastee<u>kee</u> sa<u>koo</u>la

plate πιάτο n <u>pya</u>to 39, 148

platform αποβάθρα f apo<u>va</u>thra 73, 76, 77

platinum πλατίνα f pla<u>tee</u>na 149

play, to παίζω <u>pe</u>zo 110, 121; *(music)* παίζω (μουσική) <u>pe</u>zo (moosee<u>kee</u>) 111; ~**ground** παιδική χαρά f pethee<u>kee</u> kha<u>ra</u> 113; ~**group** παιδικός σταθμός m pethee<u>kos</u> stath<u>mos</u> 113

playing field γήπεδο n <u>yee</u>peTHo 115

playwright δραματουργός f THramatoor<u>ghos</u> 110

pleasant ευχάριστο ef<u>kha</u>reesto 14

please παρακαλώ paraka<u>lo</u> 10

plug πρίζα f <u>pree</u>za 148

plumber υδραυλικός eethravlee<u>kos</u>

pneumonia πνευμονία f pnevmo<u>nee</u>a 165

point: Point! δείξτε! <u>THee</u>kste 11

poison δηλητήριο n THeelee<u>tee</u>reeo 140

poisonous δηλητηριώδης THeeleetee<u>ree</u>othees

police αστυνομία f asteeno<u>mee</u>a 92, 152; ~ **certificate** πιστοποιητικό αστυνομίας n peestopee-ee<u>tee</u>ko asteeno<u>mee</u>as 153; ~ **station** αστυνομικό τμήμα n asteenomee<u>ko</u> <u>tmee</u>ma 96, 131, 152

pond λιμνούλα f
leemnoola 107
popcorn ποπ-κορν
"popcorn" 110
popular δημοφιλής
THeemofeelees 157
porter αχθοφόρος akhthoforos 71
portion μερίδα f mereeTHa 40
possible: as soon as possible
όσο το δυνατόν πιο σύντομα
oso to THeenaton peeo seendoma
post (mail)**: ~ office** ταχυδρομείο n
takheeTHromeeo 96, 131, 154;
~box ταχυδρομικό κουτί n
takheeTHromeeko kootee 154; **~card**
κάρτα f karta 150, 154, 156
potatoes πατάτες fpl patates 38
pottery αγγειοπλαστική f
angeeoplasteekee
poultry πουλερικά poolereeka 46, 158
pound (sterling) λίρα (στερλίνα) f
leera (sterleena) 67, 138
power cut διακοπή ρεύματος f
THeeakopee revmatos
pregnant, to be είμαι έγκυος
eeme engeeos 163
prescribe, to γράφω συνταγή ghrafo
seendayee 165
prescription συνταγή γιατρού f
seendayee yatroo 140, 141
present (gift) δώρο n THoro
press, to σιδερώνω
seeTHerono 137
pretty όμορφο omorfo 101
priest ιερέας ee-ereas
prison φυλακή f feelakee
private bathroom ιδιωτικό μπάνιο n
eeTHeeooteeko baneeo
problem πρόβλημα n provleema 88
program πρόγραμμα n proghrama 109;
~ of events οδηγός θεαμάτων
oTHeeghos theamaton 108
prohibited: is it prohibited?
απαγορεύεται; apaghorevete

promenade deck κατάστρωμα n
katastroma
pronounce, to προφέρω profero 11
Protestant Διαμαρτυρόμενος
THeeamarteeromenos
public: ~ building δημόσιο κτίριο n
THeemoseeo kteereeo 96; **~ holiday**
δημόσια αργία f THeemoseea
aryeea 219
pullover πουλόβερ n poolover 144
pump τρόμπα, αεραντλία f tromba,
aerandleea 83
puncture (flat)**: I have a ~** παθαίνω
λάστιχο patheno lasteekho 88
purple μωβ mov 143
purpose σκοπός m skopos 66
put: where can I put ...? Πού να
βάλω ...; poo na valo

Q **quality** ποιότητα f peeoteeta 134
quantity ποσότητα f
posoteeta 134
quarantine καραντίνα f karandeena
quarter, a ένα τέταρτο ena tetarto 217;
~ past ... ... και τέταρτο ... ke tetarto
220; **~ to ...** ... παρά τέταρτο ... para
tetarto 220
quay προβλήτα, αποβάθρα f provleeta,
apovathra
queen (cards) ντάμα f dama; (chess)
βασίλισσα f vaseeleesa
question ερώτηση f eroteesee
queue ουρά f oora
queue, to περιμένω στην ουρά
pereemeno steen oora 112
quick γρήγορο ghreeghoro 14; **quickly**
γρήγορα ghreeghora 17
quiet ήσυχο eeseekho 14; **quieter** πιο
ήσυχο peeo eeseekho 24, 126

R **rabbi** ραββίνος m raveenos
race track [race course]
ιπποδρόμιο n eepoTHromeeo 114

racket *(tennis, squash)* ρακέτα f
raketa 115

radio ραδιόφωνο n raTHeeofono 25

rail station σιδηροδρομικός σταθμός m
seeTHeeroTHromeekos stathmos 73

rain, to βρέχει vrekhee 122

raincoat αδιάβροχο n aTHeeavrokho 145

rapids ρεύμα ποταμού f revma
potamoo 107

rare *(steak)* με το αίμα του, σενιάν me to
ema too, seneean; *(unusual)* σπάνιος
spaneeos

rash εξάνθημα n eksantheema 162

ravine ρεματιά f remateea 107

razor blades ξυραφάκια n
kseerafakeea 142

razor ξυραφάκι n kseerafakee

ready έτοιμος eteemos 89, 151;
it's ready είναι έτοιμο eene eteemo
137; **are you ready?** Είστε έτοιμος;
eeste eteemos

real *(genuine)* αληθινός aleetheenos 149

really? αλήθεια; aleetheea 19

receipt απόδειξη f apoTHeeksee 32, 89,
136, 137, 151

reception *(hotel)* ρεσεψιόν f resepseeon

reclaim tag ετικέτα παραλαβής
αποσκευών eteeketa paralavees
aposkevon 71

recommend, to συστήνω seesteeno 21,
35; **can you recommend?** μπορείτε να
συστήσετε; boreete na seesteesete 97;
what do you recommend? τι
συστήνετε; tee seesteenete? 37

record *(lp)* δίσκος m THeeskos 157; **~
store** δισκάδικο n THeeskaTHeeko 131

red κόκκινος kokeenos 143; **~ wine**
κόκκινο κρασί n kokeeno krasee 40

reduction μειωμένο εισιτήριο n
meeomeno eeseeteereeo 74, 100

refund επιστροφή χρημάτων f
epeestrofee khreematon 137

refuse bag σακκούλα σκουπιδιών f
sakoola skoopeeTHeeon 148

refuse tip σκουπιδότοπος
m skoopeeTHotopos

region περιοχή f
pereeokhee 106

registration number αριθμός
κυκλοφορίας m areethmos
keekloforeeas 88, 93

registration plates πινακίδες fpl
peenakeeTHes 87

regular *(gas [petrol])* απλή aplee 87; *(size
of drink)* μέτριο metreeo 110

religion θρησκεία f threeskeea

remember: I don't remember Δεν
θυμάμαι THen theemame

rent, to νοικιάζω neekeeazo 29, 86; **I'd
like to rent ...** θα ήθελα να νοικιάσω ...
tha eethela na nekeeaso

repair, to επισκευάζω epeeskevazo 89;
διορθώνω THeeorthono 137

repairs επισκευές fpl
epeeskeves 89, 137

repeat, to επαναλαμβάνω
epanalamvano 94, 128; **please repeat
that** παρακαλώ επαναλάβετέ το
parakalo epanalavete to 11

replacement part ανταλλακτικό n
andalakteeko 137

report, to αναφέρω anafero 152

require: it is required χρειάζεται
khreeazete 111

reservation κράτηση f krateesee
22, 68, 77, 112

reserve, to κλείνω kleeno 21, 36, 109;
I'd like to reserve ... θα ήθελα να
κλείσω ... tha eethela na kleeso 74

restaurant εστιατόριο n esteeatoreeo 35

retired, to be συνταξιούχος
seendakseeookhos 121

return, to επιστρέφω epeestrefo 75, 81,
98; **~ ticket** εισιτήριο με επιστροφή
eeseeteereeo me epeestrofee 68, 74, 79

reverse the charges με χρέωση του
παραλήπτη me khreeosee too
paraleeptee 127

revolting αηδιαστικό aeeтнeeasteeko 14

rheumatism ρευματισμοί mpl revmateezmee

rib πλευρό n plevro 166

right (*correct*) σωστός sostos 14, 77, 79, 80, 94; **that's right** σωστά sosta

right (*not left*): **on the ~** στα δεξιά sta тнekseea 76, 95; **~handed** δεξιόχειρας тнekseeokheeras

right of way προτεραιότητα f protereoteeta 93, 106

rip-off n κλεψιά klepseea 101

river ποταμός m potamos 107

road δρόμος m тнromos 94; **~ assistance** οδική βοήθεια f отнeekee voeetheea 88; **~ sign** πινακίδα f, σήμα n peenakeeтнa seema 93

roasted ψητός pseetos

robbery ληστεία f leesteea

rock climbing αναρρίχηση f anareekheesee

rocks βράχια npl vrakheea

rolls ψωμάκια n psomakeea 43; **is this the road for ...** Αυτός είναι ο δρόμος για ...; aftos eene o тнromos ya

romantic ρομαντικό romandeeko 101

roof (*house/car*) σκεπή f, στέγη f skepee, steyee; **~-rack** σχάρα αυτοκινήτου f skhara aftokeeneetoo

rook (*chess*) πύργος m peerghos

room δωμάτιο n тнomateeo 21; **~ service** υπηρεσία δωματίου f eepeereseea тнomateeoo 26

rope σχοινί n skheenee

round (*adj*) στρογγυλός strongeelos 134

round (*of golf*) παιχνίδι n pekhneeтнee 115

roundtrip (*ticket*) εισιτήριο με επιστροφή eeseeteereeo me epeestrofee 68, 74, 79

route διαδρομή f тнeeaтнromee 106

rowing κωπηλασία f kopeelaseea

rubbish σκουπίδια npl skoopeeтнya 28

rucksack σακκίδιο n sakeeтнeeo 145

rude, to be είμαι αγενής eeme ayenees

run: **~ out** (*fuel*) μένω από meno apo 88; **~ into: I ran into ...** χτύπησα ... khteepeesa 93

rush hour ώρα αιχμής f ora ekhmees

S **safe** (*lock-up*) θυρίδα f тнeereeтнa 27

safe (*not dangerous*) ασφαλής asfalees 116; **to feel ~** αισθάνομαι ασφαλής esthanome asfalees 65

sailing boat ιστιοπλοϊκό n eesteeoploeeko 116

salad σαλάτα f salata

sales rep αντιπρόσωπος πωλήσεων andeeprosopos poleeseon

sales tax ΦΠΑ fee pee a 24

salt αλάτι n alatee 38, 39, 160

salty αλμυρό almeero

same ίδιος eeтнeeos 75; **the same again please** το ίδιο παρακαλώ to eeтнeeo parakalo

sand άμμος f amos; **sandy** (*beach*) με άμμο me amo 116

sandals πέδιλα npl peтнeela 145

sandwich σάντουιτς n "sandwich" 40

sanitary towels σερβιέττες f servee-etes 142

satellite TV δορυφορική τηλεόραση f тнoreeforeekee teeleorasee 22

satin σατέν n saten

satelite TV δορυφορική τηλεόραση f тнoreeforeekee teeleorasee

Saturday Σάββατο n savato 218

sauce σάλτσα f saltsa 38

saucepan κατσαρόλα f katsarola 29

sauna σάουνα f saoona

sausages λουκάνικα npl lookaneeka 40

saw (*tool*) πριόνι n preeonee

say: how do you say ...? Πώς λέγεται ...; pos leyete; **what did he say?** Τί είπε; tee eepe

scarf κασκώλ n kaskol 144

scenic route γραφική διαδρομή ghrafeek<u>ee</u> тнeeaтн<u>ro</u>mee 106

scheduled flight προγραμματισμένη πτήση f proghramatee<u>zm</u>enee pt<u>ee</u>see

sciatica ισχυαλγία f eeskheeal<u>yee</u>a 165

scientist επιστήμονας epee<u>stee</u>monas

scissors ψαλίδι n psal<u>ee</u>THee 148

Scotland Σκωτία f sk<u>o</u>teea 119

Scottish n Σκωτσέζος skots<u>e</u>zos

screw βίδα f v<u>ee</u>THa

screwdriver κατσαβίδι n katsav<u>ee</u>THee 148

sea θάλασσα f th<u>a</u>lassa 107; **~food** θαλασσινά thalass<u>ee</u>na 45

seafront προκυμαία f prokeem<u>ea</u>

seasoning αλατοπίπερο n alatop<u>ee</u>pero 38

seat θέση f th<u>e</u>see 74, 77, 109

second δεύτερος тн<u>e</u>fteros 217; **~ class** δεύτερη θέση тн<u>e</u>fteree th<u>e</u>see 74; **~-hand shop** κατάστημα μεταχειρισμένων ειδών n kat<u>a</u>steema metakheereez<u>m</u>enon ee<u>тн</u>on 131

secretary γραμματέας ghramat<u>e</u>as

security guard φύλακας m f<u>ee</u>lakas

sedative ηρεμιστικό n eeremeest<u>ee</u>ko

see, to βλέπω vl<u>e</u>po 34, 37; **~ again** ξαναβλέπω ksanavl<u>e</u>po 126

self-employed, to be ελεύθερος επαγγελματίας el<u>e</u>ftheros epangelmat<u>ee</u>as 121

self-service σελφ-σέρβις n "self-service" 87

send, to στέλνω st<u>e</u>lno 88, 155

senior citizen συνταξιούχος seendaksee<u>oo</u>khos 74

separately ξεχωριστά ksekhoreest<u>a</u> 42

September Σεπτέμβριος m sept<u>e</u>mvreeos 218

service λειτουργία f leetoor<u>yee</u>a 105; **is ~ included?** συμπεριλαμβάνεται η υπηρεσία; seembereelamv<u>a</u>nete ee eepeer<u>e</u>seea 42; **~ charge** ποσοστό υπηρεσίας n posos<u>to</u> eepeer<u>e</u>seeas

set menu μενού α λα καρτ n men<u>oo</u> ala kart 37

seven επτά ep<u>ta</u> 216

seventeen δεκαεπτά тнekaep<u>ta</u> 216

seventy εβδομήντα ενтн<u>o</u>meenda 217

sex (act) σεξ n "sex"

shade απόχρωση f ap<u>o</u>khrosee 143; **shady** έχει σκιά <u>e</u>khee skee<u>a</u> 31

shampoo σαμπουάν n samp<u>oo</u>an 142; **~ and set** σαμπουάν και χτένισμα n samp<u>oo</u>an ke kht<u>e</u>neezma 147

shape σχήμα n skh<u>ee</u>ma 134

shaving brush βούρτσα ξυρίσματος f v<u>oo</u>rtsa ksee<u>ree</u>zmatos

shaving cream κρέμα ξυρίσματος f kr<u>e</u>ma ksee<u>ree</u>zmatos

sheet (bedding) σεντόνι n send<u>o</u>nee 28

shelf ράφι n r<u>a</u>fee

ship πλοίο n pl<u>ee</u>o

shirt πουκάμισο n pook<u>a</u>meeso 144

shock (electric) ηλεκτρικό σοκ n eelektr<u>ee</u>ko sok

shoe: shoes παπούτσια npl pap<u>oo</u>tseea 145; **~ store** κατάστημα υποδημάτων n kat<u>a</u>steema eeroтн<u>ee</u>maton 130; **~ laces** κορδόνια παπουτσιών npl korт<u>ho</u>neea papootsee<u>on</u>; **~ polish** λούστρο παπουτσιών n l<u>oo</u>stro papootsee<u>on</u>; **~ repair** διόρθωση παπουτσιών f тнee<u>o</u>rthosee papootsee<u>on</u>

shop (store) κατάστημα n kat<u>a</u>steema 130

shopping: to go ~ πάω ψώνια p<u>a</u>o ps<u>o</u>neea; **~ area** εμπορική περιοχή f emboreek<u>ee</u> pereeokh<u>ee</u> 99; **~ mall [centre]** εμπορική περιοχή f emboreek<u>ee</u> pereeokh<u>ee</u> 130

shore (sea/lake) ακτή f akt<u>ee</u>

short κοντό kond<u>o</u> 14, 146; **~-sighted** μύωπας m<u>ee</u>opas 167

shorts σόρτς n "shorts" 144

shoulder ώμος m omos 166

show, to: show! δείξετε! THeeksete 18; **can you show me?** μπορείτε να μου δείξετε; boreete na moo THeeksete 94, 106, 133

shower gel αφρόλουτρο για ντουζ n afrolootro ya dooz

shower το ντουζ n to dooz 26, 30

shut (adj) κλειστό kleesto 14

shut: when do you shut? Πότε κλείνετε; pote kleenete

shutter παραθυρόφυλλο n paratheerofeelo 25

sick, to feel αισθάνομαι άρρωστος esthanome arostos 163

sick: I'm going to be θα κάνω εμετό tha kano emeto

side (of road) μεριά f merya 95; **~ street** παράδρομος m paraTHromos 95

sights αξιοθέατα npl akseeotheata

sightseeing tour ξενάγηση στα αξιοθέατα ksenayeese sta akseeotheata 97

sign (road) σήμα n seema 95

signpost σήμα τροχαίας n seema trokheas

silk μετάξι n metaksee

silver ασήμι n aseemee 149; **~-plate** επάργυρο eparyeero 149

singer τραγουδιστής (τραγουδίστρια) traghooTHeestees (traghooTHeestreea) 157

single μονός monos 81; **~ room** μονό δωμάτιο mono THomateeo 21; **to be ~** (unmarried) είμαι ελεύθερος eeme eleftheros 120; **~ ticket** απλό εισιτήριο n aplo eeseeteereeo 68, 79

sink (bathroom) νιπτήρας m neepteeras 25

sister αδελφή f aTHelfee 120

sit, to κάθομαι kathome 36, 77, 126

six έξι eksee 216

sixteen δεκαέξι THekaeksee 216

sixty εξήντα ekseenda 217

size μέγεθος n meyethos 115, 146

skates παγοπέδιλα npl paghopeTHeela 117

skating rink παγοδρόμιο n paghoTHromeeo

ski σκι n "ski" 117; **~ boots** μπότες του σκι fpl botes too "ski" 117; **~ poles** μπαστούνια του σκι bastooneea too "ski" 117; **~-lift** τελεφερίκ n telefereek 117; **~-school** σχολή σκι f skholee too "ski" 117; **skiing** σκι n "ski" 117

skin δέρμα n THerma 166

skirt φούστα f foosta 144

sledge έλκηθρο n elkeethro

sleep, to κοιμάμαι keemame 167; **sleeping bag** υπνόσακκος m eepnosakos 31; **sleeping car** βαγκόν-λι n vagon-lee 77; **sleeping pill** υπνωτικό χάπι n eepnoteeko khapee

slice φέτα f feta 159

slippers παντόφλες fpl pandofles 145

slope (ski) πλαγιά f playa 117

slow αργό argho 14; **slowly** αργά argha 11, 17, 94; **slow down!** Κόψτε ταχύτητα! kopste takheeteeta

SLR camera μονοοπτική ρεφλέξ φωτογραφική μηχανή f monoopteekee refleks fotoghrafeekee meekhanee 151

small μικρός meekros 14, 24, 40, 110, 117, 134; **~ change** ψιλά npl pseela 136

smell: there's a bad smell Μυρίζει άσχημα meereezee askheema

smoke, to καπνίζω kapneezo 126; **I don't smoke** Δεν καπνίζω THen kapneezo; **it's too smoky** Έχει πολύ καπνίλα ekhee polee kapneela; **smoking** καπνίζοντες kapneezondes 36; **smoking area** περιοχή για καπνίζοντες pereeokhee ya kapneezondes 69

snack bar κυλικείο n keelee<u>keeo</u> 73

sneakers αθλητικά παπούτσια npl athleetee<u>ka</u> pa<u>poo</u>tseea

snorkel αναπνευστήρας m anapnefs<u>tee</u>ras

snow, to χιονίζει kheeo<u>nee</u>zee 122

snowed in, to be έχω κλειστεί από το χιόνι <u>e</u>kho klees<u>tee</u> a<u>po</u> to kheeo<u>nee</u>

snowplow χιονοκαθαριστήρας m kheeonokatharees<u>tee</u>ras

soap powder απορρυπαντικό n aporeepandee<u>ko</u>

soap σαπούνι sa<u>poo</u>nee 27, 142

soccer ποδόσφαιρο n po<u>THo</u>sfero 114

socket πρίζα f <u>pree</u>za

socks κάλτσες fpl <u>kalt</u>ses 144

soda [soft drink] αναψυκτικό n anapseektee<u>ko</u> 110, 160

sofa καναπές m kana<u>pes</u>; **~-bed** καναπές-κρεββάτι m kana<u>pes</u>-kre<u>va</u>tee

sole (shoes) σόλα f <u>so</u>la

something κάτι <u>ka</u>tee 14

sometimes μερικές φορές meree<u>kes</u> fo<u>res</u> 13

son γιος m yos 120, 162

soon σύντομα <u>see</u>ndoma 13; **as soon as possible** όσο το δυνατόν πιο σύντομα <u>o</u>so to THeena<u>ton</u> pee<u>o</u> <u>see</u>ndoma 161

sore: it's ~ πονάει po<u>na</u>ee; **~ throat** πονόλαιμος m po<u>no</u>lemos 141, 163

sorry! συγγνώμη seegh<u>no</u>mee 10

sort είδος n <u>ee</u>THos 134

soup σούπα f <u>soo</u>pa 44

sour ξινός ksee<u>nos</u> 41

South Africa Νότια Αφρική f <u>no</u>teea afree<u>kee</u>

South African Νοτιοαφρικανός noteeoafreeka<u>nos</u>

south νότια <u>no</u>teea 95

souvenir σουβενίρ n "souvenir" 98, 156; **~ store** κατάστημα σουβενίρ n ka<u>ta</u>steema "souvenir" 131

souvlaki/gyros stand σουβλατζίδικο n soovlatzee<u>THee</u>ko 35

spa ιαματικά λουτρά npl eeamatee<u>ka</u> loo<u>tra</u> 107

space χώρος m <u>kho</u>ros 30

spade (shovel) φτυαράκι n fteea<u>ra</u>kee 157

spades (cards) μπαστούνι n ba<u>stoo</u>nee

spare (extra) επιπλέον, έξτρα epee<u>ple</u>on, "extra"

speak, to μιλώ mee<u>lo</u> 11, 18, 41, 67, 128; **do you speak English?** μιλάτε Αγγλικά; mee<u>la</u>te anglee<u>ka</u>? 11

special requirements ειδικές ανάγκες f ee<u>THee</u>kes a<u>na</u>nges 39

specialist ειδικός ee<u>THee</u>kos 164

specimen δείγμα n <u>THee</u>ghma 164

spectacles γυαλιά n yalee<u>a</u>

speed, to τρέχω <u>tre</u>kho 93

spell: it is spelled γράφεται <u>ghra</u>fete 11

spend, to ξοδεύω kso<u>THe</u>vo

spices μπαχαρικά npl bakharee<u>ka</u> 48

spicy καυτό ka<u>fto</u>

spin-dryer στεγνωτήριο n steghno<u>tee</u>reeo

spine σπονδυλική στήλη f spon<u>THee</u>lee<u>kee</u> <u>stee</u>lee 166

spoon κουτάλι n koo<u>ta</u>lee 39, 41, 148

sport αθλητισμός athleetee<u>zmos</u> 114; **sports club** αθλητικός όμιλος athleetee<u>kos</u> <u>o</u>meelos 115; **sports ground** (αθλητικό) στάδιο n (athleetee<u>ko</u>) <u>sta</u>THeeo 96; **sporting goods store** κατάστημα αθλητικών n ka<u>ta</u>steema athleetee<u>kon</u> 131

spring άνοιξη f <u>a</u>neeksee 219

square τετράγωνος te<u>tra</u>ghonos 134

stadium στάδιο n <u>sta</u>THeeo 96

stain λεκές m le<u>kes</u>

stairs σκάλες f <u>ska</u>les

stale μπαγιάτικο ba<u>ya</u>teeko 14

stamp γραμματόσημο n ghrama<u>to</u>seemo 150, 154

start, to αρχίζω
arkh**ee**zo 98, 112
statement *(legal)* δήλωση
(νομική) f THe**e**losee
(nome**ee**kee) 93
station σταθμός m
stath**mos** 73, 96
statue άγαλμα n **a**ghalma 99
stay, to μένω m**e**no 23, 65, 123
sterilizing solution αποστειρωτικό
διάλυμα n aposteerotee**ko**
THee**a**leema 142
stern *(ship)* πρύμνη f pr**ee**mnee
sting τσίμπημα n ts**ee**mbeema 162
stolen, to be κλάπηκε **kl**apeeke 71
stomach στομάχι n sto**ma**khee 166;
~ache στομαχόπονος m
stoma**kho**ponos 163
stop *(bus/tram)* στάση f st**a**see 79, 80
stop, to σταματώ stama**to** 77, 98; **~ at**
σταματώ στο/στη stama**to** sto/
stee 76, 78
store *(shop)* κατάστημα n ka**ta**steema
130; **~ guide** οδηγός καταστήματος m
oTHee**ghos** kata**stee**matos 132
stove κουζίνα f koo**zee**na 28, 29
straight ahead ευθεία/ίσια
efth**ee**a/**ee**seea 95
strange παράξενο par**a**kseno 101
straw *(drinking)* καλαμάκι n kala**ma**kee
stream ρυάκι f ree**a**kee 107
string σπάγγος m sp**a**gos
striped *(patterned)* ριγέ ree**ye**
student φοιτητής (φοιτήτρια) feetee**tees**
(fee**tee**treea) 74, 100
study, to σπουδάζω spoo**THa**zo 121
style ρυθμός m reeth**mos** 104
subtitled, to be με υπότιτλους me
eepoteet**loos** 110
subway *(metro)* μετρό n (υπόγειος
σιδηρόδρομος, ηλεκτρικός) m "metro"
(ee**po**yeeos seeTHee**ro**THromos,
eelektree**kos**) 80; **~ station** σταθμός
μετρό m stath**mos** "metro" 80, 96

suede σουέτ soo**et**
sugar ζάχαρη f z**a**kharee 38, 39, 160
suggest, to προτείνω prot**ee**no 123
suit *(men's)* κουστούμι n koos**too**mee
144; *(women's)* ταγιέρ n ta**yer** 144
suitable κατάλληλος kat**a**leelos 117, 140
summer καλοκαίρι n kalo**ke**ree 219
sun: ~glasses γυαλιά ήλιου n yalee**a**
eeleeoo 144; **~-tan cream/lotion**
κρέμα/λάδι ήλιου kr**e**ma/l**a**THee
eeleeoo 142; **~burn** έγκαυμα ηλίου n
engavma eel**ee**oo 141; **~shade**
ομπρέλλα f ombr**e**la 116; **~stroke**
ηλίαση f eel**ee**asee 163; **to be sunny**
έχει ήλιο **e**khee **ee**leeo 122
Sunday Κυριακή f keeree**a**kee 218
superb έξοχο **e**ksokho 101
supermarket σουπερμάρκετ n
"supermarket" 131, 158
supervision επίβλεψη f ep**ee**vlepsee 113
supplement επιβάρυνση f
epee**va**reensee 74
suppositories υπόθετα n ee**po**theta 165
sure: are you sure? Είστε σίγουρος;
eeste s**ee**ghooros
surname επίθετο n ep**ee**theto
sweatshirt αθλητική μπλούζα f
athleetee**kee** bl**oo**za 144
sweet *(taste)* γλυκός ghlee**kos**
sweets *(candy)* καραμέλες fpl
kara**me**les 150
swelling πρήξιμο n pr**ee**kseemo 162
swimming κολύμβηση f kol**ee**mveesee
114; **~ pool** πισίνα f pee**see**na 22, 26,
116; **~ trunks** μαγιό n ma**yo** 144
swimsuit ολόσωμο μαγιό n ol**o**somo
ma**yo** 144
switch on/off, to ανοίγω/κλείνω
an**ee**gho/kl**ee**no
swollen πρησμένος pree**zme**nos
symptoms συμπτώματα npl
seem**pto**mata 163
synagogue συναγωγή f seenagho**yee**

T T-shirt μπλουζάκι n bloo<u>za</u>kee 144, 156

table τραπέζι n tra<u>pe</u>zee 36, 112; **~ cloth** τραπεζομάντηλο n trapezo<u>man</u>deelo; **~ tennis** πινγκ-πονγκ n peeng-pong

tablet χάπι n <u>kha</u>pee 140

take, to παίρνω <u>per</u>no 24, 78, 165; **I'll take it** θα το πάρω tha to <u>pa</u>ro 24, 135; **~ away** παίρνω (σπίτι) <u>per</u>no <u>spee</u>tee 40; **~ photographs** παίρνω φωτογραφίες <u>per</u>no fotohra<u>fee</u>-es 98; **how long does it take?** πόσο διαρκεί; <u>po</u>so THee<u>ar</u>kee 78; **it takes time** παίρνει ώρα/κάνει ώρα <u>per</u>nee <u>o</u>ra / <u>ka</u>nee <u>o</u>ra 84

taken (occupied) πιασμένος pia<u>zme</u>nos 77

talk, to μιλώ mee<u>lo</u>

tall ψηλό pse<u>lo</u> 14

tampons ταμπόν n ta<u>mbon</u> 142

tan μαύρισμα n <u>ma</u>vreezma

tap (water) βρύση f <u>vree</u>see 25

taxi ταξί n ta<u>ksee</u> 70, 71, 84; **~ rank** πιάτσα ταξί f <u>pia</u>tsa ta<u>ksee</u> 96; **~ driver** ταξιτζής m taksee<u>tzees</u>

tea τσάι n <u>tsae</u> 40; **~ bags** φακελάκια τσαγιού n fake<u>la</u>keea tsa<u>yoo</u> 160; **~spoon** κουταλάκι n koota<u>la</u>kee 148

teacher δάσκαλος m <u>THa</u>skalos

team ομάδα f o<u>ma</u>THa 114

teat (for baby bottle) ρώγα f <u>ro</u>gha

teddy bear αρκουδάκι n arkoo<u>THa</u>kee 157

teenager έφηβος m <u>e</u>feevos

telephone τηλέφωνο n tee<u>le</u>fono 22, 70, 73, 92, 127; **~ bill** λογαριασμός τηλεφώνου m logharya<u>zmos</u> tee<u>le</u>fonoo 32; **~ booth** τηλεφωνικός θάλαμος m teelefonee<u>kos</u> <u>tha</u>lamos 127; **~ directory** τηλεφωνικός κατάλογος m teelefonee<u>kos</u> <u>ka</u>taloghos 127; **~ number** αριθμός τηλεφώνου m aree<u>thmos</u> tee<u>le</u>fonoo 127

tell: tell me! πείτε μου!/ πέστε μου moo / <u>pe</u>ste moo 79

temperature (body) θερμοκρασία f thermokra<u>see</u>a 164

temple ναός na<u>os</u> 99

temporarily προσωρινά prosoree<u>na</u> 89

temporary προσωρινός prosoree<u>nos</u>

ten δέκα <u>THe</u>ka 216

tennis τέννις n "tennis" 114; **~ court** γήπεδο τέννις n <u>yee</u>peTHo "tennis" 115

tent σκηνή f skee<u>nee</u> 30, 31; **~ pegs** παλούκι n pa<u>loo</u>kee 31; **~ pole** στύλος της σκηνής m <u>stee</u>los tees skee<u>nees</u> 31

terrible φοβερό fove<u>ro</u> 101

tetanus τέτανος m <u>te</u>tanos 164

thank you ευχαριστώ efhare<u>esto</u> 10; **thanks for your help** ευχαριστώ για τη βοήθειά σας efhare<u>esto</u> ya tee vo<u>ee</u>theea sas 94

that one εκείνο e<u>kee</u>no 16, 134

theater θέατρο n <u>the</u>atro 96, 110; (ancient) (αρχαίο) θέατρο n (ar<u>kheo</u>) <u>the</u>atro 99

theft κλοπή f klo<u>pee</u> 71, 153

their τους toos 16

theirs δικό τους THee<u>ko</u> toos 16

them αυτούς af<u>toos</u> 16

then (time) τότε <u>to</u>te 13

there εκεί e<u>kee</u> 12, 17; **there is ...** υπάρχει ... ee<u>par</u>khee 17

thermometer θερμόμετρο n ther<u>mo</u>metro

thermos flask θερμός n ther<u>mos</u>

these αυτά af<u>ta</u> 134

thick χοντρό kho<u>ndro</u> 14

thief κλέφτης <u>kle</u>ftees

thin λεπτό le<u>pto</u> 14

think: I think νομίζω no<u>mee</u>zo 42, 77; **~ about it** το σκέφτομαι to <u>ske</u>ftome 135

third (adj.) τρίτος <u>tree</u>tos 217; (n) ένα τρίτο <u>e</u>na <u>tree</u>to 217

thirsty διψάω тнеepsao

thirteen δεκατρία
THEkatreea 216

thirty τριάντα
treeanda 216

this one αυτό afto 16, 134

those εκείνα ekeena 134

thousand χίλια kheeleea 217

three τρεις, τρία trees, treea 216

throat λαιμός m lemos 166

thrombosis θρόμβωση f thromvosee

thumb αντίχειρας m andeekheeras 166

thundery, to be έχει καταιγίδες ekhee
kateyeeTHes 122

Thursday Πέμπτη f pemptee 218

ticket εισιτήριο n eeseeteereeo 68, 69, 75,
77, 79, 80, 100, 114; **~ office** γραφείο
εισιτηρίων n ghrafeeo eeseeteereeon 73

tie γραβάτα f ghravata 144

tight στενός stenos 117

tights καλτσόν n kaltson 144

till receipt απόδειξη f aροTHeeksee

time: on ~ στην ώρα του steen ora too
76; **free ~** ελεύθερος χρόνος m
eleftheros khronos 98; **~table**
δρομολόγιο n тнromologheeo 75

tin opener ανοιχτήρι n
aneekhteeree 148

tire (on wheel) λάστιχο n lasteekho 83

tired, to be είμαι κουρασμένος eeme
koorazmenos

tissues χαρτομάντηλα n
khartomandeela 142

to (place) στο(-η) sto(-ee) 12

toaster τοστιέρα f tostee-era

tobacco καπνός m kapnos 150;
tobacconist καπνοπωλείο n
kapnopoleeo 131

today σήμερα seemera 124, 218

toe δάχτυλο ποδιού n тнakhteelo
poтнyoo 166

toilet(s) τουαλέττα f tooaleta 25, 26, 29,
73, 96, 98; **toilet paper** χαρτί υγείας n
khartee eeyeeas 25, 29, 142

toiletries καλλυντικά n
kaleendeeka 142

tomorrow αύριο avreeo 84, 124, 218

tongue γλώσσα f ghlosa 166

tonight απόψε apopse 110, 124

tonsillitis αμυγδαλίτιδα f
ameeghтнaleeteeтнa

tonsils αμυγδαλές fpl ameeghтнales

too (extreme) πολύ polee 17, 93; **~ much**
πάρα πολύ para polee 15

tooth δόντι n тнondee 168; **~brush**
οδοντόβουρτσα f oтнondovoortsa 142;
~paste οδοντόπαστα f oтнondopasta
142; **~ache** πονόδοντος m
poноTHondos

top πάνω pano; **~ floor** ο επάνω όροφος
m o epano orofos

torch φακός m fakos 31

torn, to be (muscle) είναι σχισμένος
eene skheezmenos 164

tough (food) σκληρός skleeros 41

tour guide ξεναγός ksenaghos

tour ξενάγηση f ksenayeesee 97

tourist τουρίστας tooreestas

tow rope σχοινί για ρυμούλκηση n
skheenee ya reemoolkeesee

towards προς pros 12

tower πύργος(m) peerghos 99

town πόλη f polee 70, 94; **~ hall**
Δημαρχείο(n) тнeemarkheeo 99

toy παιχνίδι n pekhneeтнee 157

traditional παραδοσιακός
paraтноseeakos 35

traffic κίνηση f keeneesee

trailer τροχόσπιτο n
trokhospeeto 30, 81

train τραίνο n treno 75, 76, 77, 80; **~
times** δρομολόγιο τραίνου n
тнromoloyeeo trenoo 75

training shoes αθλητικά παπούτσια npl
athleeteeka papootseea 145

transfer, to μεταφέρω metafero

transit, in στην μεταφορά
stee metafora 71

translate, to μεταφράζω meta**fra**zo 11

translation μετάφραση f me**ta**frasee

translator μεταφραστής metafra**stees**

trash σκουπίδια npl skoo**pee**THya 28;
~**cans** τενεκέδες mpl tene**ke**THes 30

travel: ~ agency ταξιδιωτικό γραφείο n takseeTHeeoteeko ghra**fee**o 131;
~ **sickness** ναυτία f **naf**teea 141

traveler's check [traveller's cheque] ταξιδιωτικές επιταγές takseeTHeeotee**kes** epeeta**yes** 136, 138

tray δίσκος m **THees**kos

tree δέντρο n **THen**dro 106

trim διόρθωμα n **THee**orthoma 147

trolley καροτσάκι n karo**tsa**kee 158

trolley-bus τρόλλεϋ n "trolley" 78, 79

trousers παντελόνι n pande**lo**nee 144;
trouser press σιδερωτήριο n seeTHero**tee**reeo

true: that's not true Αυτό δεν είναι αλήθεια af**to** THen **ee**ne a**lee**theea

try on, to δοκιμάζω THokee**ma**zo 146

Tuesday Τρίτη f **tree**tee 218

tumor όγκος m **ong**os 165

tunnel τούνελ n **too**nel

Turkey Τουρκία f toor**kee**a

turn: turn! στρίψτε! **streep**ste 95; ~ **off** σβήνω **svee**no 25; ~ **on** ανάβω a**na**vo 25; ~ **down** (volume, heat) χαμηλώνω khamee**lo**no; ~ **up** (volume, heat) ανεβάζω ane**va**zo

turning στενό n ste**no** 95

TV τηλεόραση f teele**o**rasee 22, 25

twelve δώδεκα **THO**THeka 216

twenty είκοσι **ee**kosee 216

twice δύο φορές THeeo fo**res** 217

twin beds δύο κρεββάτια (pl.) THeeo kreva**tee**a 21

two δύο **THee**o 216; ~-**door car** δίπορτο αυτοκίνητο n THee**por**to afto**kee**neeto 86

typical τυπικός teepee**kos** 37

tyre λάστιχο n **las**teekho 83

U **U.K.** Ηνωμένο Βασίλειο n eeno**me**no va**see**leeo

U.S. Ηνωμένες Πολιτείες fpl eeno**me**nes politee**tee**-es 119

ugly άσχημο **as**kheemo 14, 101

ulcer έλκος n **el**kos

uncle θείος m **thee**os 120

unconscious αναίσθητος a**nes**theetos 92

underdone όχι καλά ψημένο **o**khee ka**la** psee**me**no 41

underpass υπόγεια διάβαση f ee**po**yeea THee**a**vasee 76, 96

understand, to καταλαβαίνω katala**ve**no 11; **do you understand?** καταλαβαίνετε; katala**ve**nete 11; **I don't understand** δεν καταλαβαίνω THen katala**ve**no 11, 67

uneven (ground) ανώμαλος a**no**malos 31

unfortunately δυστυχώς THeestee**khos** 19

uniform στολή f sto**lee**

unit μονάδα f mo**na**THa 155

United States Ηνωμένες Πολιτείες fpl eeno**me**nes politee**tee**-es

university Πανεπιστήμιο n panepee**stee**meeo

unleaded petrol αμόλυβδη βενζίνη f a**mo**leevTHee ven**zee**nee 74

unlimited mileage απεριόριστα χιλιόμετρα apereeo**ree**sta kheelee**o**metra

unpleasant δυσάρεστο THee**sa**resto 14

until ως, μέχρι os, **me**khree 221

upper (berth) πάνω (κουκέτα) **pa**no (koo**ke**ta) 74

upset stomach στομαχόπονος m stoma**kho**ponos 141

upstairs επάνω e**pa**no 12

urgent επείγον e**pee**ghon 161

urine ούρα npl **oo**ra 164

use, to χρησιμοποιώ
khreeseemopeeo 139
useful χρήσιμος
khreeseemos

V vacancy ελεύθερο
δωμάτιο n
eleftherο THoμateeo 21
vacant ελεύθερο eleftherο 14
vacate, to αδειάζω aTHyazo 32
vacation διακοπές fpl THeeakopes 123;
on ~ για διακοπές ya THeeakopes 66;
~ resort τόπος διακοπών topos
THeeakopon
vaccinated against έχω κάνει εμβόλιο
για ... ekho kanee emvoleeo ya 164
vaccination εμβόλιο n emvoleeo
valid ισχύει eeskhee-ee 75
valley κοιλάδα f keelaTHa 107
valuable πολύτιμος poleeteemos
value αξία f akseea 155
vanilla (flavor) βανίλια vaneeleea 40
VAT ΦΠΑ fee pee a 24
vegetable λαχανικό n lakhaneeko 47, 158
vegetarian χορτοφάγος khortofaghos 39
vein φλέβα f fleva 166
velvet βελούδο n velooTHo
venereal disease αφροδισιακό νόσημα n
afroTHeeseeako noseema 165
very πολύ polee 17
video ταινία βίντεο f teneea "video";
~ game παιχνίδι βίντεο n
pekhneeTHee "video"; **~ recorder (VCR)**
βίντεο n "video"
village χωριό f khoryo 107
vineyard αμπελώνας m ambelonas 107
visit επίσκεψη f epeeskepsee 119;
visiting hours ώρες επισκεπτηρίου f
ores epeeskepteereeoo 167
vitamin tablets βιταμίνες fpl
veetameenes 141
volleyball βόλεϋ n "volley" 114
vomit, to κάνω εμετό
kano emeto 163

W wait, to περιμένω pereemeno
76, 89, 140; **wait!** περιμένετε!
pereemenete 98
waiter! Γκαρσόν! garson 37
waitress! Δεσποινίς! THespeenees 37
wake to: wake (me)! ξυπνήσετε!
kseepneesete 27
Wales Ουαλλία f ooaleea 119
walk περπατώ perpato 65; **walking
boots** μπότες πεζοπορίας fpl botes
pezoporeeas 145
wall τοίχος m teekhos
wallet πορτοφόλι n portofolee 42
want, to θέλω thelo 18
ward (hospital) πτέρυγα f ptereegha 167
warm χλιαρό khleearo 14; (weather)
ζεστός zestos 122
washing machine πλυντήριο n
pleendeereeo 29
washing powder απορρυπαντικό n
aporeepandeeko 148
washing-up liquid υγρό πιάτων n
eeghro piaton 148
wasp σφήκα f sfeeka
watch ρολόι n roloee; **~ strap** λουρί
ρολογιού n looree roloyoo
water νερό n nero 87; **~ heater**
θερμοσίφωνας m thermoseefonas 28;
~-skis θαλάσσια σκι npl thalaseea
"ski" 116; **~skiing** θαλάσσιο σκι n
thalaseeo "ski"; **~proof** αδιάβροχο n
aTHeeavrokho
waterfall καταρράχτης m
katarakhtees 107
wave κύμα n keema
waxing χαλάουα f khalaooa 147
way: I've lost my way έχασα το δρόμο
μου ekhasa to THromo moo 94
we εμείς emees
weak: I feel weak αισθάνομαι αδύναμος
esthanome aTHeenamos
wear: he/she was wearing φορούσε
foroose 152

weather καιρός keros 122; ~ forecast
πρόβλεψη καιρού provlepsee keroo 122

wedding γάμος m ghamos; ~ ring
δακτυλίδι γάμου n тнakteeleetnee
ghamoo

Wednesday Τετάρτη f tetartee 218

week εβδομάδα f evтноматна 23, 218

well-done (steak) καλοψημένο
kalopseemeno

Welsh (adj) ουαλλέζικος ooalezeekos;
(n) Ουαλλός ooalos

west δυτικά тнeeteeka 95

wetsuit στολή δύτη f stolee тнeetee

what? τι; tee 18; what time ...? τι ώρα
...; tee ora 68, 76, 78, 81; what's the
time? τι ώρα είναι; tee ora eene 220;
what kind of ...? τι είδους ...; tee
eетноos ... 37; what sort of ...? τι
είδους ...; tee eетноos 106

wheelchair αναπηρική καρέκλα f
anapeereekee karekla

when? πότε; pote? 13

where? πού; poo 12; where is ...? πού
είναι ...; poo eene 99; where are you
from? από πού είσαι/είστε (formal);
apo poo eese/eeste (formal) 119

which? ποιό; peeo 16; which stop?
ποιά στάση; pia stasee 80

white άσπρος aspros 143; ~ wine
άσπρο κρασί n aspro krasee 40

who? ποιός peeos 16

whose? ποιανού/-ής; peeanoo/-ees 16

why? γιατί; yatee 15

wide φαρδύ farтнee 14

wife γυναίκα f yeeneka 120, 162

window παράθυρο n paratheero 25, 77;
(in shop) βιτρίνα f veetreena 134, 149;
~ seat θέση στο παράθυρο f тнesee
sto paratheero 74

wine κρασί n krasee 40

winery οινοποιεία f eenopee-eea 107

winter χειμώνας m kheemonas 219

with με me 17

withdraw, to κάνω
ανάληψη kano
analeepsee 139

without χωρίς khorees 17

witness μάρτυρας
marteeras 93

wood (material) ξύλο n kseelo

wood δάσος f тнasos 107

work, to δουλεύω тнoolevo 83, 89, 121;
it doesn't work δεν δουλεύει тнen
тнoolevee 25

worry: I'm worried ανησυχώ
aneeseekho

worse χειρότερο kheerotero 14

worst ο χειρότερος o kheeroteros

wound (cut) πληγή f pleeyee 162

write (down), to γράφω ghrafo 136

writing pad μπλοκ n blok 150

wrong λάθος lathos 14, 136; ~ number
λάθος νούμερο lathos noomero 128

X Y Z

x-ray ακτινογραφία f
akteenoghrafeea 164

yacht γιωτ n "yacht"

year χρόνος m khronos 218

yellow κίτρινος keetreenos 143

yes ναι ne 10

yesterday χτες khtes 218

yogurt γιαούρτι n yaoortee 43, 160

you (informal sing) εσύ esee;
(plural or formal sing) εσείς esees

young νέος neos 14

your (sing/plur) σου/σας soo/sas

yours: it's yours (informal/formal) είναι
δικό σου/σας eene тнeeko soo/sas

youth hostel ξενώνας νεότητας m
ksenonas neoteetas 29

zebra crossing διάβαση πεζών f
тнeeavasee pezon

zero μηδέν meeтнen

zipper [zip] φερμουάρ n fermooar

zoo ζωολογικός κήπος m zo-oloyeekos
keepos 113

zoology ζωολογία f zo-oloyeea

Glossary
Greek - English

The Greek-English glossary covers all the areas where you may need to decode written Greek: hotels, public buildings, restaurants, stores, ticket offices, airports, and stations. The Greek is written in large type to help you identify the character(s) from the signs you see around you.

General ΓΕΝΙΚΑ

ΑΡΙΣΤΕΡΑ	areester*a*	LEFT
ΔΕΞΙΑ	THeksee*a*	RIGHT
ΕΙΣΟΔΟΣ	ees*o*THos	ENTRANCE
ΕΞΟΔΟΣ	*e*ksoTHos	EXIT
ΤΟΥΑΛΕΤΕΣ	tooal*e*tes	TOILETS
ΑΝΔΡΩΝ	anTHr*on*	MEN (TOILETS)
ΓΥΝΑΙΚΩΝ	gheenek*on*	WOMEN (TOILETS)
ΑΠΑΓΟΡΕΥΕΤΑΙ ΤΟ ΚΑΠΝΙΣΜΑ	apaghor*e*vete to *k*apneesma	NO SMOKING
ΚΙΝΔΥΝΟΣ	*kee*nTHeenos	DANGER
ΑΠΑΓΟΡΕΥΤΑΙ Η ΕΙΣΟΔΟΣ	apaghor*e*vete ee *ee*soTHos	NO ENTRY
ΕΛΞΑΤΕ	*e*lksate	PULL
ΩΘΗΣΑΤΕ	ooth*ee*sate	PUSH
ΕΠΙΤΡΕΠΕΤΑΙ	epeetr*e*pete	ALLOWED
ΑΠΑΓΟΡΕΥΕΤΑΙ	apaghor*e*vete	FORBIDDEN

ΤΜΗΜΑ ΑΠΟΛΕΣΘΕΝΤΩΝ ΑΝΤΙΚΕΙΜΕΝΩΝ	_tmeema apolesthendon andeekeemenon_	LOST PROPERTY
ΑΠΑΓΟΡΕΥΕΤΑΙ Η ΚΟΛΥΜΒΗΣΗ	_apaghorevete ee koleemveesee_	NO SWIMMING
ΠΟΣΙΜΟ ΝΕΡΟ	_poseemo nero_	DRINKING WATER
ΙΔΙΩΤΙΚΟΣ ΧΩΡΟΣ	_eeTHeeoteekos khoros_	PRIVATE
ΜΗΝ ΠΕΤΑΤΕ ΣΚΟΥΠΙΔΙΑ	_meen petate skoopeeTHya_	NO LITTER
ΠΡΟΣΟΧΗ ΣΚΥΛΟΣ	_prosokhee skeelos_	BEWARE OF THE DOG
ΥΠΟΓΕΙΑ ΔΙΑΒΑΣΗ	_eepogheea THeeavasee_	UNDERPASS/ SUBWAY
ΠΡΟΣΕΞΤΕ ΤΟ ΣΚΑΛΟΠΑΤΙ	_proseksete to skalopatee_	MIND THE STEP
ΦΡΕΣΚΟ-ΒΑΜΜΕΝΟ	_freskovameno_	WET PAINT
ΠΡΩΤΗ ΘΕΣΗ	_protee thesee_	FIRST CLASS
ΔΕΥΤΕΡΗ ΘΕΣΗ	_THefteree thesee_	SECOND CLASS

Road Signs
ΟΔΙΚΕΣ ΠΙΝΑΚΙΔΕΣ

Greek	Pronunciation	English
ΕΞΟΔΟΣ ΟΧΗΜΑΤΩΝ	eksoтнos okheematon	EXIT IN USE
ΚΡΑΤΑΤΕ ΤΗ ΔΕΞΙΑ	kratate tee тнekseea	KEEP RIGHT
ΚΡΑΤΑΤΕ ΤΗΝ ΑΡΙΣΤΕΡΑ	kratate teen areestera	KEEP LEFT
ΜΟΝΟΔΡΟΜΟΣ	monoтнromos	ONE WAY
ΑΠΑΓΟΡΕΥΕΤΑΙ Η ΠΡΟΣΠΕΡΑΣΗ	apaghorevete ee prosperasee	NO PASSING
ΑΠΑΓΟΡΕΥΕΤΑΙ Η ΣΤΑΘΜΕΥΣΗ/ ΤΟ ΠΑΡΚΑΡΙΣΜΑ	apaghorevete ee stathmefsee/ to parkareesma	NO PARKING
ΕΘΝΙΚΗ ΟΔΟΣ	ethneekee oтнos	FREEWAY [MOTORWAY]
ΔΙΟΔΙΑ	тнeeотнeea	TOLL
ΚΟΜΒΟΣ	komvos	JUNCTION
ΠΑΡΑΚΑΜΠΤΗΡΙΟΣ	parakampteereeos	DETOUR
ΠΡΟΣ ΛΙΜΕΝΑ	pros leemena	TO PORT
ΠΡΟΣ ΚΕΝΤΡΟ	pros kendro	DOWNTOWN

Airport/Station
ΑΕΡΟΔΡΟΜΙΟ/
ΣΙΔΗΡΟΔΡΟΜΙΚΟΣ ΣΤΑΘΜΟΣ

Greek	Pronunciation	English
ΠΛΗΡΟΦΟΡΙΕΣ	pleeroforee-es	INFORMATION
ΠΛΑΤΦΟΡΜΑ 1	platforma 1	PLATFORM 1
ΕΞΟΔΟΣ/ΠΥΛΗ 1	eksoτΗos/peelee 1	GATE 1
ΤΕΛΩΝΕΙΟ	teloneeo	CUSTOMS
ΤΜΗΜΑ ΑΛΛΟΔΑΠΩΝ	tmeema alloτΗapon	IMMIGRATION
ΑΦΙΞΕΙΣ	afeeksees	ARRIVALS
ΑΝΑΧΩΡΗΣΕΙΣ	anakhoreesees	DEPARTURES
ΠΑΡΑΛΑΒΗ ΑΠΟΣΚΕΥΩΝ	paralavee aposkevon	LUGGAGE RECLAIM
ΛΕΩΦΟΡΕΙΟ/ ΤΡΕΝΟ	leoforeeo/ treno	BUS/TRAIN
ΕΝΟΙΚΙΑΣΗ ΑΥΤΟΚΙΝΗΤΩΝ	eneekeeasee aftokeeneeton	CAR RENTAL
ΠΡΟΣ ΗΛΕΚΤΡΙΚΟΝ/ ΜΕΤΡΟ	pros eelektreekon/ metro	SUBWAY [METRO]
ΕΛΕΓΧΟΣ ΔΙΑΒΑΤΗΡΙΩΝ	eelenkhos τΗeeavateereeon	PASSPORT CONTROL

Hotel / Restaurant
ΞΕΝΟΔΟΧΕΙΟ/ ΕΣΤΙΑΤΟΡΙΟ

ΠΛΗΡΟΦΟΡΙΕΣ	pleerofo<u>ree</u>-es	INFORMATION
ΡΕΣΕΨΙΟΝ/ ΥΠΟΔΟΧΗ	resepse<u>on</u>/ eepoτH<u>okhee</u>	RECEPTION
ΚΛΕΙΣΜΕΝΟ	klee<u>sme</u>no	RESERVED
ΕΞΟΔΟΣ ΚΙΝΔΥΝΟΥ	<u>ekso</u>τHos keen<u>THee</u>noo	EMERGENCY/ FIRE EXIT
ΖΕΣΤΟ (ΝΕΡΟ)	<u>ze</u>sto (<u>ne</u>ro)	HOT (WATER)
ΚΡΥΟ (ΝΕΡΟ)	<u>kree</u>o (<u>ne</u>ro)	COLD (WATER)
ΜΟΝΟ ΓΙΑ ΠΡΟΣΩΠΙΚΟ	<u>mo</u>no ya prosope<u>e</u>ko	STAFF ONLY
ΒΕΣΤΙΑΡΙΟ	vestee<u>a</u>reeo	COATCHECK [CLOAKROOM]
ΤΑΡΑΤΣΑ/ΚΗΠΟΣ	ta<u>ra</u>tsa/<u>kee</u>pos	TERRACE/GARDEN
ΜΠΑΡ	"bar"	BAR
ΖΑΧΑΡΟ- ΠΛΑΣΤΕΙΟ	zakharopla<u>stee</u>o	CAKE SHOP

Stores ΚΑΤΑΣΤΗΜΑΤΑ

ΑΝΟΙΧΤΟ	*aneekhto*	OPEN
ΚΛΕΙΣΤΟ	*kleesto*	CLOSED
ΤΜΗΜΑ	*tmeema*	DEPARTMENT
ΟΡΟΦΟΣ	*orofos*	FLOOR
ΥΠΟΓΕΙΟ	*eepogheeo*	BASEMENT
ΑΣΑΝΣΕΡ/ ΑΝΕΛΚΥΣΤΗΡΑΣ	*asanser/ anelkeesteeras*	ELEVATOR [LIFT]
ΚΥΛΙΟΜΕΝΕΣ ΣΚΑΛΕΣ	*keeleeomenes skales*	ESCALATOR
ΤΑΜΕΙΟ	*tameeo*	CASHIER
ΕΚΠΤΩΣΕΙΣ	*ekptosees*	DISCOUNT
ΟΡΟΦΟΣ	*orofos*	FLOOR
ΗΜΙΟΡΟΦΟΣ/ ΜΕΣΟΠΑΤΩΜΑ	*eemeeorofos/ mesopatoma*	MEZZANINE
ΠΩΛΕΙΤΑΙ	*poleete*	FOR SALE

Greek	Pronunciation	English
ΕΛΕΥΘΕΡΑ ΕΙΣΟΔΟΣ/Η ΕΙΣΟΔΟΣ ΔΩΡΕΑΝ	_elefthera eesoTHos/ ee eesoTHos THorean_	ADMISSION FREE
ΕΝΗΛΙΚΕΣ	_eneeleekes_	ADULTS
ΠΑΙΔΙΑ (ΑΚΑΤΑΛΛΗΛΟ ΓΙΑ ΠΑΙΔΙΑ)	_peTHya (akataleelo ya peTHya)_	CHILDREN (CHILDREN NOT ALLOWED)
ΦΟΙΤΗΤΙΚΑ/ ΜΑΘΗΤΙΚΑ	_feeteeteeka/ matheeteeka_	CONCESSIONS (students/ pupils)
ΣΟΥΒΕΝΙΡ/ ΕΙΔΗ ΔΩΡΩΝ	_sooveneer/ eeTHee THoron_	SOUVENIRS/ GIFTS
ΚΥΛΙΚΕΙΟ/ ΑΝΑΨΥΚΤΙΚΑ•ΚΑΦΕΣ	_keeleekeeo/ anapseekteeka•kafes_	REFRESHMENTS
ΜΗΝ ΑΓΓΙΖΕΤΕ	_meen angeezete_	DO NOT TOUCH
ΑΠΑΓΟΡΕΥΕΤΑΙ Η ΦΩΤΟΓΡΑΦΗΣΗ	_apaghorevete ee fotoghrafeesee_	NO PHOTOGRAPHY
ΗΣΥΧΙΑ!	_eeseekheea_	SILENCE
ΑΠΑΓΟΡΕΥΕΤΑΙ Η ΠΡΟΣΒΑΣΗ	_apaghorevete ee prosvasee_	NO ACCESS
ΕΚΔΟΣΗ ΕΙΣΙΤΗΡΙΩΝ	_ekTHosee eeseeteereeon_	TICKETS

Public Buildings
ΔΗΜΟΣΙΑ ΚΤΙΡΙΑ

Greek	Pronunciation	English
ΝΟΣΟΚΟΜΕΙΟ	nosokomeeo	HOSPITAL
ΙΑΤΡΟΣ/ΙΑΤΡΕΙΟ	eeatros/eeatreeo	DOCTOR
ΟΔΟΝΤΙΑΤΡΟΣ/ ΟΔΟΝΤΙΑΤΡΕΙΟ	oTHondeeatros/ oTHondeeatreeo	DENTIST
ΑΣΤΥΝΟΜΙΑ	asteenomeea	POLICE
ΤΡΑΠΕΖΑ	trapeza	BANK
ΤΑΧΥΔΡΟΜΕΙΟ	takheeTHromeeo	POST OFFICE
ΚΟΛΥΜΒΗΤΗΡΙΟ/ ΠΙΣΙΝΑ	koleemveeteereeo/ peeseena	SWIMMING POOL
ΔΗΜΑΡΧΕΙΟ	THeemarkheeo	TOWN HALL
ΤΑΞΙ	taksee	TAXI STAND
ΜΟΥΣΕΙΟ	mooseeo	MUSEUM
ΝΟΜΑΡΧΕΙΑ	nomarkheea	COUNTY HALL
ΚΙΝΗΜΑΤΟ-ΓΡΑΦΟΣ	keenematoghrafos	MOVIE THEATER [CINEMA]
ΘΕΑΤΡΟ	theatro	THEATER
ΛΟΥΝΑ ΠΑΡΚ	loona park	FAIR SITE

Numbers

GRAMMAR

The Greek numbers 1, 3, and 4 – and the corresponding 21, 23, 24, 31, etc. – have different forms depending on the gender of the word that follows. Number 1 has three forms, while 3 and 4 have two forms. These are shown in parentheses below.

0	μηδέν *meeтHen*	18	δεκαοκτώ *тHekaokto*
1	ένας (μια, ένα) *enas (meea/mia, ena)*	19	δεκαεννέα *тHekaenea*
2	δύο *тHeeo*	20	είκοσι *eekosee*
3	τρεις (τρία) *trees (treea)*	21	είκοσι ένα *eekosee ena*
4	τέσσερις (τέσσερα) *teserees (tesera)*	22	είκοσι δύο *eekosee тHeeo*
5	πέντε *pende*	23	είκοσι τρία *eekosee treea*
6	έξι *eksee*	24	είκοσι τέσσερα *eekosee tesera*
7	επτά *epta*	25	είκοσι πέντε *eekosee pende*
8	οκτώ *okhto*	26	είκοσι έξι *eekosee eksee*
9	εννέα *enea*	27	είκοσι επτά *eekosee epta*
10	δέκα *тHeka*	28	είκοσι οκτώ *eekosee okto*
11	έντεκα *endeka*	29	είκοσι εννέα *eekosee enea*
12	δώδεκα *тHoтHeka*	30	τριάντα *treeanda*
13	δεκατρία *тHekatreea*	31	τριάντα ένα *treeanda ena*
14	δεκατέσσερα *тHekatesera*		
15	δεκαπέντε *тHekapende*		
16	δεκαέξι *тHekaeksee*		
17	δεκαεπτά *тHekaepta*		

32	τριάντα δύο *tree*anda THEEo	second	δεύτερος THEFteros
40	σαράντα sa*ran*da	third	τρίτος
50	πενήντα pe*nee*nda		*tree*tos
60	εξήντα ek*see*nda	fourth	τέταρτος *tetartos*
70	εβδομήντα evTHO*mee*nda	fifth	πέμπτος *pem*tos
80	ογδόντα o*ghtho*nda	once	μια φορά mia *fo*ra
90	ενενήντα ene*nee*nda	twice	δύο φορές THEEo *fo*res
100	εκατό eka*to*	three times	τρείς φορές trees *fo*res
101	εκατόν ένα eka*ton* *e*na	a half	μισό *mee*so
102	εκατόν δύο eka*ton* THEEo	half an hour	μισή ώρα mee*see* ora
200	διακόσια THEEa*ko*seea	half a tank	μισό ντεπόζιτο *mee*so depo*zee*to
300	τριακόσια trea*ko*seea	a quarter	ένα τέταρτο ena *te*tarto
400	τετρακόσια tetra*ko*seea	a third	ένα τρίτο ena *tree*to
500	πεντακόσια penda*ko*seea	a pair of …	ένα ζευγάρι … ena zev*gha*ree
600	εξακόσια eksa*ko*seea	a dozen …	μια ντουζίνα mia doo*zee*na
700	εφτακόσια efta*ko*seea	1999	χίλια εννιακόσια ενενήντα εννέα *khee*leea eneea*ko*seea ene*nee*nda e*ne*a
800	οχτακόσια okhta*ko*seea		
900	εννιακόσια eneea*ko*seea		
1,000	χίλια *khee*leea		
10,000	δέκα χιλιάδες THEka khee*lee*aTHes	2003	δύο χιλιάδες τρία THEEo khee*lee*aTHes *tree*a
1,000,000	ένα εκατομμύριο *e*na ekato*mee*reeo		
first	πρώτος *pro*tos		

Days Ημέρες

Monday	Δευτέρα	*THeftera*
Tuesday	Τρίτη	*treetee*
Wednesday	Τετάρτη	*tetartee*
Thursday	Πέμπτη	*pemtee*
Friday	Παρασκευή	*paraskevee*
Saturday	Σάββατο	*savato*
Sunday	Κυριακή	*keeyakee*

Months Μήνες

January	Ιανουάριος	*eeanoogreeos*
February	Φεβρουάριος	*fevrooareos*
March	Μάρτιος	*marteeos*
April	Απρίλιος	*apreeleeos*
May	Μάιος	*maeeos*
June	Ιούνιος	*eeooneeos*
July	Ιούλιος	*eeooleeos*
August	Αύγουστος	*avghoostos*
September	Σεπτέμβριος	*septemvreeos*
October	Οκτώβριος	*oktovreeos*
November	Νοέμβριος	*noemvreeos*
December	Δεκέμβριος	*THekemvreeos*

Dates Ημερομηνίες

It's ...	Είναι ...	*eene*
July 10	δέκα Ιουλίου	*THeka eeooleeoo*
yesterday	χτες	*khtes*
today	σήμερα	*seemera*
tomorrow	αύριο	*avreeo*
this ...	αυτό τον/αυτή την ...	*afto ton/aftee teen*
last ...	τον προηγούμενο/την προηγούμενη ...	*ton proeeghoomeno/teen proeeghoomenee*
next ...	τον επόμενο/την επόμενη ...	*ton epomeno/teen epomenee*
week/month/year	εβδομάδα/μήνα/χρόνο	*evTHomaTHa/meena/khrono*

Seasons Εποχές

spring	η άνοιξη *ee aneeksee*
summer	το καλοκαίρι *to kalokeree*
fall [autumn]	το φθινόπωρο *to ftheenoporo*
winter	ο χειμώνας *o kheemonas*
in spring	την άνοιξη *teen aneeksee*
during the summer	κατά τη διάρκεια του καλοκαιριού *kata tee THeearkeea too kalokeryoo*

Greetings Χαιρετισμοί

Happy birthday!	Να τα εκατοστήσετε! *na ta ekatosteesete*
Best wishes! (on namedays)	Χρόνια πολλά! *khroneea pola*
Merry Christmas!	Καλά Χριστούγεννα! *kala khreestooyena*
Happy New Year!	Ευτυχισμένος ο Καινούριος Χρόνος! *efteekheezmenos o kenooryos khronos*
Congratulations!	Συγχαρητήρια *seenkhareeteereea*
Good luck!/All the best!	Καλή επιτυχία! *kalee epeeteekheea*

Public holidays Δημόσιες αργίες

1 January	Πρωτοχρονιά *protokhroneea*	New Year's Day
6 January	Θεοφάνεια *theofaneea*	Epiphany
25 March	Ευαγγελισμός/Εθνική εορτή *evangeleesmos/ethneekee eortee*	Annunciation/Anniversary of start of Greek War of Independence
2nd Mon. in May	Πρωτομαγιά *protomaya*	May Day
15 August	Κοίμηση της Θεοτόκου *keemeesee tees theotokoo*	Assumption
28 October	Εθνική εορτή *ethneekee eortee*	Anniversary of Greece's rejection of Mussolini's ultimatum and entry into WW2
25 December	Χριστούγεννα *khreestooyena*	Christmas Day
26 December	Αγίου Στεφάνου *agheeoo stefanoo*	St. Stephen's Day

Movable feasts:
Easter Πάσχα *paskha* ; First day of Lent Καθαρή Δευτέρα *katharee THeftera*;
50 days after Easter Sunday Αγίου Πνεύματος *ayeeoo pnevmatos*;
Each city or town has a patron saint. Their name day is a local public holiday.

Time Η ώρα

Excuse me. Can you tell me the time?	Συγγνώμη. Τί ώρα είναι; *seeghnomee. tee ora eene*
It's ...	Είναι ... *eene*
five past one	μία και πέντε *mia ke pende*
ten past two	δύο και δέκα *THeeo ke THeka*
a quarter past three	τρεις και τέταρτο *trees ke tetarto*
twenty past four	τέσσερις και είκοσι *teserees ke eekosee*
twenty-five past five	πέντε και είκοσι πέντε *pende ke eekosee pende*
half past six	έξι και μισή *eksee ke meesee*
twenty-five to seven	επτά παρά είκοσι πέντε *epta para eekosee pende*
twenty to eight	οκτώ παρά είκοσι *okhto para eekosee*
a quarter to nine	εννέα παρά τέταρτο *enea para tetarto*
ten to ten	δέκα παρά δέκα *THeka para THeka*
five to eleven	έντεκα παρά πέντε *endeka para pende*
twelve o'clock	δώδεκα η ώρα *THOTHeka ee ora*
noon/midnight	μεσημέρι/μεσάνυχτα *meseemeree/mesaneekhta*

at dawn	τα ξημερώματα *ta kseemer<u>o</u>mata*
in the morning	το πρωί *to pro<u>ee</u>*
during the day	κατά τη διάρκεια της ημέρας *kat<u>a</u> tee* *THee<u>a</u>rkeea tees eem<u>e</u>ras*
before lunch	πριν το μεσημεριανό *preen to meseemery<u>a</u>no*
after lunch	μετά το μεσημεριανό *met<u>a</u> to meseemery<u>a</u>no*
in the afternoon	το απόγευμα *to ap<u>o</u>yevma*
in the evening	το βράδυ *to vr<u>a</u>THee*
at night	τη νύχτα *tee n<u>ee</u>khta*
I'll be ready in five minutes.	Θα είμαι έτοιμος/-η σε πέντε λεπτά. *tha <u>ee</u>me <u>e</u>teemos/-ee se* *p<u>e</u>nde lept<u>a</u>*
He'll be back in 15 minutes.	Θα επιστρέψει σε ένα τέταρτο της ώρας. *tha epeestr<u>e</u>psee se ena t<u>e</u>tarto* *tees <u>o</u>ras*
She arrived half an hour ago.	Έφτασε πριν από μισή ώρα. *<u>e</u>ftase preen ap<u>o</u> mees<u>ee</u> <u>o</u>ra*
The train leaves at …	Το τραίνο φεύγει … *to tr<u>e</u>no f<u>e</u>vyee*
13:04	στις δεκατρείς και τέσσερα λεπτά *stees THekatr<u>ee</u>s ke t<u>e</u>sera lept<u>a</u>*
0:40	σαράντα λεπτά μετά τα μεσάνυχτα *sar<u>a</u>nda lept<u>a</u> met<u>a</u> ta mes<u>a</u>neekhta*
10 minutes late / early	δέκα λεπτά αργότερα/νωρίτερα *THeka lept<u>a</u> argh<u>o</u>tera/nor<u>ee</u>tera*
from 9:00 to 5:00	από τις εννέα ως τις πέντε *ap<u>o</u> tees en<u>e</u>a os tees p<u>e</u>nde*
between 8:00 and 2:00	μεταξύ οκτώ και δύο
I'll be leaving by …	Θα φύγω στις … *tha f<u>ee</u>vgho stees*
Will you be back before … ?	Θα επιστρέψετε πριν τις … ; *tha epeestr<u>e</u>psete preen tees*
We'll be here until …	Θα είμαστε εδώ ως τις … *tha <u>ee</u>maste eTH<u>o</u> os tees*

221

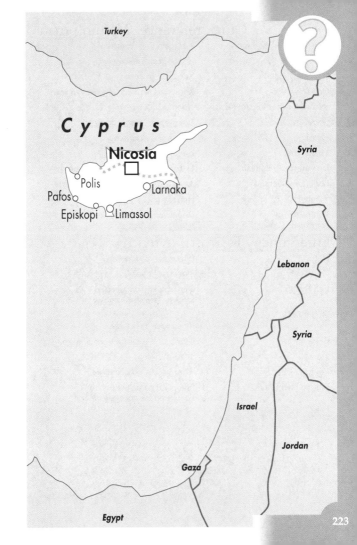

Quick reference Με μια ματιά

Good morning.	Καλημέρα.	*kaleemera*
Good afternoon.	Καλησπέρα.	*kaleespera*
Hello.	Χαίρετε.	*kherete*
Good-bye.	Χαίρεται/Γειά σας.	*kherete/ya sas*
Excuse me (getting attention).	Παρακαλώ!	*parakalo*
Sorry!	Συγγνώμη.	*seeghnomee*
Please.	Παρακαλώ.	*parakalo*
Thank you.	Ευχαριστώ.	*efkhareesto*
Do you speak English?	Μιλάτε Αγγλικά;	*meelate angleeka*
I don't understand	Δεν καταλαβαίνω	*тнen katalaveno*
Where is ... ?	Πού είναι ... ;	*poo eene*
Where are the bathrooms [toilets]?	Πού είναι οι τουαλέττες;	*poo eene ee tooaletes*

Emergency Έκτακτη ανάγκη

Help!	Βοήθεια!	*voeetheea*
Go away!	Φύγετε!	*feeyete*
Call the police!	Φωνάξτε την αστυνομία!	*fonakste teen asteenomeea*
Stop thief!	Σταματήστε τον κλέφτη!	*stamateeste ton kleftee*
Get a doctor!	Φωνάξτε ένα γιατρό!	*fonakste ena yatro*
Fire!	Φωτιά!	*foteea*
I'm lost.	Έχω χαθεί.	*ekho khathee*
Can you help me?	Μπορείτε να με βοηθήσετε;	*boreete na me voeetheesete*

Emergency ☎

Fire 199	Medical 166	Police 100	Tourist Police 171

Embassies ☎

	Embassy (Athens)	Embassy (Cyprus)
U.K.	723 6211	(2) 473 131-7
U.S.	721 2951	(2) 476 100
Canada	723 9511	*represented by U.S.*